KT-386-484

DSA ™
DRIVING STANDARDS AGENCY
SAFE DRIVING FOR LIFE

the official
theory test
for car drivers

Approved by
Plain
English
Campaign

London: TSO

Written and compiled by the Publications Unit of the Driving Standards Agency (DSA).

Questions and answers are compiled by the Question Development Team of the DSA.

Published with the permission of the Driving Standards Agency on behalf of the Controller of Her Majesty's Stationery Office.

First published 1996
Sixth edition 2003

ISBN 011 552347 2

A CIP catalogue record for this book is available from the British Library.

Other titles in the Driving Skills series

The Official Theory Test for Motorcyclists

The Official Theory Test for Drivers of Large Vehicles

Driving - the essential skills

The Official Driving Test

The Official Guide to Accompanying Learner Drivers

Motorcycle Riding – the essential skills

Official Motorcycling – CBT, theory and practical test

Driving Buses and Coaches – the official DSA syllabus

Driving Goods Vehicles – the official DSA syllabus

The Official Guide to Tractor and Specialist Vehicle Driving Tests

The Official DSA Guide for Driving Instructors

The Official Theory Test CD-ROM – for car drivers and motorcyclists

The Official Theory Test CD-ROM – for motorcyclists

The Official Theory Test CD-ROM – for drivers of large vehicles

Acknowledgements

The Driving Standards Agency would like to thank their staff and the following organisations for their contribution to the production of this publication:

    Transport Research Laboratory
    Department for Transport
    Driver & Vehicle Testing Agency, Northern Ireland

Every effort has been made to ensure that the information contained in this publication is accurate at the time of going to press. The Stationery Office cannot be held responsible for any inaccuracies.

Information in this book is for guidance only.

All metric and imperial conversions in this book are approximate.

ontents

cknowledgements   ii

ormation   iii

out DSA and DVTA   iv

ecial message from the Chief Driving Examiner   1

he theory test

Getting started   3

The theory test   4

Preparing for your theory test   5

Booking your theory test   7

Provision for special needs   8

Taking your theory test   9

After your theory test   14

he questions and answers

How to use this part of the book   15

Alertness   16

Attitude   30

Safety and your vehicle   50

Safety margins   82

Hazard awareness   102

Vulnerable road users   144

Other types of vehicle   180

Vehicle handling   194

Motorway rules   218

Rules of the road   238

Road and traffic signs   268

Documents   340

Accidents   352

Vehicle loading   378

seful information

Acceptable forms of photo ID   385

Theory test centres in Great Britain and Northern Ireland   386

Service standards   388

Complaints guide   388

Compensation code   389

The Driving Standards Agency (DSA) is an executive agency of the Department for Transport. You'll see its logo at test centres.

DSA aims to promote road safety through the advancement of driving standards, by

- establishing and developing high standards and best practice in driving and riding on the road; before people start to drive, as they learn, and after they pass their test
- ensuring high standards of instruction for different types of driver and rider
- conducting the statutory theory and practical tests efficiently, fairly and consistently across the country
- providing a centre of excellence for driver training and driving standards
- developing a range of publications and other publicity material designed to promote safe driving for life.

DVTA

The Driver & Vehicle Testing Agency (DVTA) is an executive agency within the Department of the Environment for Northern Ireland. Its primary aim is to promote and improve road safety through the advancement of driving standards and implementation of the Government's policies for improving the mechanical standards of vehicles.

DSA Website

www.driving-tests.co.uk

DVTA Website

www.doeni.gov.uk/dvta

Information

Theory and Practical Tests
DSA Bookings and Enquiries: 0870 01 01 372
DVTA (Northern Ireland) Booking and Enquiries: 0845 600 6700

Faxes: 0870 01 04 372
Minicom: 0870 01 06 372
Welsh speakers: 0870 01 00 372

Postal applications for theory tests to:
Driving Standards Agency or Driver and Vehicle Testing Agency
PO Box 148
Salford M5 3SY

Driving Standards Agency
(Headquarters)
Stanley House
Talbot Street
Nottingham NG1 5GU

Tel: 0115 901 2500
Fax: 0115 901 2510

Driver & Vehicle Testing Agency
(Headquarters)
Balmoral Road
Belfast BT12 6QL

Tel: 02890 681831
Fax: 02890 665520

Driver Vehicle Licensing Agency
(GB Licence Enquiries)

Tel: 0870 240 0009
Fax: 01792 783071
Minicom: 01792 782787

Driver and Vehicle Licensing Northern Ireland
Customer Services
Tel: 02870 341469
02890 250 500 (24 hours)
Minicom: 02870 341 380

Website addresses
DSA: www.driving-tests.co.uk
DVTA: www.doeni.gov.uk/dvta

A special message from the Chief Driving Examiner

With the ever-increasing volume of traffic on the roads today, it's important to make sure that new drivers have a broad spread of driving knowledge. Since July 1996 all new drivers have had to pass a separate theory test before obtaining a full driving licence. In November 2002 the original multiple choice test was extended to include a hazard perception part. The introduction of the theory test has been a major step towards improving road safety in the UK.

All aspects of the theory test are continually monitored, and the question bank is regularly updated to take account of changes to legislation and best driving practices. This book contains the whole theory test question bank, set out in an easy-to-read style, with explanations as to why the answers are correct.

However, to prepare properly for the test, you should study the source material; this consists of

The Highway Code

Know Your Traffic Signs

Driving – the essential skills

To help you practise for the multiple choice questions, *The Official Theory Test CD-ROM for Car Drivers and Motorcyclists* contains the full question bank and allows you to take a mock multiple choice test.

Using these training aids will give you an extensive knowledge of driving theory, and will help you towards a better understanding of practical driving skills.

You'll never know all the answers. Throughout your driving career there will always be more to learn. Remember, any passengers you carry will be your responsibility. By being reliable, efficient and safe you'll be on your way to becoming a good driver.

Robin Cummins

The Chief Driving Examiner
Driving Standards Agency

The theory test

This part of the book explains how you get started and gives general information about the theory test.

It has advice on

- Getting started

  your licence and starting to drive on the road

- The theory test

  why is there a theory test?

- Preparing for your theory test

  details of books and other training materials

- Booking your theory test

  various ways of booking your test

- Provision for special needs

  how we provide for those with reading and hearing difficulties, physical disabilities and languages other than English

- Taking your theory test

  arriving at the test centre, and information about the multiple choice and hazard perception parts of the test

- After your theory test

  the next stage

- The questions and answers

  how to use the question and answer part of the book.

Getting started

Applying for your licence

You must be at least 17 years old to drive a car. As an exception, if you receive Disability Living Allowance at the higher rate, you're allowed to start driving at 16. You'll need to apply for your provisional driving licence before you can drive on the road.

Driving licences are issued by the Driver and Vehicle Licensing Agency (DVLA) but application forms D1 and D750 can be obtained from any Post Office. In Northern Ireland the issuing authority is Driver and Vehicle Licensing Northern Ireland and the form is a DL1.

These forms need to be sent to the appropriate office, which is shown on the form. You must enclose the required passport-type photographs, as all provisional licences now issued are photocard licences.

When you receive your provisional licence, check that all details are correct before you drive on the road.

If you need to contact DVLA, their telephone number is 0870 240 0009.

You will need to show your provisional licence when you take your theory test.

Residency requirements

You can't take a test or obtain a full licence unless you are normally resident in this country. Normal residence means the place where you reside because of personal or occupational ties. However, if you moved to the United Kingdom (UK) having recently been permanently resident in another state of the EC/EEA (European Economic Area), you must have been normally resident in the UK for 185 days in the 12 months prior to your application for a driving test or full driving licence.

Choosing an instructor

DSA in Great Britain, and DVTA in Northern Ireland, approve instructors who are then able to teach learner drivers in return for payment. These instructors have their standards checked regularly.

Approved Driving Instructors (ADIs) must

- pass a series of difficult examinations
- reach a high standard of instruction
- be registered with DSA or DVTA
- display an Approved Driving Instructor's certificate (except in Northern Ireland).

These professional instructors will give you guidance on

- what books to read
- your practical skills
- how to study and practise
- when you're ready for your tests
- further training after passing your practical test under the 'Pass Plus' scheme.

DSA and the main bodies representing ADIs place great emphasis on professional standards and business ethics.

A code of practice has been created, setting a framework within which all instructors should operate. Details of this can be obtained from DSA headquarters (tel: 0115 901 2500).

The theory test

The theory test is a computer-based test, and consists of two parts.

It has been devised to test your knowledge of driving theory, in particular the rules of the road and best driving practice.

Your knowledge of this information is tested in the first part of the theory test, as a series of multiple choice questions. More information about this part of the test is given on page 10 and the questions are given in the main part of the book, beginning on page 16.

There is now a second part of the theory test called the hazard perception part, more information about this is given on page 12.

Foreign licence holders:

If you hold a foreign driving licence issued outside the EEA, first check with the Driver Vehicle Licensing Agency (tel: 0870 240 0009) to see whether you can exchange your driving licence. If you cannot exchange your licence, you will need to take a theory and practical driving test.

Frequently asked questions

Can I take the practical test first?

No. You have to pass your theory test before you can book a practical test.

Does everyone have to take the theory test?

UK licence holders:

Most people in the UK who are learning to drive will have to sit a theory test. However, you won't have to if

- you're upgrading within the same category i.e. B (car) to B+E (car with trailer)
- you already have a full B1 entitlement because you have a full motorcycle licence issued before 1 February 2001.

Any particular enquiries about whether you have to take a theory test should be addressed to the Theory Test Unit, Driving Standards Agency, Stanley House, 56 Talbot Street, Nottingham, NG1 5GU. Tel: 0115 901 2500.

Preparing for your theory test

Although you have to pass your theory test before you can take your practical test, it's recommended that you start studying for your theory test, but don't actually take it until you have some practical experience of driving.

To prepare for the multiple choice part of the theory test, we strongly recommend that you study the books from which the questions are taken as well as the questions themselves. These books are:

The Highway Code – this is essential reading for all drivers. It contains the most up-to-date advice on road safety and the laws which apply to all road users.

Know Your Traffic Signs – this contains most of the signs and road markings that you are likely to come across.

Driving – the essential skills – this is the official reference, giving practical advice and best driving practice for all drivers.

These books will help you to answer the questions correctly and will also help you when studying for your practical test. The information in them will be relevant throughout your driving life so make sure you always have an up-to-date copy that you can refer to.

need to get !

got all Ready

Other study aids

The Official Theory Test CD-ROM for Car Drivers and Motorcyclists – this is an alternative way of preparing for the multiple choice part of the theory test. It contains all the questions and answers and also allows you to take mock tests.

RoadSense – the official guide to hazard perception for all drivers. We recommend that you prepare for the hazard perception part of the theory test by studying and working through *RoadSense*, preferably with your instructor.

All the training materials listed are available by mail order from 0870 241 4523. The books, together with relevant books from other publishers, are also available from good bookshops.

Frequently asked questions

Why do the questions keep changing?

To make sure that all candidates are being tested fairly, questions and video clips are under continuous review. Some of the questions may be changed as a result of customer feedback. They may also be changed to reflect revised legislation, and the publications listed above are updated to reflect such changes.

Can I take a mock test?

You can take a mock test online at www.driving-tests.co.uk.

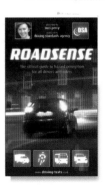

It's important that you study, not just to pass the test, but to become a safer driver.

Booking your theory test

The easiest ways to book your test are online or by telephone, but it can also be booked by post.

Online or by telephone

If you book by either of these methods, you'll be given the date and time of your test immediately.

You can book your theory test online at www.driving-tests.co.uk or www.dsa.gov.uk.

To book by telephone, call 0870 0101 372 (0845 600 6700 for Northern Ireland) between 8 am and 6 pm Monday to Friday.

If you're deaf and use a minicom machine, call 0870 0106 372 and if you are a Welsh speaker, call 0870 0100 372.

You will need your

- DVLA or DVLNI driving licence number
- credit or debit card details. Please note that the person who books the test must be the card holder. We accept Visa, Access, Switch, Delta, Solo and Electron.

You'll be given a booking number and sent an appointment letter that you should receive within eight days.

By post

If you prefer to book by post, you'll need to fill in an application form. These are available from theory test centres or driving test centres, or your instructor may have one.

You should normally receive an appointment letter within ten days of posting your application form.

Frequently asked questions

Where can I take the test?

There are over 150 theory test centres throughout England, Scotland and Wales, and six in Northern Ireland. Most people have a test centre within 20 miles of their home, but this will vary depending on the density of population in your area.

You can find a list of test centres on page 386.

When are test centres open?

Test centres are usually open on weekdays, some evenings and Saturdays.

What if I don't receive an acknowledgement?

If you don't receive an acknowledgement within the time specified above, please telephone the booking office to check that an appointment has been made.

We can't take responsibility for postal delays. If you miss your test appointment you'll lose your fee.

How do I cancel or postpone my test?

To cancel or postpone your theory test appointment you should contact the booking office at least **three clear working days** before your test date, otherwise you'll lose your fee.

Only in exceptional circumstances, such as documented ill-health or family bereavement, can this rule be waived.

Provision for special needs

Every effort is made to ensure that the theory test can be taken by all candidates.

It's important that you state your needs when you book your test so that the necessary arrangements can be made.

Reading difficulties

There's an English language voiceover, on a headset, to help you if you have reading difficulties or dyslexia.

You can ask for up to twice the normal time to take the multiple choice part of the test.

You will be asked to provide a letter from an appropriate person (such as a teacher, psychologist or doctor, or possibly an independent person who knows about your reading ability). Please check with the Special Needs section on the normal booking number (see page 7) if you're unsure about who to ask.

We can't guarantee to return any original documents, so please send copies only.

Hearing difficulties

The introduction to both the multiple choice and hazard perception parts of the test can be delivered in British Sign Language (BSL) by an on-screen signer if you're deaf or have other hearing difficulties.

A BSL interpreter or lip speaker can be provided if requested at the time of booking.

Physical disabilities

If you have a physical disability which would make it difficult for you to use a mouse button to respond to the clips in the hazard perception part of the test, we may be able to make special arrangements for you to use a different method if you let us know when you book your test.

If you need wheelchair access and your nearest test centre doesn't provide this, then we may be able to arrange for you to take your test at another location (for example a library or another test centre).

Languages other than English

You can listen through a headset to the test being read out in one of 20 languages other than English. These are: Albanian, Arabic, Bengali, Cantonese, Dari, Farsi, Gujarati, Hindi, Kashmiri, Kurdish, Mirpuri, Polish, Portuguese, Punjabi, Pushto, Spanish, Tamil, Turkish, Urdu and Welsh.

Northern Ireland tests are available in Cantonese, Bengali and Urdu only.

In Wales, and at theory test centres on the Welsh borders, you can take your theory test with Welsh text on screen.

To take your test in a language other than those listed above, you may bring a translator with you to certain theory test centres. The translator must be approved by DSA and you must make arrangements when you book your test. You have to arrange and pay for the services of the translator yourself.

Tests with translators can be taken at the following test centres: Aldershot, Birkenhead, Birmingham, Cardiff, Derby, Edinburgh, Glasgow, Ipswich, Leeds, Milton Keynes, Palmers Green and Preston.

Taking your theory test

Arriving at the test centre

You must make sure that when you arrive at the test centre you have all the relevant documents with you, or you won't be able to take your test and you'll lose your fee.

You'll need

- your signed photocard licence and paper counterpart, or
- your signed driving licence and photo identity (if you don't have a photocard licence). The types of photo identity which are acceptable can be found on page 385.

All documents must be original. We can't accept photocopies.

The test centre staff will check your documents and make sure that you take the right category of test.

Make sure that you arrive in plenty of time so you aren't rushed. If you arrive after the session has started you may not be allowed to take the test.

Remember
- **No photo**
- **No licence**

NO TEST

You'll then be ready to start your test. It's a computer-based test and is made up of a multiple choice part and a hazard perception part.

Multiple choice questions

You'll begin by taking the multiple choice part of the theory test. This consists of 35 multiple choice questions and you select your answers for this part of the test by simply touching the screen. This 'touch screen' has been carefully designed to make it easy to use.

Before you start this part of your test you'll be given the opportunity to work through a practice session for up to 15 minutes to get used to the system. Staff at the test centre will be available to help you if you have any difficulties.

The questions will cover a variety of topics relating to road safety, the environment and documentation. Only one question will appear on the screen at a time.

Most questions will ask you to mark one correct answer from four possible answers given. Some questions may ask for two or more correct answers from a selection, but this is shown clearly on the screen. If you try to move on without marking the correct number of answers you'll be reminded that more answers are needed.

To answer, you need to touch the box alongside the answer or answers you think are correct. If you change your mind and don't want that answer to be selected, touch it again. You can then choose another answer.

shows the question number

shows your name and category of test

shows the time remaining, it will flash when you have 5 minutes left

shows how many answers are required

shows the question

touch the screen to indicate which answer(s) are correct

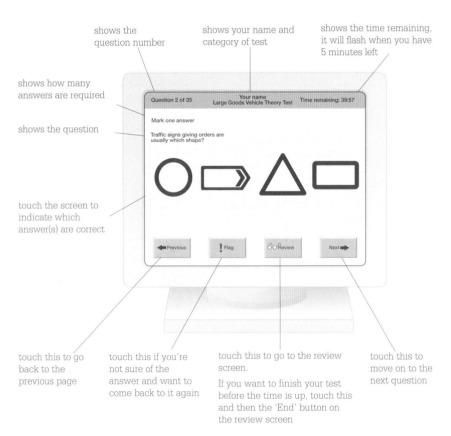

touch this to go back to the previous page

touch this if you're not sure of the answer and want to come back to it again

touch this to go to the review screen.

If you want to finish your test before the time is up, touch this and then the 'End' button on the review screen

touch this to move on to the next question

Take your time and read the questions carefully. You're given 40 minutes for this part of the test, so relax and don't rush. Some questions will take longer to answer than others, but there are no trick questions. The time remaining is displayed on screen. Extra time can be provided if you have special needs and you let us know when you book your test. You'll be able to move backwards and forwards through the questions and you can also 'flag' questions that you'd like to look at again. It's easy to change your answer if you want to.

Try to answer all the questions. If you're well prepared you shouldn't find them difficult.

Before you finish, if you have time, you can use the 'review' feature to check your answers before you end this part of the test. If you want to finish your test before the full time, press the 'review' button and then the 'end' button on the review screen.

When you press the review button you will see the following screen.

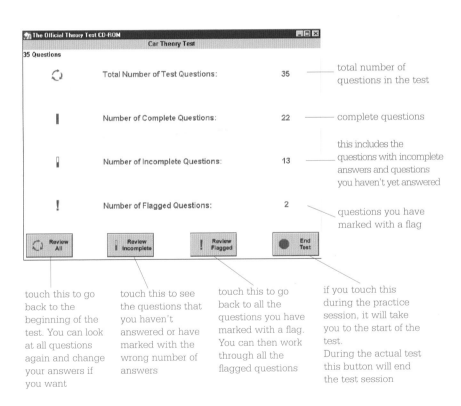

touch this to go back to the beginning of the test. You can look at all questions again and change your answers if you want

touch this to see the questions that you haven't answered or have marked with the wrong number of answers

touch this to go back to all the questions you have marked with a flag. You can then work through all the flagged questions

if you touch this during the practice session, it will take you to the start of the test.
During the actual test this button will end the test session

Hazard perception

After you've finished the multiple choice part, you may have a break of up to three minutes if you wish, before you start the hazard perception (HP) part of the test. This part of the test will consist of a series of film clips, shown from a driver's point of view.

Before you start this part of the test you'll be shown a short tutorial video that explains how the test works and gives you a chance to see a sample film clip. This will help you to understand what you need to do. You can run this video a second time if you want to.

During the HP part of the test you'll be shown 14 film clips. Each clip contains one or more developing hazards. You should respond by pressing the mouse button **as soon as you see** a hazard developing

that may result in you, the driver, having to take some action, such as changing speed or direction. The earlier you notice a developing hazard and make a response, the higher your score. There are 15 scoreable hazards in total.

Your response will not cause the scene in the video to alter in any way. However, a red flag will appear on the bottom of the screen to show that your response has been noted.

Before each clip starts, there will be a 10-second pause to allow you to familiarise yourself with the new road situation.

The HP part of the test lasts about 20 minutes. For this part of the test there is no extra time available, and you can't repeat any of the clips – you don't get a second chance to notice a hazard when you're driving on the road.

Trial questions

We're constantly checking the questions and clips to help us decide whether to use them in future tests. After each part of the test you may be given the option of doing an additional trial question or clip. You don't have to do these if you don't want to, and if you answer them they won't count towards your final score.

Customer satisfaction survey

We want to ensure our customers are completely satisfied with the service they receive. At the end of your test you'll be shown some questions designed to give us information about you and how happy you are with the service you received from us.

Your answers will be treated in the strictest confidence. They are not part of the test and they won't be used in determining your final score or for marketing purposes. You'll be asked if you want to complete the survey, there's no obligation to do so.

The result

You should receive your result at the test centre within 30 minutes of completing the test.

You'll be given a score for each part of the test (the multiple choice part and the HP part). You'll need to pass both parts to pass the theory test. If you fail one of the parts you'll have to take the whole test again.

Frequently asked questions

What's the pass mark?

To pass the multiple choice part of the theory test you must answer at least 30 questions correctly.

To pass the HP part you must reach the required pass mark. This part of the test was introduced in November 2002 and initially the pass mark was set at 38 out of a total of 75 marks. This will increase in the light of actual operational experience. You can find out the current pass mark by calling 0115 901 2500, checking on www.driving-tests.co.uk or asking your ADI.

If I don't pass, when can I take the test again?

If you fail your test, you've shown that you're not fully prepared. You'll have to wait at least three clear working days before you take the theory test again.

Good preparation will save you time and money.

Why do I have to retake both parts of the test if I only failed one?

It's really only one test. The theory test has always included questions relating to hazard awareness – the new test merely tests the same skills in a more effective way. The two parts are only presented separately in the theory test as a different scoring method is used for each.

After your theory test

When you pass your theory test you'll be given a certificate. Keep this carefully, you'll need it when you go for your practical test.

This certificate has a life of two years from the date of your test. This means that you have to take and pass the practical test within this two-year period. If you don't, you'll have to take and pass the theory test again before you can book your practical test.

Your practical driving test

Your next step is to take a practical driving test. To help you prepare for this DSA has produced a book *The Official Driving Test* and a video *The Driving Test - Inside View 2.*

The Official Driving Test explains the test requirements and the official syllabus for car drivers.

The Driving Test - Inside View 2 gives valuable advice about taking the driving test, including tips on preparation and an explanation of what examiners expect.

Pass plus

As a newly qualified driver you can take further training in the form of the Pass Plus scheme. This scheme has been introduced by DSA for new drivers who would like to improve their basic skills and safely widen their driving experience.

If you take a Pass Plus course, you may be rewarded with reduced insurance premiums.

> **Driving is a life skill**
>
> **Your driving tests are just the beginning**

The questions and answers

How to use this part of the book

The following part of the book contains all the questions that could be used in the multiple choice part of the theory test.

For easy reference, and to help you to study, the questions have been divided into topics and put into sections. Although this isn't how you'll find them in your test, it's helpful if you want to refer to particular subjects.

The questions are in the left-hand column with a choice of answers beneath. On the right-hand side of the page you'll find the correct answers and a brief explanation of why they are correct. There will also be some advice on correct driving procedures.

Don't just learn the answers. It's important that you know why the answers are correct. This will help you with your practical skills and prepare you to become a safe and confident driver.

Taking exams or tests is rarely a pleasant experience, but you can make your test less stressful by being confident that you have the knowledge to answer the questions correctly.

Make studying more enjoyable by involving friends and relations. Take part in a question-and-answer game. Test those 'experienced' drivers who've had their licence a while: they might learn something too!

Some of the questions in this book will not be used in Northern Ireland theory tests. These questions are marked as follows:

NI EXEMPT

Alertness

This section looks at alertness and attention when you're driving.

The questions will ask you about

● **Observation**

looking all around for other road users and pedestrians.

● **Anticipation**

looking ahead and giving yourself enough time to react to hazards.

● **Concentration**

being alert at all times when driving.

● **Awareness**

understanding the actions of other road users.

● **Distraction**

not becoming distracted while driving. Your attention must be on the road.

● **Boredom**

keeping your mind on your driving. Boredom can make you feel sleepy.

Q. 1.1

Mark one answer

Before you make a U-turn in the road, you should

- ▓ give an arm signal as well as using your indicators

- ▓ signal so that other drivers can slow down for you

- ▓ look over your shoulder for a final check

- ▓ select a higher gear than normal

Answer

☑ **look over your shoulder for a final check**

If you want to make a U-turn, slow down and ensure that the road is clear in both directions. Make sure that the road is wide enough to carry out the manoeuvre safely.

Q. 1.2

Mark three answers

As you approach this bridge you should

- ▓ move into the middle of the road to get a better view

- ▓ slow down

- ▓ get over the bridge as quickly as possible

- ▓ consider using your horn

- ▓ find another route

- ▓ beware of pedestrians

Answers

☑ **slow down**

☑ **consider using your horn**

☑ **beware of pedestrians**

This sign gives you a warning. The brow of the hill prevents you seeing oncoming traffic so you must be cautious.

The bridge is narrow and there may not be enough room for you to pass an oncoming vehicle at this point.

There is no footpath, so pedestrians may be walking in the road.

Consider the hidden hazards and be ready to react if necessary.

questions   *answers*

Q. 1.3

Mark one answer

When following a large vehicle you should keep well back because

- ☐ it allows you to corner more quickly
- ☐ it helps the large vehicle to stop more easily
- ☐ it allows the driver to see you in the mirrors
- ☐ it helps you to keep out of the wind

Answer

☑ **it allows the driver to see you in the mirrors**

If you're following a large vehicle but are so close to it that you can't see the exterior mirrors, the driver can't see you.

Keeping well back will also allow you to see the road ahead by looking past either side of the large vehicle.

Q. 1.4

Mark one answer

In which of these situations should you avoid overtaking?

- ☐ Just after a bend
- ☐ In a one-way street
- ☐ On a 30 mph road
- ☐ Approaching a dip in the road

Answer

☑ **Approaching a dip in the road**

As you begin to think about overtaking, ask yourself if it's really necessary. If you can't see well ahead stay back and wait for a safer place to pull out.

Q. 1.5

Mark one answer

This road marking warns

- ☐ drivers to use the hard shoulder
- ☐ overtaking drivers there is a bend to the left
- ☐ overtaking drivers to move back to the left
- ☐ drivers that it is safe to overtake

Answer

☑ **overtaking drivers to move back to the left**

You should plan your overtaking to take into account any hazards ahead. In this picture the marking indicates that you are approaching a junction. You will not have time to overtake and move back into the left safely.

Q. 1.6

Mark one answer

Your mobile phone rings while you are travelling. You should

- ▪ stop immediately
- ▪ answer it immediately
- ▪ pull up in a suitable place
- ▪ pull up at the nearest kerb

Answer

✓ **pull up in a suitable place**

Always use the safe option. It is not worth taking the risk of endangering other road users.

If you need to use a mobile phone, make sure that you pull up in a place that does not obstruct other road users. Using a message service will enable you to complete your journey without interruptions and you can catch up with your calls when you take your rest breaks.

Q. 1.7

Mark one answer

Why are these yellow lines painted across the road?

- ▪ To help you choose the correct lane
- ▪ To help you keep the correct separation distance
- ▪ To make you aware of your speed
- ▪ To tell you the distance to the roundabout

Answer

✓ **To make you aware of your speed**

These lines are often found on the approach to a roundabout or a dangerous junction. They give you extra warning to adjust your speed. Look well ahead and do this in good time.

questions   *answers*

Q. 1.8

Mark one answer

You are approaching traffic lights that have been on green for some time. You should

▪ accelerate hard
▪ maintain your speed
▪ be ready to stop
▪ brake hard

Answer

☑ **be ready to stop**

The longer traffic lights have been on green, the greater the chance of them changing. Always allow for this on approach and be prepared to stop.

Q. 1.9

Mark one answer

Which of the following should you do before stopping?

▪ Sound the horn
▪ Use the mirrors
▪ Select a higher gear
▪ Flash your headlights

Answer

☑ **Use the mirrors**

Before pulling up check the mirrors to see what is happening behind you. Also assess what is ahead and make sure you give the correct signal if it helps other road users.

Q. 1.10

Mark one answer

As a driver what does the term 'Blind Spot' mean?

▪ An area covered by your right hand mirror
▪ An area not covered by your headlamps
▪ An area covered by your left hand mirror
▪ An area not seen in your mirrors

Answer

☑ **An area not seen in your mirrors**

Modern vehicles provide the driver with well-positioned mirrors which are essential to safe driving. However, they cannot see every angle of the scene behind and to the sides of the vehicle. This is why it is essential that you check over your shoulder, so that you are aware of any hazards not reflected in your mirrors.

Q. 1.11

Mark two answers

Objects hanging from your interior mirror may

- ■ restrict your view
- ■ improve your driving
- ■ distract your attention
- ■ help your concentration

Answers

- ☑ **restrict your view**
- ☑ **distract your attention**

Ensure that you can see clearly through the windscreen of your vehicle. Stickers or hanging objects could affect your field of vision or draw your eyes away from the road.

Q. 1.12

Mark four answers

Which of the following may cause loss of concentration on a long journey?

- ■ Loud music
- ■ Arguing with a passenger
- ■ Using a mobile phone
- ■ Putting in a cassette tape
- ■ Stopping regularly to rest
- ■ Pulling up to tune the radio

Answers

- ☑ **Loud music**
- ☑ **Arguing with a passenger**
- ☑ **Using a mobile phone**
- ☑ **Putting in a cassette tape**

You should not allow yourself to be distracted when driving. You need to concentrate fully in order to be safe on the road. Loud music could mask other sounds, such as the audible warning of an emergency vehicle.

Any distraction which causes you to take your hands off the steering wheel or your eyes off the road could be dangerous.

Q. 1.13

Mark two answers

On a long motorway journey boredom can cause you to feel sleepy. You should

- ■ leave the motorway and find a safe place to stop
- ■ keep looking around at the surrounding landscape
- ■ drive faster to complete your journey sooner
- ■ ensure a supply of fresh air into your vehicle
- ■ stop on the hard shoulder for a rest

Answers

- ☑ **leave the motorway and find a safe place to stop**
- ☑ **ensure a supply of fresh air into your vehicle**

Plan your journey to include suitable rest stops. You should take all possible precautions against feeling sleepy while driving. Any lapse of concentration could have serious consequences.

questions   *answers*

Q. 1.14

Mark two answers

You are driving at dusk. You should switch your lights on

- even when street lights are not lit
- so others can see you
- only when others have done so
- only when street lights are lit

Answers

- ☑ **even when street lights are not lit**
- ☑ **so others can see you**

Your headlights and tail lights help others on the road to see you. It may be necessary to turn on your lights during the day if visibility is reduced, for example due to heavy rain. In these conditions the light might fade before the street lights are timed to switch on. Be seen to be safe.

Q. 1.15

Mark two answers

You are most likely to lose concentration when driving if you

- use a mobile phone
- listen to very loud music
- switch on the heated rear window
- look at the door mirrors

Answers

- ☑ **use a mobile phone**
- ☑ **listen to very loud music**

Distractions which cause you to take your hands off the steering wheel or your eyes off the road are potentially dangerous. You must be in full control of your vehicle at all times.

Q. 1.16

Mark four answers

Which FOUR are most likely to cause you to lose concentration while you are driving?

- Using a mobile phone
- Talking into a microphone
- Tuning your car radio
- Looking at a map
- Checking the mirrors
- Using the demisters

Answers

- ☑ **Using a mobile phone**
- ☑ **Talking into a microphone**
- ☑ **Tuning your car radio**
- ☑ **Looking at a map**

Planning your journey is important. A few sensible precautions will allow you to

- tune your radio into frequencies in your area of travel before setting off
- take planned breaks (which can be used for phone calls)
- plan your route (make notes of road numbers and junction numbers if necessary).

This will avoid the need to look at maps or use a mobile phone while driving.

Q. 1.17

Mark one answer

You should not use a mobile phone whilst driving

- until you are satisfied that no other traffic is near
- unless you are able to drive one handed
- because it might distract your attention from the road ahead
- because reception is poor when the engine is running

Answer

☑ **because it might distract your attention from the road ahead**

Driving requires your total attention and concentration at all times. Using a mobile phone will distract you and will increase your chances of having an accident.

Be safe, switch off your phone while driving and pick up any messages when you stop for a break.

Q. 1.18

Mark one answer

Your vehicle is fitted with a hands free phone system. Using this equipment whilst driving

- is quite safe as long as you slow down
- could distract your attention from the road
- is recommended by The Highway Code
- could be very good for road safety

Answer

☑ **could distract your attention from the road**

Using a hands free system doesn't mean that you can safely drive and use a mobile phone. This type of mobile phone can still distract your attention from the road. As a driver, it is your responsibility to keep yourself and other road users safe at all times.

Q. 1.19

Mark one answer

Using a hands free phone is likely to

- improve your safety
- increase your concentration
- reduce your view
- divert your attention

Answer

☑ **divert your attention**

Unlike someone in the car with you, the person on the other end of the line is unable to see the traffic situations you are dealing with. They will not stop speaking to you even if you are approaching a hazardous situation. You need to be concentrating on your driving all of the time, but especially so when dealing with a hazard.

questions   *answers*

Q. 1.20

Mark one answer

You should ONLY use a mobile phone when

- receiving a call
- suitably parked
- driving at less than 30 mph
- driving an automatic vehicle

Answer

☑ **suitably parked**

It is far more convenient for you, as well as being safer, if you have parked in a safe and convenient place before receiving or making a call or using text messaging. You will also be free to take notes or refer to papers, which would be not be possible while driving.

Q. 1.21

Mark one answer

Using a mobile phone while you are driving

- is acceptable in a vehicle with power steering
- will reduce your field of vision
- could distract your attention from the road
- will affect your vehicle's electronic systems

Answer

☑ **could distract your attention from the road**

Driving today requires all of your attention, all of the time. Any distraction, however brief, is potentially dangerous and could lead to you losing control of your vehicle.

Q. 1.22

Mark one answer

What is the safest way to use a mobile phone in your vehicle?

- Use hands free equipment
- Find a suitable place to stop
- Drive slowly on a quiet road
- Direct your call through the operator

Answer

☑ **Find a suitable place to stop**

If the use of a mobile phone causes you to drive in a careless or dangerous manner, you could be prosecuted for those offences. The penalties include an unlimited fine, disqualification and up to two years' imprisonment.

questions

answers

Q. 1.23

Mark one answer

You are driving on a wet road. You have to stop your vehicle in an emergency. You should

- ■ apply the handbrake and footbrake together
- ■ keep both hands on the wheel
- ■ select reverse gear
- ■ give an arm signal

Answer

☑ **keep both hands on the wheel**

As you drive, look well ahead and all around so that you're ready for any hazards that might occur. There may be occasions when you have to stop in an emergency. React as soon as you can whilst keeping control of the vehicle.

Q. 1.24

Mark three answers

When you are moving off from behind a parked car you should

- ■ look round before you move off
- ■ use all the mirrors on the vehicle
- ■ look round after moving off
- ■ use the exterior mirrors only
- ■ give a signal if necessary
- ■ give a signal after moving off

Answers

☑ **look round before you move off**

☑ **use all the mirrors on the vehicle**

☑ **give a signal if necessary**

Before moving off you should use all the mirrors to check if the road is clear. Look round to check the blind spots and give a signal if it is necessary to warn other road users of your intentions.

answers

Q. 1.25

Mark one answer

You are travelling along this narrow country road. When passing the cyclist you should go

◻ slowly, sounding the horn as you pass

◻ quickly, leaving plenty of room

◻ slowly, leaving plenty of room

◻ quickly, sounding the horn as you pass

Answer

☑ **slowly, leaving plenty of room**

Look well ahead and only pull out if it is safe. You will need to use all of the road to pass the cyclist, so be extra-cautious. Look out for entrances to fields where tractors or other farm machinery could be waiting to pull out.

Q. 1.26

Mark one answer

Your vehicle is fitted with a hand-held telephone. To use the telephone you should

◻ reduce your speed

◻ find a safe place to stop

◻ steer the vehicle with one hand

◻ be particularly careful at junctions

Answer

☑ **find a safe place to stop**

Your attention should be on your driving at all times. Never attempt to dial or reach out for your phone while on the move. This could mean taking your eyes off the road and at 60 mph your vehicle will travel about 27 metres every second.

Q. 1.27

Mark one answer

To answer a call on your mobile phone while travelling you should

◻ reduce your speed wherever you are

◻ stop in a proper and convenient place

◻ keep the call time to a minimum

◻ slow down and allow others to overtake

Answer

☑ **stop in a proper and convenient place**

No phone call is important enough to risk endangering lives. If you must be contactable when driving, plan your route to include breaks where you can catch up on telephone messages in safety. Always choose a proper and convenient place to take a break, such as a lay-by or service area.

Q. 1.28

Mark one answer

NI EXEMPT

Your mobile phone rings while you are on the motorway. Before answering you should

- ◼ reduce your speed to 50 mph
- ◼ pull up on the hard shoulder
- ◼ move into the left hand lane
- ◼ stop in a safe place

Answer

☑ **stop in a safe place**

When driving on motorways, you can't just pull up to answer your mobile phone. If you need to be contactable, plan your journey to include breaks so you can pick up any phone messages.

Q. 1.29

Mark one answer

You are turning right onto a dual carriageway. What should you do before emerging?

- ◼ Stop, apply the handbrake and then select a low gear
- ◼ Position your vehicle well to the left of the side road
- ◼ Check that the central reserve is wide enough for your vehicle
- ◼ Make sure that you leave enough room for a following vehicle

Answer

☑ **Check that the central reserve is wide enough for your vehicle**

Before emerging right onto a dual carriageway make sure that the central reserve is wide enough to protect your vehicle. If it's not, you should treat it as one road and check that it's clear in both directions before pulling out. Neglecting to do this could place part or all of your vehicle in the path of approaching traffic and cause an accident.

Q. 1.30

Mark one answer

You lose your way on a busy road. What is the best action to take?

- ◼ Stop at traffic lights and ask pedestrians
- ◼ Shout to other drivers to ask them the way
- ◼ Turn into a side road, stop and check a map
- ◼ Check a map, and keep going with the traffic flow

Answer

☑ **Turn into a side road, stop and check a map**

It's easy to lose your way in an unfamiliar area. If you need to check a map or ask for directions, first find a safe place to stop.

questions   answers

Q. 1.31

Mark one answer

You are waiting to emerge from a junction. The screen pillar is restricting your view. What should you be particularly aware of?

■ Lorries

■ Buses

■ Motorcyclists

■ Coaches

Answer

 Motorcyclists

Windscreen pillars can completely block your view of pedestrians, motorcyclists and pedal cyclists. You should particularly watch out for these road users; don't just rely on a quick glance. Where possible make eye contact with them so you can be sure they have seen you too.

Q. 1.32

Mark one answer

When emerging from junctions which is most likely to obstruct your view?

■ Windscreen pillars

■ Steering wheel

■ Interior mirror

■ Windscreen wipers

Answer

 Windscreen pillars

Windscreen pillars can block your view, particularly at junctions. Those road users most at risk of not being seen are cyclists, motorcyclists and pedestrians. Never rely on just a quick glance.

Q. 1.33

Mark one answer

Windscreen pillars can obstruct your view. You should take particular care when

■ driving on a motorway

■ driving on a dual carriageway

■ approaching a one-way street

■ approaching bends and junctions

Answer

 approaching bends and junctions

Windscreen pillars can obstruct your view, particularly at bends and junctions. Look out for other road users, particularly cyclists and pedestrians, as they can be hard to see.

Q. 1.34

Mark one answer

You cannot see clearly behind when reversing. What should you do?

- ☐ Open your window to look behind
- ☐ Open the door and look behind
- ☐ Look in the nearside mirror
- ☐ Ask someone to guide you

Answer

☑ **Ask someone to guide you**

If you want to turn your car around try to find a place where you have good all-round vision. If this isn't possible and you're unable to see clearly, then get someone to guide you.

Attitude

This section looks at your attitude to other road users.

The questions will ask you about

- **Consideration**

  considering other road users. Be positive but treat them as you would wish to be treated.

- **Close following**

  not following too closely. As well as being dangerous, it can feel threatening to the driver in front.

- **Courtesy**

  treating other road users as colleagues or team members. They too are trying to complete their journey safely.

- **Priority**

  being aware that rules on priority won't always be followed by other road users. Try to be calm and tolerant if other drivers or riders break the rules.

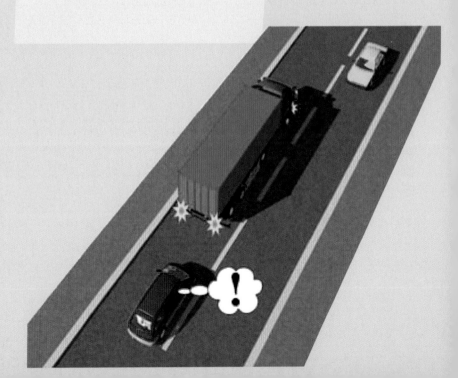

questions

answers

Q. 2.1

Mark one answer

At a pelican crossing the flashing amber light means you MUST

- ■ stop and wait for the green light
- ■ stop and wait for the red light
- ■ give way to pedestrians waiting to cross
- ■ give way to pedestrians already on the crossing

Answer

☑ **give way to pedestrians already on the crossing**

Pelican crossings are signal-controlled crossings operated by pedestrians. Push-button controls change the signals. Pelican crossings have no red-and-amber stage before green. Instead, they have a flashing amber light, which means you must give way to pedestrians already on the crossing, but if it is clear, you may continue.

Q. 2.2

Mark one answer

You should never wave people across at pedestrian crossings because

- ■ there may be another vehicle coming
- ■ they may not be looking
- ■ it is safer for you to carry on
- ■ they may not be ready to cross

Answer

☑ **there may be another vehicle coming**

If people are waiting to use a pedestrian crossing, slow down and be prepared to stop. Don't wave them across the road since another driver may not

- • have seen them
- • have seen your signal
- • be able to stop safely.

Q. 2.3

Mark one answer

At a puffin crossing what colour follows the green signal?

- ■ Steady red
- ■ Flashing amber
- ■ Steady amber
- ■ Flashing green

Answer

☑ **Steady amber**

Puffin crossings have infra-red sensors which detect when pedestrians are crossing and hold the red traffic signal until the crossing is clear. The use of a sensor means there is no flashing amber phase as there is with a pelican crossing.

questions   answers

Q. 2.4

Mark one answer

You could use the 'Two-Second Rule'

- before restarting the engine after it has stalled
- to keep a safe gap from the vehicle in front
- before using the 'Mirror-Signal-Manoeuvre' routine
- when emerging on wet roads

Answer

 to keep a safe gap from the vehicle in front

To measure this, choose a fixed reference point such as a bridge, sign or tree. When the vehicle ahead passes the object, say to yourself 'Only a fool breaks the two-second rule.' If you reach the object before you finish saying this, you're TOO CLOSE.

Q. 2.5

Mark one answer

'Tailgating' means

- using the rear door of a hatchback car
- reversing into a parking space
- following another vehicle too closely
- driving with rear fog lights on

Answer

 following another vehicle too closely

'Tailgating' is used to describe this dangerous practice, often seen in fast-moving traffic and on motorways. Following the vehicle in front too closely is dangerous because it

- restricts your view of the road ahead
- leaves you no safety margin if the vehicle in front slows down or stops suddenly.

Q. 2.6

Mark one answer

Following this vehicle too closely is unwise because

■ your brakes will overheat

■ your view ahead is increased

■ your engine will overheat

■ your view ahead is reduced

Answer

 your view ahead is reduced

Staying back will increase your view of the road ahead. This will help you to see any hazards that might occur and allow you more time to react.

Q. 2.7

Mark one answer

You are following a vehicle on a wet road. You should leave a time gap of at least

■ one second

■ two seconds

■ three seconds

■ four seconds

Answer

 four seconds

Wet roads will reduce your tyres' grip on the road. The safe separation gap of at least two seconds in dry conditions should be doubled in wet weather.

questions   *answers*

Q. 2.8

Mark one answer

You are in a line of traffic. The driver behind you is following very closely. What action should you take?

- ◼ Ignore the following driver and continue to drive within the speed limit
- ◼ Slow down, gradually increasing the gap between you and the vehicle in front
- ◼ Signal left and wave the following driver past
- ◼ Move over to a position just left of the centre line of the road

Answer

☑ **Slow down, gradually increasing the gap between you and the vehicle in front**

It can be worrying to see that the car behind is following you too closely. Give yourself a greater safety margin by easing back from the vehicle in front.

Q. 2.9

Mark one answer

A long, heavily-laden lorry is taking a long time to overtake you. What should you do?

- ◼ Speed up
- ◼ Slow down
- ◼ Hold your speed
- ◼ Change direction

Answer

☑ **Slow down**

A long lorry with a heavy load will need more time to pass you than a car, especially on an uphill stretch of road. Slow down and allow the lorry to pass.

Q. 2.10

Mark three answers

Which of the following vehicles will use blue flashing beacons?

- ◼ Motorway maintenance
- ◼ Bomb disposal
- ◼ Blood transfusion
- ◼ Police patrol
- ◼ Breakdown recovery

Answers

☑ **Bomb disposal**

☑ **Blood transfusion**

☑ **Police patrol**

When you see emergency vehicles with blue flashing beacons move out of the way as soon as it is safe to do so.

Q. 2.11

Mark three answers

Which THREE of these emergency services might have blue flashing beacons?

- Coastguard
- Bomb disposal
- Gritting lorries
- Animal ambulances
- Mountain rescue
- Doctors' cars

Answers

- ☑ **Coastguard**
- ☑ **Bomb disposal**
- ☑ **Mountain rescue**

When attending an emergency these vehicles will be travelling at speed. You should help their progress by pulling over and allowing them to pass. Do so safely. Don't stop suddenly or in a dangerous position.

Q. 2.12

Mark one answer

When being followed by an ambulance showing a flashing blue beacon you should

- pull over as soon as safely possible to let it pass
- accelerate hard to get away from it
- maintain your speed and course
- brake harshly and immediately stop in the road

Answer

- ☑ **pull over as soon as safely possible to let it pass**

Pull over in a place where the ambulance can pass safely. Check that there are no bollards or obstructions in the road that will prevent it from doing so.

Q. 2.13

Mark one answer

What type of emergency vehicle is fitted with a green flashing beacon?

- Fire engine
- Road gritter
- Ambulance
- Doctor's car

Answer

- ☑ **Doctor's car**

A green flashing beacon on a vehicle means the driver or passenger is a doctor on an emergency call. Give way to them if it's safe to do so. Be aware that the vehicle may be travelling quickly or may stop in a hurry.

questions *answers*

Q. 2.14

Mark one answer

A flashing green beacon on a vehicle means

- police on non-urgent duties
- doctor on an emergency call
- road safety patrol operating
- gritting in progress

Answer

✓ **doctor on an emergency call**

If you see a vehicle with a flashing green beacon approaching, allow it to pass when you can do so safely. Be aware that someone's life could depend on the driver making good progress through traffic.

Q. 2.15

Mark one answer

A vehicle has a flashing green beacon. What does this mean?

- A doctor is answering an emergency call
- The vehicle is slow-moving
- It is a motorway police patrol vehicle
- A vehicle is carrying hazardous chemicals

Answer

✓ **A doctor is answering an emergency call**

A doctor attending an emergency may show a green flashing beacon on their vehicle. Give way to them when you can do so safely as they will need to reach their destination quickly. Be aware that they might pull over suddenly.

Q. 2.16

Mark one answer

Diamond-shaped signs give instructions to

- tram drivers
- bus drivers
- lorry drivers
- taxi drivers

Answer

✓ **tram drivers**

These signs only apply to trams. They are directed at tram drivers but you should know their meaning so that you're aware of the priorities and are able to anticipate the actions of the driver.

Q. 2.17

Mark one answer

On a road where trams operate, which of these vehicles will be most at risk from the tram rails?

▪ Cars

▪ Cycles

▪ Buses

▪ Lorries

Answer

 Cycles

The narrow wheels of a bicycle can become stuck in the tram rails, causing the cyclist to stop suddenly, wobble or even lose balance altogether.

The tram lines are also slippery which could cause a cyclist to slide or fall off.

Q. 2.18

Mark one answer

What should you use your horn for?

▪ To alert others to your presence

▪ To allow you right of way

▪ To greet other road users

▪ To signal your annoyance

Answer

 To alert others to your presence

Your horn must not be used between 11.30 pm and 7 am in a built-up area or when you are stationary, unless a moving vehicle poses a danger. Its function is to alert other road users to your presence.

Q. 2.19

Mark one answer

You are in a one-way street and want to turn right. You should position yourself

▪ in the right-hand lane

▪ in the left-hand lane

▪ in either lane, depending on the traffic

▪ just left of the centre line

Answer

 in the right-hand lane

If you're travelling in a one-way street and wish to turn right you should take up a position in the right-hand lane. This will enable other road users not wishing to turn to proceed on the left. Indicate your intention and take up your position in good time.

Q. 2.20

Mark one answer

You wish to turn right ahead. Why should you take up the correct position in good time?

☐ To allow other drivers to pull out in front of you

☐ To give a better view into the road that you're joining

☐ To help other road users know what you intend to do

☐ To allow drivers to pass you on the right

Answer

☑ **To help other road users know what you intend to do**

If you wish to turn right into a side road take up your position in good time. Move to the centre of the road when it's safe to do so. This will allow vehicles to pass you on the left. Early planning will show other traffic what you intend to do.

Q. 2.21

Mark one answer

At which type of crossing are cyclists allowed to ride across with pedestrians?

☐ Toucan

☐ Puffin

☐ Pelican

☐ Zebra

Answer

☑ **Toucan**

A toucan crossing is designed to allow pedestrians and cyclists to cross at the same time. Look out for cyclists approaching the crossing at speed.

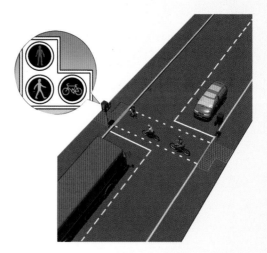

Q. 2.22

Mark one answer

A bus is stopped at a bus stop ahead of you. Its right-hand indicator is flashing. You should

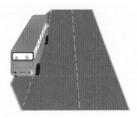

▪ flash your headlights and slow down

▪ slow down and give way if it is safe to do so

▪ sound your horn and keep going

▪ slow down and then sound your horn

Answer

☑ **slow down and give way if it is safe to do so**

Give way to buses whenever you can do so safely, especially when they signal to pull away from bus stops. Look out for people leaving the bus and crossing the road.

Q. 2.23

Mark one answer

You are travelling at the legal speed limit. A vehicle comes up quickly behind, flashing its headlights. You should

▪ accelerate to make a gap behind you

▪ touch the brakes sharply to show your brake lights

▪ maintain your speed to prevent the vehicle from overtaking

▪ allow the vehicle to overtake

Answer

☑ **allow the vehicle to overtake**

Don't enforce the speed limit by blocking another vehicle's progress. This will only lead to the other driver becoming more frustrated. Allow the other vehicle to pass when you can do so safely.

39

questions   *answers*

Q. 2.24

Mark one answer

You should ONLY flash your headlights to other road users

- ☐ to show that you are giving way
- ☐ to show that you are about to turn
- ☐ to tell them that you have right of way
- ☐ to let them know that you are there

Answer

☑ **to let them know that you are there**

You should only flash your headlights to warn others of your presence. Don't use them to

- greet others
- show impatience
- give up your priority.

Other road users could misunderstand your signal.

Q. 2.25

Mark one answer

You are approaching unmarked crossroads. How should you deal with this type of junction?

- ☐ Accelerate and keep to the middle
- ☐ Slow down and keep to the right
- ☐ Accelerate looking to the left
- ☐ Slow down and look both ways

Answer

☑ **Slow down and look both ways**

Be extra-cautious, especially when your view is restricted by hedges, bushes, walls and large vehicles etc. In the summer months these junctions can become more difficult to deal with when growing foliage may obscure your view.

Q. 2.26

Mark one answer

You are approaching a pelican crossing. The amber light is flashing. You must

- ☐ give way to pedestrians who are crossing
- ☐ encourage pedestrians to cross
- ☐ not move until the green light appears
- ☐ stop even if the crossing is clear

Answer

☑ **give way to pedestrians who are crossing**

While the pedestrians are crossing don't encourage them to cross by waving or flashing your headlights: other road users may misunderstand your signal.

Don't harass them by creeping forward or revving your engine.

Q. 2.27
Mark one answer

At puffin crossings which light will not show to a driver?

- ■ Flashing amber
- ■ Red
- ■ Steady amber
- ■ Green

Answer
 Flashing amber

A flashing amber light is shown at pelican crossings, but puffin crossings are different. They are controlled electronically and automatically detect when pedestrians are on the crossing. The phase is shortened or lengthened according to the position of the pedestrians.

Q. 2.28
Mark one answer

A two-second gap between yourself and the car in front is sufficient when conditions are

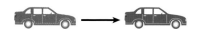

- ■ wet
- ■ good
- ■ damp
- ■ foggy

Answer
 good

In good, dry conditions an alert driver who's driving a vehicle with tyres and brakes in good condition needs to keep a distance of at least two seconds from the car in front.

Q. 2.29
Mark one answer

You are driving on a clear night. There is a steady stream of oncoming traffic. The national speed limit applies. Which lights should you use?

- ■ Full beam headlights
- ■ Sidelights
- ■ Dipped headlights
- ■ Fog lights

Answer
 Dipped headlights

Use the full beam headlights only when you can be sure that you won't dazzle other road users.

questions

answers

Q. 2.30

Mark one answer

You are driving behind a large goods vehicle. It signals left but steers to the right. You should

- slow down and let the vehicle turn
- drive on, keeping to the left
- overtake on the right of it
- hold your speed and sound your horn

Answer

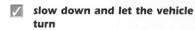 **slow down and let the vehicle turn**

Large, long vehicles need extra room when making turns at junctions. They may move out to the right in order to make a left turn. Keep well back and don't attempt to pass on the left.

Q. 2.31

Mark one answer

You are driving along this road. The red van cuts in close in front of you. What should you do?

- Accelerate to get closer to the red van
- Give a long blast on the horn
- Drop back to leave the correct separation distance
- Flash your headlights several times

Answer

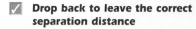 **Drop back to leave the correct separation distance**

There are times when other drivers make incorrect or ill-judged decisions. Be tolerant and try not to retaliate or react aggressively. Always consider the safety of other road users, your passengers and yourself.

Q. 2.32

Mark one answer

You are waiting in a traffic queue at night. To avoid dazzling following drivers you should

▓ apply the handbrake only

▓ apply the footbrake only

▓ switch off your headlights

▓ use both the handbrake and footbrake

Answer

✓ **apply the handbrake only**

You should consider the driver behind; brake lights can dazzle. However, if you are driving in fog it's safer to keep your foot on the footbrake. In this case it will give the vehicle behind extra warning of your presence.

Q. 2.33

Mark one answer

You are driving in traffic at the speed limit for the road. The driver behind is trying to overtake. You should

▓ move closer to the car ahead, so the driver behind has no room to overtake

▓ wave the driver behind to overtake when it is safe

▓ keep a steady course and allow the driver behind to overtake

▓ accelerate to get away from the driver behind

Answer

✓ **keep a steady course and allow the driver behind to overtake**

Keep a steady course to give the driver behind an opportunity to overtake safely. If necessary, slow down. Reacting incorrectly to another driver's impatience can lead to danger.

Q. 2.34

Mark one answer

You are driving at night on an unlit road following a slower moving vehicle. You should

▓ flash your headlights

▓ use dipped beam headlights

▓ switch off your headlights

▓ use full beam headlights

Answer

✓ **use dipped beam headlights**

If you follow another vehicle with your headlights on full beam they could dazzle the driver. Leave a safe distance and ensure that the light from your dipped beam falls short of the vehicle in front.

questions   *answers*

Q. 2.35

Mark one answer

A bus lane on your left shows no times of operation. This means it is

☐ not in operation at all

☐ only in operation at peak times

☐ in operation 24 hours a day

☐ only in operation in daylight hours

Answer

☑ **in operation 24 hours a day**

Don't drive or park in a bus lane when it's in operation. This can cause disruption to traffic and delays to public transport.

Q. 2.36

Mark two answers

You are driving along a country road. A horse and rider are approaching. What should you do?

☐ Increase your speed

☐ Sound your horn

☐ Flash your headlights

☐ Drive slowly past

☐ Give plenty of room

☐ Rev your engine

Answers

☑ **Drive slowly past**

☑ **Give plenty of room**

It's important that you reduce your speed. Passing too closely at speed could startle the horse and unseat the rider.

Q. 2.37

Mark one answer

A person herding sheep asks you to stop. You should

- ☐ ignore them as they have no authority
- ☐ stop and switch off your engine
- ☐ continue on but drive slowly
- ☐ try and get past quickly

Answer

☑ **stop and switch off your engine**

Allow the sheep to clear the road before you proceed. Animals are unpredictable and startle easily; they could turn and run into your path or into the path of another moving vehicle.

Q. 2.38

Mark one answer

When overtaking a horse and rider you should

- ☐ sound your horn as a warning
- ☐ go past as quickly as possible
- ☐ flash your headlights as a warning
- ☐ go past slowly and carefully

Answer

☑ **go past slowly and carefully**

Horses can become startled by the sound of a car engine or the rush of air caused by passing too closely. Keep well back and only pass when it is safe; leave them plenty of room. You may have to use the other side of the road to go past: if you do, first make sure there is no oncoming traffic.

Q. 2.39

Mark one answer

You are approaching a zebra crossing. Pedestrians are waiting to cross. You should

- ☐ give way to the elderly and infirm only
- ☐ slow down and prepare to stop
- ☐ use your headlights to indicate they can cross
- ☐ wave at them to cross the road

Answer

☑ **slow down and prepare to stop**

Zebra crossings have

- flashing amber beacons on both sides of the road
- black and white stripes on the crossing
- white zigzag markings on both sides of the crossing.

Where you can see pedestrians are waiting to cross, slow down and prepare to stop.

questions
answers

Q. 2.40

Mark one answer

You are driving a slow moving vehicle on a narrow winding road. You should

- keep well out to stop vehicles overtaking dangerously
- wave following vehicles past you if you think they can overtake quickly
- pull in safely when you can, to let following vehicles overtake
- give a left signal when it is safe for vehicles to overtake you

Answer

☑ **pull in safely when you can, to let following vehicles overtake**

Try not to hold up a queue of traffic. Other road users may become impatient and this could lead to reckless actions. If you're driving a slow moving vehicle and the road is narrow, look for a safe place to pull in. DON'T wave other traffic past since this could be dangerous if you or they haven't seen an oncoming vehicle.

Q. 2.41

Mark one answer

You are driving a slow moving vehicle on a narrow road. When traffic wishes to overtake you should

- take no action
- put your hazard warning lights on
- stop immediately and wave it on
- pull in safely as soon as you can do so

Answer

☑ **pull in safely as soon as you can do so**

If you're driving a slow moving vehicle and a queue of traffic builds up behind you, look for a safe place to pull in.

Letting other vehicles pass reduces frustration and sets a good example.

Q. 2.42

Mark one answer

You are driving a slow-moving vehicle on a narrow winding road. In order to let other vehicles overtake you should

- wave to them to pass
- pull in when you can
- show a left turn signal
- keep left and hold your speed

Answer

☑ **pull in when you can**

Don't frustrate other road users by driving for long distances with a queue of traffic behind you. This could lead them into losing concentration or making ill-judged decisions.

questions   answers

Q. 2.43

Mark one answer

A vehicle pulls out in front of you at a junction. What should you do?

- Swerve past it and sound your horn
- Flash your headlights and drive up close behind
- Slow down and be ready to stop
- Accelerate past it immediately

Answer

☑ **Slow down and be ready to stop**

Try to be ready for the unexpected. Plan ahead and learn to anticipate hazards. You'll then give yourself more time to react to any problems that might occur.

Be tolerant of the behaviour of other road users who don't behave correctly.

Q. 2.44

Mark one answer

You stop for pedestrians waiting to cross at a zebra crossing. They do not start to cross. What should you do?

- Be patient and wait
- Sound your horn
- Carry on
- Wave them to cross

Answer

☑ **Be patient and wait**

If you stop for pedestrians and they don't start to cross don't wave them across or sound your horn.

This could be dangerous if another vehicle is approaching and hasn't seen or heard your signal.

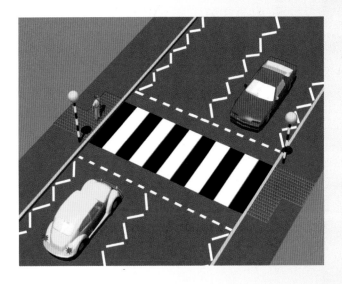

questions *answers*

Q. 2.45

Mark one answer

You are following this lorry. You should keep well back from it to

- give you a good view of the road ahead
- stop following traffic from rushing through the junction
- prevent traffic behind you from overtaking
- allow you to hurry through the traffic lights if they change

Answer

☑ **give you a good view of the road ahead**

By keeping well back you will increase your width of vision around the rear of the lorry. This will allow you to see further down the road and be prepared for any hazards.

Q. 2.46

Mark one answer

You are approaching a red light at a puffin crossing. Pedestrians are on the crossing. The red light will stay on until

- you start to edge forward on to the crossing
- the pedestrians have reached a safe position
- the pedestrians are clear of the front of your vehicle
- a driver from the opposite direction reaches the crossing

Answer

☑ **the pedestrians have reached a safe position**

The electronic device will automatically detect that the pedestrians have reached a safe position. Don't proceed until the green light shows it is safe for vehicles to do so.

Q. 2.47

Mark one answer

Which instrument panel warning light would show that headlights are on full beam?

Answer

You should be aware of where all the warning lights and visual aids are on the vehicle you are driving. If you are driving a vehicle for the first time you should take time to check all the controls.

Safety and your vehicle

This section looks at safety and your vehicle.

The questions will ask you about

- **Fault detection**

  being able to detect minor faults on your vehicle.

- **Defects and their effects on safety**

  being aware that an unroadworthy vehicle might endanger your passengers or other road users.

- **Use of safety equipment**

  making sure you have any necessary training.

- **Emissions**

  making sure your vehicle complies with current emissions regulations.

- **Noise**

  being aware that vehicles are noisy. Prevent excessive noise, especially at night.

- **Vehicle security**

  taking sensible precautions to avoid vehicle theft and break-ins.

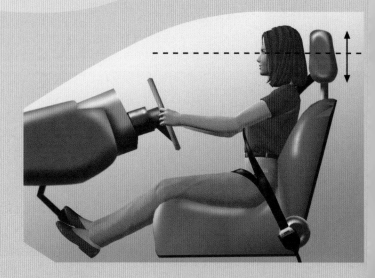

questions

answers

Q. 3.1

Mark one answer

Which of these, if allowed to get low, could cause an accident?

■ Antifreeze level

■ Brake fluid level

■ Battery water level

■ Radiator coolant level

Answer

☑ **Brake fluid level**

You should carry out frequent checks on all fluid levels but particularly brake fluid. As the friction material on your brake shoes or pads wears down, the brake fluid level will fall. If it falls below the minimum mark on the fluid reservoir, air could enter the hydraulic system and this would lead to loss of braking efficiency.

Q. 3.2

Mark two answers

Which TWO are badly affected if the tyres are under-inflated?

■ Braking

■ Steering

■ Changing gear

■ Parking

Answers

☑ **Braking**

☑ **Steering**

Your tyres are your only contact with the road so it is very important to ensure that they are free from defects, have sufficient tread depth and are correctly inflated. Correct tyre pressures help reduce the risk of skidding and provide a safer and more comfortable drive or ride.

Q. 3.3

Mark three answers

Motor vehicles can harm the environment. This has resulted in

■ air pollution

■ damage to buildings

■ reduced health risks

■ improved public transport

■ less use of electrical vehicles

■ using up natural resources

Answers

☑ **air pollution**

☑ **damage to buildings**

☑ **using up natural resources**

Exhaust emissions are harmful to health and this form of pollution, together with vibration from heavy traffic, causes damage to buildings.

Petrol and diesel fuels come from a finite and non-renewable source. Anything you can do to reduce the amount of these fuels that you use will help the environment.

questions   *answers*

Q. 3.4

Mark three answers

Excessive or uneven tyre wear can be caused by faults in which THREE?

- ☐ The gearbox
- ☐ The braking system
- ☐ The accelerator
- ☐ The exhaust system
- ☐ Wheel alignment
- ☐ The suspension

Answers

- ☑ **The braking system**
- ☑ **Wheel alignment**
- ☑ **The suspension**

Regular servicing will help to detect faults at an early stage and this will avoid the risk of minor faults becoming serious or even dangerous.

Q. 3.5

Mark one answer

You must NOT sound your horn

- ☐ between 10 pm and 6 am in a built-up area
- ☐ at any time in a built-up area
- ☐ between 11.30 pm and 7 am in a built-up area
- ☐ between 11.30 pm and 6 am on any road

Answer

- ☑ **between 11.30 pm and 7 am in a built-up area**

Vehicles can be noisy. Every effort must be made to prevent excessive noise, especially in built-up areas at night. Don't

- rev the engine
- sound the horn

unnecessarily.

It is illegal to sound your horn in a built-up area between 11.30 pm and 7 am, except when another vehicle poses a danger.

questions
answers

Q. 3.6

Mark three answers

The pictured vehicle is 'environmentally friendly' because it

- reduces noise pollution
- uses diesel fuel
- uses electricity
- uses unleaded fuel
- reduces parking spaces
- reduces town traffic

Answers

- ☑ **reduces noise pollution**
- ☑ **uses electricity**
- ☑ **reduces town traffic**

Trams are powered by electricity and therefore do not emit exhaust fumes. They are also much quieter than petrol or diesel engines and can carry a large number of passengers.

Q. 3.7

Mark one answer

Supertrams or Light Rapid Transit (LRT) systems are environmentally friendly because

- they use diesel power
- they use quieter roads
- they use electric power
- they do not operate during rush hour

Answer

- ☑ **they use electric power**

This means that they do not emit toxic fumes, which add to city pollution problems. They are also a lot quieter and smoother to ride on.

Q. 3.8

Mark one answer

'Red routes' in major cities have been introduced to

- raise the speed limits
- help the traffic flow
- provide better parking
- allow lorries to load more freely

Answer

- ☑ **help the traffic flow**

Traffic jams today are often caused by the volume of traffic. However, inconsiderate parking can lead to the closure of an inside lane or traffic having to wait for oncoming vehicles. Driving slowly in traffic increases fuel consumption and causes a build-up of exhaust fumes.

questions

answers

Q. 3.9

Mark one answer

In some narrow residential streets you will find a speed limit of

■ 20 mph

■ 25 mph

■ 35 mph

■ 40 mph

Answer

 20 mph

In some built-up areas, you may find the speed limit reduced to 20 mph. Driving at a slower speed will help give you the time and space to see and deal safely with hazards such as pedestrians and parked cars.

Q. 3.10

Mark one answer

Road humps, chicanes, and narrowings are

■ always at major road works

■ used to increase traffic speed

■ at toll-bridge approaches only

■ traffic calming measures

Answer

 traffic calming measures

Traffic calming measures help keep vehicle speeds low in sensitive areas.

A pedestrian is much more likely to survive an accident with a motor vehicle travelling at 20 mph than at 40 mph.

Q. 3.11

Mark one answer

The purpose of a catalytic converter is to reduce

■ fuel consumption

■ the risk of fire

■ toxic exhaust gases

■ engine wear

Answer

 toxic exhaust gases

Catalytic converters are designed to reduce toxic emissions by up to 90%. They work more efficiently when the engine has reached its normal working temperature.

Q. 3.12

Mark one answer

Catalytic converters are fitted to make the

- ▪ engine produce more power
- ▪ exhaust system easier to replace
- ▪ engine run quietly
- ▪ exhaust fumes cleaner

Answer

 **exhaust fumes cleaner**

Harmful gases in the exhaust system pollute the atmosphere. These gases are reduced by up to 90% if a catalytic converter is fitted. Cleaner air benefits everyone, especially people who live or work near congested roads.

Q. 3.13

Mark one answer

It is essential that tyre pressures are checked regularly. When should this be done?

- ▪ After any lengthy journey
- ▪ After travelling at high speed
- ▪ When tyres are hot
- ▪ When tyres are cold

Answer

When tyres are cold

When you check the tyre pressures do so when the tyres are cold. This will give you a more accurate reading. The heat generated from a long journey will raise the pressure inside the tyre.

Q. 3.14

Mark one answer

When should you NOT use your horn in a built-up area?

- ▪ Between 8 pm and 8 am
- ▪ Between 9 pm and dawn
- ▪ Between dusk and 8 am
- ▪ Between 11.30 pm and 7 am

Answer

Between 11.30 pm and 7 am

Only sound your horn to prevent an accident. If you need to let someone know you are there, you could flash your headlights instead.

questions   *answers*

Q. 3.15

Mark one answer

You will use more fuel if your tyres are

- under-inflated
- of different makes
- over-inflated
- new and hardly used

Answer

✓ **under-inflated**

Check your tyre pressures frequently – normally once a week. If pressures are lower than those recommended by the manufacturer, there will be more 'rolling resistance'. The engine will have to work harder to overcome this, leading to increased fuel consumption.

Q. 3.16

Mark two answers

How should you dispose of a used battery?

- Take it to a local authority site
- Put it in the dustbin
- Break it up into pieces
- Leave it on waste land
- Take it to a garage
- Burn it on a fire

Answers

✓ **Take it to a local authority site**

✓ **Take it to a garage**

Batteries contain acid which is hazardous and must be disposed of safely.

Q. 3.17

Mark one answer

What is most likely to cause high fuel consumption?

- Poor steering control
- Accelerating around bends
- Staying in high gears
- Harsh braking and accelerating

Answer

✓ **Harsh braking and accelerating**

Accelerating and braking gently and smoothly will help to save fuel, reduce wear on your vehicle and is better for the environment.

questions

answers

Q. 3.18

Mark one answer

The fluid level in your battery is low. What should you top it up with?

- Battery acid
- Distilled water
- Engine oil
- Engine coolant

Answer

 Distilled water

Some modern batteries are maintenance-free. Check your vehicle handbook and, if necessary, make sure that the plates in each battery cell are covered.

Q. 3.19

Mark one answer

You need top up your battery. What level should you fill to?

- The top of the battery
- Half-way up the battery
- Just below the cell plates
- Just above the cell plates

Answer

 Just above the cell plates

Top up the battery with distilled water and make sure each cell plate is covered.

Q. 3.20

Mark one answer

You have too much oil in your engine. What could this cause?

- Low oil pressure
- Engine overheating
- Chain wear
- Oil leaks

Answer

 Oil leaks

Too much oil in the engine will create excess pressure and could damage engine seals and cause oil leaks. Any excess oil should be drained off.

questions

answers

Q. 3.21

Mark one answer

You are parking on a two way road at night. The speed limit is 40 mph. You should park on the

- left with parking lights on
- left with no lights on
- right with parking lights on
- right with dipped headlights on

Answer

✓ **left with parking lights on**

On a two way road you may only park at night, without leaving the vehicle's lights on, if you're facing in the direction of the traffic flow, the road has a speed limit of 30 mph or less and you're at least 10 metres (32 feet) away from any junction.

Q. 3.22

Mark one answer

You are parked on the road at night. Where must you use parking lights?

- Where there are continuous white lines in the middle of the road
- Where the speed limit exceeds 30 mph
- Where you are facing oncoming traffic
- Where you are near a bus stop

Answer

✓ **Where the speed limit exceeds 30 mph**

When parking at night, park in the direction of the traffic. This will enable other road users to see the reflectors on the rear of your vehicle. Use your parking lights if the speed limit is over 30 mph.

Q. 3.23

Mark four answers

Which FOUR of these MUST be in good working order for your car to be roadworthy?

- Temperature gauge
- Speedometer
- Windscreen washers
- Windscreen wiper
- Oil warning light
- Horn

Answers

✓ **Speedometer**

✓ **Windscreen washers**

✓ **Windscreen wiper**

✓ **Horn**

You should also regularly check

- lights (you may need to get someone to help you with this)
- indicators
- battery electrolyte level (if necessary)
- steering
- oil
- water and other fluid levels
- suspension.

questions

Q. 3.24

Mark one answer

New petrol-engined cars must be fitted with catalytic converters. The reason for this is to

- ■ control exhaust noise levels
- ■ prolong the life of the exhaust system
- ■ allow the exhaust system to be recycled
- ■ reduce harmful exhaust emissions

Answer

☑ **reduce harmful exhaust emissions**

We should all be concerned about the effect traffic has on our environment. Fumes from vehicles are polluting the air around us. Catalytic converters act like a filter, removing some of the toxic waste from exhaust gases.

Q. 3.25

Mark one answer

What can cause heavy steering?

- ■ Driving on ice
- ■ Badly worn brakes
- ■ Over-inflated tyres
- ■ Under-inflated tyres

Answer

☑ **Under-inflated tyres**

If your tyres don't have enough air in them they'll drag against the surface of the road and this makes the steering feel heavy.

As well as steering, under-inflated tyres can affect

- braking
- cornering
- fuel consumption.

It is an offence to drive with tyres that are not properly inflated.

Q. 3.26

Mark two answers

Driving with under-inflated tyres can affect

- ■ engine temperature
- ■ fuel consumption
- ■ braking
- ■ oil pressure

Answers

☑ **fuel consumption**

☑ **braking**

Keeping your vehicle's tyres correctly inflated is a legal requirement.

Driving with correctly inflated tyres will use less fuel and your vehicle will brake more safely.

questions answers

Q. 3.27

Mark two answers

Excessive or uneven tyre wear can be caused by faults in the

- gearbox
- braking system
- suspension
- exhaust system

Answers

- ☑ **braking system**
- ☑ **suspension**

Uneven wear on your tyres can be caused by the condition of your vehicle. Having it serviced regularly will ensure that the brakes, steering and wheel alignment are maintained in good order.

Q. 3.28

Mark one answer

The main cause of brake fade is

- the brakes overheating
- air in the brake fluid
- oil on the brakes
- the brakes out of adjustment

Answer

- ☑ **the brakes overheating**

If your vehicle is fitted with drum brakes they can get hot and lose efficiency. This happens when they're used continually, such as on a long, steep, downhill stretch of road. Using a lower gear will assist the braking and help prevent the vehicle gaining momentum.

Q. 3.29

Mark one answer

Your anti-lock brakes warning light stays on. You should

- check the brake fluid level
- check the footbrake free play
- check that the handbrake is released
- have the brakes checked immediately

Answer

- ☑ **have the brakes checked immediately**

Only drive to a garage if it is safe to do so. Consult the vehicle handbook or garage before driving the vehicle.

Q. 3.30

Mark one answer

What does this instrument panel light mean when lit?

▪ Gear lever in park

▪ Gear lever in neutral

▪ Handbrake on

▪ Handbrake off

Answer

✓ **Handbrake on**

If you are not sure about any lights or switches in your vehicle check the vehicle manual. You should be aware that a light on the instrument panel could be a warning about the condition of your vehicle.

Q. 3.31

Mark one answer

While driving, this warning light on your dashboard comes on. It means

▪ a fault in the braking system

▪ the engine oil is low

▪ a rear light has failed

▪ your seat belt is not fastened

Answer

✓ **a fault in the braking system**

Don't ignore this warning light. A fault in your braking system could have dangerous consequences.

Q. 3.32

Mark one answer

It is important to wear suitable shoes when you are driving. Why is this?

▪ To prevent wear on the pedals

▪ To maintain control of the pedals

▪ To enable you to adjust your seat

▪ To enable you to walk for assistance if you break down

Answer

✓ **To maintain control of the pedals**

When you're going to drive, ensure that you're wearing suitable clothing.

Comfortable shoes will ensure that you have proper control of the foot pedals.

questions

answers

Q. 3.33

Mark one answer

A properly adjusted head restraint will

- make you more comfortable
- help you to avoid neck injury
- help you to relax
- help you to maintain your driving position

Answer

✓ **help you to avoid neck injury**

The restraint should be adjusted so that it gives maximum protection to the head. This will help in the event of a rear-end collision.

Q. 3.34

Mark one answer

What will reduce the risk of neck injury resulting from a collision?

- An air-sprung seat
- Anti-lock brakes
- A collapsible steering wheel
- A properly adjusted head restraint

Answer

✓ **A properly adjusted head restraint**

If you're involved in a collision, head restraints will reduce the risk of neck injury. They must be properly adjusted. Make sure they aren't positioned too low – in an accident this could cause damage to the neck.

Q. 3.35

Mark one answer

You are driving a friend's children home from school. They are both under 14 years old. Who is responsible for making sure they wear a seat belt?

- An adult passenger
- The children
- You, the driver
- Your friend

Answer

✓ **You, the driver**

Child passengers should always be secured and safe. They should be encouraged to fasten their seat belts themselves from an early age so that it becomes a matter of routine. As the driver you must check that the seat belts are fastened securely; it's your responsibility.

Q. 3.36

Mark one answer

Car passengers MUST wear a seat belt if one is available, unless they are

- ▓ under 14 years old
- ▓ under 1.5 metres (5 feet) in height
- ▓ sitting in the rear seat
- ▓ exempt for medical reasons

Answer

☑ **exempt for medical reasons**

If you have adult passengers it is their responsibility to wear a seat belt, but you should still remind them to put them on as they get in the car.

Q. 3.37

Mark one answer

You are testing your suspension. You notice that your vehicle keeps bouncing when you press down on the front wing. What does this mean?

- ▓ Worn tyres
- ▓ Tyres under-inflated
- ▓ Steering wheel not located centrally
- ▓ Worn shock absorbers

Answer

☑ **Worn shock absorbers**

If you find that your vehicle bounces as you drive around a corner or bend in the road, the shock absorbers might be worn. Press down on the front wing and if the vehicle continues to bounce, take it to be checked by a qualified mechanic.

Q. 3.38

Mark one answer

A roof rack fitted to your car will

- ▓ reduce fuel consumption
- ▓ improve the road handling
- ▓ make your car go faster
- ▓ increase fuel consumption

Answer

☑ **increase fuel consumption**

If you are carrying anything on a roof rack, make sure that any cover is securely fitted and does not flap about while driving. Aerodynamically designed roof boxes are available which reduce wind resistance and in turn fuel consumption.

questions

answers

Q. 3.39

Mark one answer

It is illegal to drive with tyres that

- have been bought second-hand
- have a large deep cut in the side wall
- are of different makes
- are of different tread patterns

Answer

 have a large deep cut in the side wall

When checking your tyres for cuts and bulges in the side walls don't forget the inner walls (ie. those facing each other under the vehicle).

Q. 3.40

Mark one answer

The legal minimum depth of tread for car tyres over three quarters of the breadth is

- 1 mm
- 1.6 mm
- 2.5 mm
- 4 mm

Answer

✓ **1.6 mm**

Tyres must have sufficient depth of tread to give them a good grip on the road surface. The legal minimum for cars is 1.6 mm.

This depth should be across the central three quarters of the breadth of the tyre and around the entire circumference.

Q. 3.41

Mark one answer

You are carrying two 13 year old children and their parents in your car. Who is responsible for seeing that the children wear seat belts?

- The children's parents
- You, the driver
- The front-seat passenger
- The children

Answer

✓ **You, the driver**

Seat belts save lives and reduce the risk of injury. If you are carrying passengers under 14 years of age it's your responsibility as the driver to ensure that their seat belts are fastened or they are seated in an approved child restraint.

Q. 3.42

Mark one answer

When a roof rack is not in use it should be removed. Why is this?

■ It will affect the suspension

■ It is illegal

■ It will affect your braking

■ It will waste fuel

Answer

☑ **It will waste fuel**

We are all responsible for the environment we live in. If each driver takes responsibility for conserving fuel, together it will make a difference.

Q. 3.43

Mark two answers

You have a loose filler cap on your diesel fuel tank. This will

■ waste fuel and money

■ make roads slippery for other road users

■ improve your vehicles fuel consumption

■ increase the level of exhaust emissions

Answers

☑ **waste fuel and money**

☑ **make roads slippery for other road users**

Diesel fuel is especially slippery if spilled on a wet road. At the end of a dry spell of weather you should be aware that the road surfaces may have a high level of diesel spillage that hasn't been washed away by rain.

Q. 3.44

Mark three answers

How can you, as a driver, help the environment?

■ By reducing your speed

■ By gentle acceleration

■ By using leaded fuel

■ By driving faster

■ By harsh acceleration

■ By servicing your vehicle properly

Answers

☑ **By reducing your speed**

☑ **By gentle acceleration**

☑ **By servicing your vehicle properly**

Rapid acceleration and heavy braking lead to greater fuel consumption. They also increase wear and tear on your vehicle.

Having your vehicle regularly serviced means your engine will maintain its efficiency, produce cleaner emissions and lengthen its life.

questions

answers

Q. 3.45

Mark three answers

To help the environment, you can avoid wasting fuel by

- having your vehicle properly serviced
- making sure your tyres are correctly inflated
- not over-revving in the lower gears
- driving at higher speeds where possible
- keeping an empty roof rack properly fitted
- servicing your vehicle less regularly

Answers

- ✓ **having your vehicle properly serviced**
- ✓ **making sure your tyres are correctly inflated**
- ✓ **not over-revving in the lower gears**

If you don't have your vehicle serviced regularly, the engine will not burn all the fuel efficiently. This will cause excess gases to be discharged into the atmosphere.

Q. 3.46

Mark three answers

To reduce the volume of traffic on the roads you could

- use public transport more often
- share a car when possible
- walk or cycle on short journeys
- travel by car at all times
- use a car with a smaller engine
- drive in a bus lane

Answers

- ✓ **use public transport more often**
- ✓ **share a car when possible**
- ✓ **walk or cycle on short journeys**

Walking or cycling are good ways to get exercise. Using public transport also gives the opportunity for exercise if you walk to the railway station or bus stop. Leave the car at home whenever you can.

Q. 3.47

Mark three answers

Which THREE of the following are most likely to waste fuel?

- Reducing your speed
- Carrying unnecessary weight
- Using the wrong grade of fuel
- Under-inflated tyres
- Using different brands of fuel
- A fitted, empty roof rack

Answers

- ✓ **Carrying unnecessary weight**
- ✓ **Under-inflated tyres**
- ✓ **A fitted, empty roof rack**

Wasting fuel costs you, the driver, hard-earned cash. It also causes unnecessary pollution to the atmosphere.

Failing to carry out basic maintenance checks, such as tyre pressures, can affect the handling of your vehicle as well as increasing fuel consumption. It is also an offence for which you can be prosecuted.

questions

answers

Q. 3.48

Mark one answer

To avoid spillage after refuelling, you should make sure that

■ your tank is only 3/4 full

■ you have used a locking filler cap

■ you check your fuel gauge is working

■ your filler cap is securely fastened

Answer

☑ **your filler cap is securely fastened**

When learning to drive it is a good idea to practise filling your car with fuel. Ask your instructor if you can use a petrol station and fill the fuel tank yourself. You need to know where the filler cap is located on the car you are driving in order to park on the correct side of the pump. Take care not to overfill the tank or spill fuel. Make sure you secure the filler cap as soon as you have replaced the fuel nozzle.

Q. 3.49

Mark three answers

Which THREE things can you, as a road user, do to help the environment?

■ Cycle when possible

■ Drive on under-inflated tyres

■ Use the choke for as long as possible on a cold engine

■ Have your vehicle properly tuned and serviced

■ Watch the traffic and plan ahead

■ Brake as late as possible without skidding

Answers

☑ **Cycle when possible**

☑ **Have your vehicle properly tuned and serviced**

☑ **Watch the traffic and plan ahead**

Although the car is a convenient form of transport it can also cause damage to health and the environment, especially when used on short journeys. Before you travel consider other types of transport. Walking and cycling are better for your health and public transport can be quicker, more convenient and less stressful than driving.

Q. 3.50

Mark three answers

As a driver you can cause MORE damage to the environment by

■ choosing a fuel efficient vehicle

■ making a lot of short journeys

■ driving in as high a gear as possible

■ accelerating as quickly as possible

■ having your vehicle regularly serviced

■ using leaded fuel

Answers

☑ **making a lot of short journeys**

☑ **accelerating as quickly as possible**

☑ **using leaded fuel**

For short journeys it may be quicker to walk, or cycle, which is far better for your health. Time spent stationary in traffic with the engine running is damaging to health, the environment and expensive in fuel costs.

questions answers

Q. 3.51

Mark one answer

Extra care should be taken when refuelling, because diesel fuel when spilt is

- sticky
- odourless
- clear
- slippery

Answer

✓ **slippery**

If you are using diesel or are at a pump which has a diesel facility be aware that there may be spilt fuel on the ground. Fuel contamination on the soles of your shoes may cause them to slip when using the foot pedals.

Q. 3.52

Mark one answer

To help protect the environment you should NOT

- remove your roof rack when unloaded
- use your car for very short journeys
- walk, cycle, or use public transport
- empty the boot of unnecessary weight

Answer

✓ **use your car for very short journeys**

Try not to use your car as a matter of routine. For shorter journeys, consider walking or cycling instead – this is much better for both you and the environment.

Q. 3.53

Mark three answers

Which THREE does the law require you to keep in good condition?

- Gears
- Transmission
- Headlights
- Windscreen
- Seat belts

Answers

✓ **Headlights**

✓ **Windscreen**

✓ **Seat belts**

Also check the

- lights – get someone to help you check the brake lights
- indicators
- battery – this may be maintenance-free and not need topping up
- steering – check for 'play' in the steering
- oil
- water
- suspension.

Once you've moved off, check that the speedometer is working.

Q. 3.54

Mark one answer

Driving at 70 mph uses more fuel than driving at 50 mph by up to

- 10%
- 30%
- 75%
- 100%

Answer

✓ **30%**

Your vehicle will be cheaper to run if you avoid heavy acceleration. The higher the engine revs, the more fuel you will use.

Q. 3.55

Mark one answer

Your vehicle pulls to one side when braking. You should

- change the tyres around
- consult your garage as soon as possible
- pump the pedal when braking
- use your handbrake at the same time

Answer

✓ **consult your garage as soon as possible**

The brakes on your vehicle must be effective and properly adjusted. If your vehicle pulls to one side when braking, take it to be checked by a qualified mechanic. Don't take risks.

Q. 3.56

Mark one answer

As a driver you can help reduce pollution levels in town centres by

- driving more quickly
- using leaded fuel
- walking or cycling
- driving short journeys

Answer

✓ **walking or cycling**

Using a vehicle for short journeys means the engine does not have time to reach its normal running temperature. When an engine is running below its normal running temperature it produces increased amounts of pollution.

Walking and cycling do not create pollution and have health benefits as well.

questions   answers

Q. 3.57

Mark one answer

Unbalanced wheels on a car may cause

- ▪ the steering to pull to one side
- ▪ the steering to vibrate
- ▪ the brakes to fail
- ▪ the tyres to deflate

Answer

 the steering to vibrate

If your wheels are out of balance it will cause the steering to vibrate at certain speeds. It is not a fault that will rectify itself. You will have to take your vehicle to a garage or tyre fitting firm as this is specialist work.

Q. 3.58

Mark two answers

Turning the steering wheel while your car is stationary can cause damage to the

- ▪ gearbox
- ▪ engine
- ▪ brakes
- ▪ steering
- ▪ tyres

Answers

✓ **steering**

✓ **tyres**

Turning the steering wheel when the car is not moving can cause unnecessary wear to the tyres and steering mechanism. This is known as 'dry' steering.

Q. 3.59

Mark one answer

How can you reduce the chances of your car being broken into when leaving it unattended?

- ▪ Take all contents with you
- ▪ Park near a taxi rank
- ▪ Place any valuables on the floor
- ▪ Park near a fire station

Answer

✓ **Take all contents with you**

When leaving your car take all valuables with you if you can, otherwise lock them out of sight.

Q. 3.60

Mark one answer

You have to leave valuables in your car. It would be safer to

- ■ put them in a carrier bag
- ■ park near a school entrance
- ■ lock them out of sight
- ■ park near a bus stop

Answer

☑ **lock them out of sight**

If you have to leave valuables in your car, always lock them out of sight. If you can see them, so can a thief.

Q. 3.61

Mark one answer

How could you deter theft from your car when leaving it unattended?

- ■ Leave valuables in a carrier bag
- ■ Lock valuables out of sight
- ■ Put valuables on the seats
- ■ Leave valuables on the floor

Answer

☑ **Lock valuables out of sight**

If you can see valuables in your car so can a thief. If you can't take them with you lock them out of sight or you risk losing them, as well as having your car damaged.

Q. 3.62

Mark one answer

Which of the following may help to deter a thief from stealing your car?

- ■ Always keeping the headlights on
- ■ Fitting reflective glass windows
- ■ Always keeping the interior light on
- ■ Etching the car number on the windows

Answer

☑ **Etching the car number on the windows**

Having your car registration number etched on all your windows is a cheap and effective way to deter professional car thieves.

questions   answers

Q. 3.63

Mark one answer

How can you help to prevent your car radio being stolen?

▪ Park in an unlit area

▪ Hide the radio with a blanket

▪ Park near a busy junction

▪ Install a security coded radio

Answer

☑ **Install a security coded radio**

A security coded radio can deter thieves as it is likely to be of little use when removed from the vehicle.

Q. 3.64

Mark one answer

Which of the following should not be kept in your vehicle?

▪ A first aid kit

▪ A road atlas

▪ The tax disc

▪ The vehicle documents

Answer

☑ **The vehicle documents**

Never leave the vehicles documents inside it. They would help a thief dispose of the vehicle more easily.

Q. 3.65

Mark one answer

What should you do when leaving your vehicle?

▪ Put valuable documents under the seats

▪ Remove all valuables

▪ Cover valuables with a blanket

▪ Leave the interior light on

Answer

☑ **Remove all valuables**

When leaving your vehicle unattended it is best to take valuables with you. If you can't, then lock them out of sight in the boot. If you can see valuables in your car, so can a thief.

questions answers

Q. 3.66

Mark one answer

You are parking your car. You have some valuables which you are unable to take with you. What should you do?

 Park near a police station

■ Put them under the drivers seat

■ Lock them out of sight

■ Park in an unlit side road

Answer

☑ **Lock them out of sight**

Your vehicle is like a shop window for thieves. Either remove all valuables or lock them out of sight.

Q. 3.67

Mark one answer

Which of these is most likely to deter the theft of your vehicle?

 An immobiliser

■ Tinted windows

■ Locking wheel nuts

■ A sun screen

Answer

☑ **An immobiliser**

An immobiliser makes it more difficult for your vehicle to be driven off by a thief. It is a particular deterrent to opportunist thieves.

Q. 3.68

Mark one answer

Wherever possible, which one of the following should you do when parking at night?

 Park in a quiet car park

■ Park in a well lit area

■ Park facing against the flow of traffic

■ Park next to a busy junction

Answer

☑ **Park in a well lit area**

If you are away from home, try to avoid leaving your vehicle unattended in poorly-lit areas. If possible park in a secure, well-lit car park.

questions   answers

Q. 3.69

Mark one answer

When parking and leaving your car you should

- park under a shady tree
- remove the tax disc
- park in a quiet road
- engage the steering lock

Answer

✓ **engage the steering lock**

When you leave your car always engage the steering lock. This increases the security of your vehicle, as the ignition key is needed to release the steering lock.

Q. 3.70

Mark one answer

Rear facing baby seats should NEVER be used on a seat protected with

- an airbag
- seat belts
- head restraints
- seat covers

Answer

✓ **an airbag**

NEVER fit a rear-facing baby seat in a seat protected by an airbag. In an accident the airbag would hit the baby seat with great force and the child would be at risk of receiving serious or possibly fatal injuries.

Q. 3.71

Mark one answer

When leaving your vehicle parked and unattended you should

- park near a busy junction
- park in a housing estate
- remove the key and lock it
- leave the left indicator on

Answer

✓ **remove the key and lock it**

An unlocked car is an open invitation to thieves.

Leaving the keys in the ignition not only makes your car easy to steal, it could also invalidate your insurance.

Q. 3.72

Mark one answer

How can you lessen the risk of your vehicle being broken into at night?

- ■ Leave it in a well lit area
- ■ Park in a quiet side road
- ■ Don't engage the steering lock
- ■ Park in a poorly lit area

Answer

☑ **Leave it in a well lit area**

Having your vehicle broken into or stolen can be very distressing and inconvenient. Avoid leaving your vehicle unattended in poorly lit areas.

Q. 3.73

Mark one answer

To help keep your car secure you could join a

- ■ vehicle breakdown organisation
- ■ vehicle watch scheme
- ■ advanced drivers scheme
- ■ car maintenance class

Answer

☑ **vehicle watch scheme**

The vehicle watch scheme helps reduce the risk of having your car stolen. By displaying high visibility vehicle watch stickers in your car you are inviting the police to stop your vehicle if seen in use between midnight and 5 am.

Q. 3.74

Mark two answers

Which TWO of the following will improve fuel consumption?

- ■ Reducing your road speed
- ■ Planning well ahead
- ■ Late and harsh braking
- ■ Driving in lower gears
- ■ Short journeys with a cold engine
- ■ Rapid acceleration

Answers

☑ **Reducing your road speed**

☑ **Planning well ahead**

Harsh braking, constant gear changes and harsh acceleration increase fuel consumption. An engine uses less fuel when travelling at a constant low speed.

You need to look well ahead so you are able to anticipate hazards early. Easing off the accelerator and timing your approach, at junctions, for example, could actually improve the fuel consumption of your vehicle.

questions answers

Q. 3.75

Mark one answer

You service your own vehicle. How should you get rid of the old engine oil?

- Take it to a local authority site
- Pour it down a drain
- Tip it into a hole in the ground
- Put it into your dustbin

Answer

 Take it to a local authority site

It is illegal to pour engine oil down any drain. Oil is a pollutant and harmful to wildlife. Dispose of it safely at an authorised site.

Q. 3.76

Mark one answer

On your vehicle, where would you find a catalytic converter?

- In the fuel tank
- In the air filter
- On the cooling system
- On the exhaust system

Answer

 On the exhaust system

Although carbon dioxide is still produced, a catalytic converter reduces the toxic and polluting gases by up to 90%. Unleaded fuel must be used in vehicles fitted with a catalytic converter.

Q. 3.77

Mark one answer

Why do MOT tests include a strict exhaust emission test?

- To recover the cost of expensive garage equipment
- To help protect the environment against pollution
- To discover which fuel supplier is used the most
- To make sure diesel and petrol engines emit the same fumes

Answer

✓ **To help protect the environment against pollution**

Emission tests are carried out to ensure your vehicle's engine is operating efficiently. This ensures the pollution produced by the engine is kept to a minimum.

If your vehicle is not serviced regularly, it may fail the annual MOT test.

Q. 3.78

Mark three answers

To reduce the damage your vehicle causes to the environment you should

- ■ use narrow side streets
- ■ avoid harsh acceleration
- ■ brake in good time
- ■ anticipate well ahead
- ■ use busy routes

Answers

- ☑ **avoid harsh acceleration**
- ☑ **brake in good time**
- ☑ **anticipate well ahead**

By looking well ahead and recognising hazards early you can avoid last-minute harsh braking. Watch the traffic flow and look well ahead for potential hazards so you can control your speed accordingly. Avoid over-revving the engine and accelerating harshly as this increases wear to the engine and uses more fuel.

Q. 3.79

Mark one answer

Your vehicle has a catalytic converter. Its purpose is to reduce

- ■ exhaust noise
- ■ fuel consumption
- ■ exhaust emissions
- ■ engine noise

Answer

- ☑ **exhaust emissions**

Catalytic converters reduce the harmful gases given out by the engine. The gases are changed by a chemical process as they pass through a special filter.

Q. 3.80

Mark two answers

A properly serviced vehicle will give

- ■ lower insurance premiums
- ■ you a refund on your road tax
- ■ better fuel economy
- ■ cleaner exhaust emissions

Answers

- ☑ **better fuel economy**
- ☑ **cleaner exhaust emissions**

When you purchase your vehicle, check at what intervals you should have it serviced. This can vary depending on model and manufacturer. Use the service manual and keep it up to date. The cost of a service may well be less than the cost of running a poorly maintained vehicle.

questions answers

Q. 3.81

Mark one answer

You enter a road where there are road humps. What should you do?

- ▪ Maintain a reduced speed throughout
- ▪ Accelerate quickly between each one
- ▪ Always keep to the maximum legal speed
- ▪ Drive slowly at school times only

Answer

✅ **Maintain a reduced speed throughout**

The humps are there for a reason – to reduce the speed of the traffic. Don't accelerate harshly between them as this means you will only have to brake harshly to negotiate the next hump. Harsh braking and accelerating uses more fuel.

Q. 3.82

Mark one answer

When should you especially check the engine oil level?

- ▪ Before a long journey
- ▪ When the engine is hot
- ▪ Early in the morning
- ▪ Every 6000 miles

Answer

✅ **Before a long journey**

During long journeys an engine can use more oil than on shorter trips. Insufficient oil is potentially dangerous: it can lead to excessive wear and expensive repairs.

Most cars have a dipstick to allow the oil level to be checked. If not, you should refer to the vehicle's handbook. Also make checks on

- • fuel
- • water
- • tyres.

questions   *answers*

Q. 3.83

Mark one answer

You are having difficulty finding a parking space in a busy town. You can see there is space on the zigzag lines of a zebra crossing. Can you park there?

 No, unless you stay with your car

■ Yes, in order to drop off a passenger

■ Yes, if you do not block people from crossing

■ No, not in any circumstances

Answer

☑ **No, not in any circumstances**

It's an offence to park there. You will be causing an obstruction by obscuring the view of both pedestrians and drivers.

Q. 3.84

Mark one answer

When leaving your car unattended for a few minutes you should

 leave the engine running

■ switch the engine off but leave the key in

■ lock it and remove the key

■ park near a traffic warden

Answer

☑ **lock it and remove the key**

Always switch off the engine, remove the key and lock your car, even if you are only leaving it for a few minutes.

Q. 3.85

Mark one answer

When parking and leaving your car for a few minutes you should

 leave it unlocked

■ lock it and remove the key

■ leave the hazard warning lights on

■ leave the interior light on

Answer

☑ **lock it and remove the key**

Always remove the key and lock your car even if you only leave it for a few minutes.

questions

answers

Q. 3.86

Mark one answer

When leaving your car to help keep it secure you should

- leave the hazard warning lights on
- lock it and remove the key
- park on a one way street
- park in a residential area

Answer

✓ **lock it and remove the key**

To help keep your car secure when you leave it, you should always remove the key from the ignition, lock it and take the key with you. Don't make it easy for thieves.

Q. 3.87

Mark one answer

When leaving your vehicle where should you park if possible?

- Opposite a traffic island
- In a secure car park
- On a bend
- At or near a taxi rank

Answer

✓ **In a secure car park**

Whenever possible leave your car in a secure car park. This will help stop thieves.

Q. 3.88

Mark one answer

You are leaving your vehicle parked on a road. When may you leave the engine running?

- If you will be parking for less than five minutes
- If the battery is flat
- When in a 20 mph zone
- Never on any occasion

Answer

✓ **Never on any occasion**

When you leave your vehicle parked on a road

- switch off the engine
- make sure that there aren't any valuables visible
- shut all the windows
- lock the vehicle
- set the alarm if it has one
- use an anti-theft device such as a steering wheel lock.

questions   answers

Q. 3.89

Mark three answers

In which THREE places would parking your vehicle cause danger or obstruction to other road users?

- In front of a property entrance
- At or near a bus stop
- On your driveway
- In a marked parking space
- On the approach to a level crossing

Answers

- ☑ **In front of a property entrance**
- ☑ **At or near a bus stop**
- ☑ **On the approach to a level crossing**

Don't park your vehicle where parking restrictions apply. Think carefully before you slow down and stop. Look at road markings and signs to ensure that you aren't parking illegally.

Q. 3.90

Mark three answers

In which THREE places would parking cause an obstruction to others?

- Near the brow of a hill
- In a lay-by
- Where the kerb is raised
- Where the kerb has been lowered for wheelchairs
- At or near a bus stop

Answers

- ☑ **Near the brow of a hill**
- ☑ **Where the kerb has been lowered for wheelchairs**
- ☑ **At or near a bus stop**

Think about the effect your parking will have on other road users. Don't forget that not all vehicles are the size of a car. Large vehicles will need more room to pass and might need more time too.

Parking out of the view of traffic, such as before the brow of a hill, causes unnecessary risks. Think before you park.

Q. 3.91

Mark one answer

You are away from home and have to park your vehicle overnight. Where should you leave it?

- Opposite another parked vehicle
- In a quiet road
- Opposite a traffic island
- In a secure car park

Answer

- ☑ **In a secure car park**

When leaving your vehicle unattended, use a secure car park whenever possible.

Safety margins

This section looks at safety margins and how they can be affected by different weather and road conditions.

The questions will ask you about

- **Stopping distances**

  leaving enough room to stop in all conditions.

- **Road surfaces**

  being aware of uneven or slippery surfaces.

- **Skidding**

  being aware of the importance of preventing a skid. You should also know how to react if you lose control of your vehicle.

- **Weather conditions**

  being aware that weather conditions will have an effect on how your vehicle behaves.

Q. 4.1

Mark one answer

Braking distances on ice can be

- ▓ twice the normal distance
- ▓ five times the normal distance
- ▓ seven times the normal distance
- ▓ ten times the normal distance

Answer

 ten times the normal distance

In icy and snowy weather, your stopping distance will increase by up to ten times compared to good, dry conditions.

Take extra care when braking, accelerating and steering, to cut down the risk of skidding.

Q. 4.2

Mark one answer

Freezing conditions will affect the distance it takes you to come to a stop. You should expect stopping distances to increase by up to

- ▓ two times
- ▓ three times
- ▓ five times
- ▓ ten times

Answer

☑ **ten times**

Your tyre grip is greatly reduced on icy roads and you need to allow up to ten times the normal stopping distance.

Q. 4.3

Mark two answers

In very hot weather the road surface can get soft. Which TWO of the following will be affected most?

- ▓ The suspension
- ▓ The grip of the tyres
- ▓ The braking
- ▓ The exhaust

Answers

☑ **The grip of the tyres**

☑ **The braking**

Only a small part of your tyres is in contact with the road. This is why you must consider the surface you're travelling on, and alter your speed to suit the road conditions.

questions

answers

Q. 4.4

Mark one answer

Where are you most likely to be affected by a sidewind?

- On a narrow country lane
- On an open stretch of road
- On a busy stretch of road
- On a long, straight road

Answer

 On an open stretch of road

In windy conditions, care must be taken on exposed roads. A strong gust of wind can blow you off course. Watch out for other road users who are particularly likely to be affected, such as

- cyclists
- motorcyclists
- high-sided lorries
- vehicles towing trailers.

Q. 4.5

Mark one answer

In windy conditions you need to take extra care when

- using the brakes
- making a hill start
- turning into a narrow road
- passing pedal cyclists

Answer

 passing pedal cyclists

You should always give cyclists plenty of room when overtaking. When it's windy, a sudden gust could blow them off course.

Q. 4.6

Mark one answer

What is the shortest stopping distance at 70 mph?

- 53 metres (175 feet)
- 60 metres (197 feet)
- 73 metres (240 feet)
- 96 metres (315 feet)

Answer

 96 metres (315 feet)

Note that this is the shortest distance. It will take at least this distance to think, brake and stop in good conditions.

questions

answers

Q. 4.7

Mark one answer

What is the shortest overall stopping distance on a dry road from 60 mph?

- 53 metres (175 feet)
- 58 metres (190 feet)
- 73 metres (240 feet)
- 96 metres (315 feet)

Answer

✓ **73 metres (240 feet)**

This distance is the equivalent of 18 car lengths. Try pacing out 73 metres and then look back. It's probably further than you think.

Q. 4.8

Mark one answer

Your indicators may be difficult to see in bright sunlight. What should you do?

- Put your indicator on earlier
- Give an arm signal as well as using your indicator
- Touch the brake several times to show the stop lights
- Turn as quickly as you can

Answer

✓ **Give an arm signal as well as using your indicator**

You should always ensure that other road users are aware of your intentions. If you think your indicator might not be seen, then give an arm signal as well.

Q. 4.9

Mark two answers

In very hot weather the road surface can get soft. Which TWO of the following will be affected most?

- The suspension
- The steering
- The braking
- The exhaust

Answers

✓ **The steering**

✓ **The braking**

Take care when braking or cornering. Tyre grip is reduced on soft tarmac.

questions

answers

Q. 4.10

Mark one answer

When approaching a right-hand bend you should keep well to the left. Why is this?

- To improve your view of the road
- To overcome the effect of the road's slope
- To let faster traffic from behind overtake
- To be positioned safely if you skid

Answer

☑ **To improve your view of the road**

Doing this will give you an earlier view around the bend and enable you to see any hazards sooner.

It also reduces the risk of collision with an oncoming vehicle that may have drifted over the centre line while taking the bend.

Q. 4.11

Mark three answers

You should not overtake when

- intending to turn left shortly afterwards
- in a one-way street
- approaching a junction
- going up a long hill
- the view ahead is blocked

Answers

☑ **intending to turn left shortly afterwards**

☑ **approaching a junction**

☑ **the view ahead is blocked**

Before you overtake you should ask yourself if it's really necessary. Arriving safely is more important than taking unnecessary risks.

Q. 4.12

Mark one answer

You have just gone through deep water. To dry off the brakes you should

- accelerate and keep to a high speed for a short time
- go slowly while gently applying the brakes
- avoid using the brakes at all for a few miles
- stop for at least an hour to allow them time to dry

Answer

☑ **go slowly while gently applying the brakes**

Water on the brakes will act as a lubricant, causing them to work less efficiently. Using the brakes lightly as you go along will dry them out.

Q. 4.13

Mark one answer

You are on a fast, open road in good conditions. For safety, the distance between you and the vehicle in front should be

- a two-second time gap
- one car length
- 2 metres (6 feet 6 inches)
- two car lengths

Answer

☑ **a two-second time gap**

One useful method of checking that you've allowed enough room between you and the vehicle in front is the two-second rule.

To check for a two-second time gap, choose a stationary object ahead, such as a bridge or road sign. When the car in front passes the object say 'Only a fool breaks the two-second rule'. If you reach the object before you finish saying it you're too close.

Q. 4.14

Mark one answer

What is the most common cause of skidding?

- Worn tyres
- Driver error
- Other vehicles
- Pedestrians

Answer

☑ **Driver error**

A skid happens when the driver changes the speed or direction of their vehicle so suddenly that the tyres can't keep their grip on the road.

Remember that the risk of skidding on wet or icy roads is much greater than in dry conditions.

Q. 4.15

Mark one answer

You are driving on an icy road. How can you avoid wheelspin?

- Drive at a slow speed in as high a gear as possible
- Use the handbrake if the wheels start to slip
- Brake gently and repeatedly
- Drive in a low gear at all times

Answer

☑ **Drive at a slow speed in as high a gear as possible**

If you're travelling on an icy road extra caution will be required to avoid loss of control. Keeping your speed down and using the highest gear you can will reduce the risk of the tyres losing their grip on this slippery surface.

questions answers

Q. 4.16

Mark one answer

Skidding is mainly caused by

- the weather
- the driver
- the vehicle
- the road

Answer

☑ **the driver**

You should always consider the conditions and drive accordingly.

Q. 4.17

Mark two answers

You are driving in freezing conditions. What should you do when approaching a sharp bend?

- Slow down before you reach the bend
- Gently apply your handbrake
- Firmly use your footbrake
- Coast into the bend
- Avoid sudden steering movements

Answers

☑ **Slow down before you reach the bend**

☑ **Avoid sudden steering movements**

Harsh use of the accelerator, brakes or steering are likely to lead to skidding, especially on slippery surfaces. Avoid steering and braking at the same time.

In icy conditions it's very important that you constantly assess what's ahead, so that you can take appropriate action in plenty of time.

Q. 4.18

Mark one answer

You are turning left on a slippery road. The back of your vehicle slides to the right. You should

- brake firmly and not turn the steering wheel
- steer carefully to the left
- steer carefully to the right
- brake firmly and steer to the left

Answer

☑ **steer carefully to the right**

This should stop the sliding and allow you to regain control. Don't use the

- accelerator
- the brakes
- the clutch.

questions   answers

Q. 4.19

Mark one answer

You are braking on a wet road. Your vehicle begins to skid. Your vehicle does not have anti-lock brakes. What is the FIRST thing you should do?

- ▮ Quickly pull up the handbrake
- ▮ Release the footbrake fully
- ▮ Push harder on the brake pedal
- ▮ Gently use the accelerator

Answer

☑ **Release the footbrake fully**

If the skid has been caused by braking too hard for the conditions, release the brake. This will allow the wheels to turn and so limit the skid.

Skids are much easier to get into than they are to get out of. Prevention is better than cure.

Stay alert to the road and weather conditions. Never drive so fast that you can't stop within the distance that you can see to be clear.

Q. 4.20

Mark one answer

Coasting the vehicle

- ▮ improves the driver's control
- ▮ makes steering easier
- ▮ reduces the driver's control
- ▮ uses more fuel

Answer

☑ **reduces the driver's control**

'Coasting' is the term used when the clutch is held down or the gear lever is in neutral and the vehicle is allowed to freewheel. This reduces the driver's control of the vehicle. When you coast, the engine can't drive the wheels to pull you through a corner. Coasting also removes the assistance of engine braking that helps to slow the car.

Q. 4.21

Mark four answers

Before starting a journey in freezing weather you should clear ice and snow from your vehicle's

- ▮ aerial
- ▮ windows
- ▮ bumper
- ▮ lights
- ▮ mirrors
- ▮ number plates

Answers

☑ **windows**

☑ **lights**

☑ **mirrors**

☑ **number plates**

Don't travel unless you really have to. Making unnecessary journeys will increase the risk of an accident.

It is important that you can see and be seen. Make sure any snow or ice is cleared from lights, mirrors, number plates and windows.

questions   answers

Q. 4.22

Mark one answer

You are trying to move off on snow. You should use

- the lowest gear you can
- the highest gear you can
- a high engine speed
- the handbrake and footbrake together

Answer

✓ **the highest gear you can**

If you attempt to move in a low gear, such as first, the engine will rev at a higher speed. This could cause the wheels to spin and dig further into the snow.

Q. 4.23

Mark one answer

When driving in falling snow you should

- brake firmly and quickly
- be ready to steer sharply
- use sidelights only
- brake gently in plenty of time

Answer

✓ **brake gently in plenty of time**

Braking on snow can be extremely dangerous. Be gentle with both the accelerator and brake to prevent wheel-spin.

Q. 4.24

Mark one answer

The MAIN benefit of having four-wheel drive is to improve

- road holding
- fuel consumption
- stopping distances
- passenger comfort

Answer

✓ **road holding**

By driving all four wheels there is improved grip, but this does not replace the skills you need to drive safely. The extra grip helps prevent skidding when travelling on slippery or uneven roads.

questions   answers

Q. 4.25

Mark one answer

You are about to go down a steep hill. To control the speed of your vehicle you should

■ select a high gear and use the brakes carefully

■ select a high gear and use the brakes firmly

■ select a low gear and use the brakes carefully

■ select a low gear and avoid using the brakes

Answer

☑ **select a low gear and use the brakes carefully**

When travelling down a steep hill your vehicle will tend to increase speed. This will make it more difficult for you to stop. To maintain control and prevent the vehicle running away

• select a lower gear – the engine will then help to control your speed

• use the brakes carefully.

Q. 4.26

Mark one answer

How can you use the engine of your vehicle as a brake?

■ By changing to a lower gear

■ By selecting reverse gear

■ By changing to a higher gear

■ By selecting neutral gear

Answer

☑ **By changing to a lower gear**

When driving on downhill stretches of road selecting a lower gear gives increased engine braking. This will prevent excess use of the brakes, which become less effective if they overheat.

Q. 4.27

Mark two answers

You wish to park facing DOWNHILL. Which TWO of the following should you do?

■ Turn the steering wheel towards the kerb

■ Park close to the bumper of another car

■ Park with two wheels on the kerb

■ Put the handbrake on firmly

■ Turn the steering wheel away from the kerb

Answers

☑ **Turn the steering wheel towards the kerb**

☑ **Put the handbrake on firmly**

Turning the wheels towards the kerb will allow it to act as a chock, preventing any forward movement of the vehicle.

questions   *answers*

Q. 4.28

Mark one answer

You are driving in a built-up area. You approach a speed hump. You should

- ☐ move across to the left-hand side of the road
- ☐ wait for any pedestrians to cross
- ☐ slow your vehicle right down
- ☐ stop and check both pavements

Answer

☑ **slow your vehicle right down**

Many towns have speed humps to slow down traffic. They're often found where there are pedestrians, so

- slow right down when driving over them
- look out for pedestrians.

They might affect your steering and suspension if you drive too fast.

Q. 4.29

Mark one answer

You are on a long, downhill slope. What should you do to help control the speed of your vehicle?

- ☐ Select neutral
- ☐ Select a lower gear
- ☐ Grip the handbrake firmly
- ☐ Apply the parking brake gently

Answer

☑ **Select a lower gear**

Selecting a low gear when travelling downhill will help you to control your speed. The engine will assist the brakes and help prevent your vehicle gathering speed.

Q. 4.30

Mark one answer

NI EXEMPT

Your vehicle is fitted with anti-lock brakes. To stop quickly in an emergency you should

- ■ brake firmly and pump the brake pedal on and off

- ■ brake rapidly and firmly without releasing the brake pedal

- ■ brake gently and pump the brake pedal on and off

- ■ brake rapidly once, and immediately release the brake pedal

Answer

☑ **brake rapidly and firmly without releasing the brake pedal**

Once you have applied the brake keep your foot firmly on the pedal. Releasing the brake and reapplying it will disable the anti-lock brake system.

Q. 4.31

Mark one answer

Anti-lock brakes prevent wheels from locking. This means the tyres are less likely to

- ■ aquaplane

- ■ skid

- ■ puncture

- ■ wear

Answer

☑ **skid**

If an anti-lock braking system (ABS) is fitted it activates automatically when maximum braking pressure is applied or when it senses that the wheels are about to lock. ABS prevents the wheels from locking so you can continue to steer the vehicle during braking.

ABS does not remove the need for good driving practices such as anticipation and correct speed for the conditions.

Q. 4.32

Mark one answer

Anti-lock brakes reduce the chances of a skid occurring particularly when

- ■ driving down steep hills

- ■ braking during normal driving

- ■ braking in an emergency

- ■ driving on good road surfaces

Answer

☑ **braking in an emergency**

The anti-lock braking system will operate when the brakes have been applied harshly. It will reduce the chances of your car skidding, but it is not a miracle cure for careless driving.

questions   *answers*

Q. 4.33

Mark one answer

NI EXEMPT

Anti-lock brakes are most effective when you

- [ ] keep pumping the foot brake to prevent skidding
- [ ] brake normally, but grip the steering wheel tightly
- [ ] brake rapidly and firmly until you have slowed down
- [ ] apply the handbrake to reduce the stopping distance

Answer

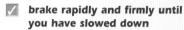 **brake rapidly and firmly until you have slowed down**

Releasing the brake before you have slowed right down will disable the system. If you have to brake in an emergency ensure that you keep your foot firmly on the brake pedal until the vehicle has stopped.

Q. 4.34

Mark one answer

NI EXEMPT

Your car is fitted with anti-lock brakes. You need to stop in an emergency. You should

- [ ] brake normally and avoid turning the steering wheel
- [ ] press the brake pedal rapidly and firmly until you have stopped
- [ ] keep pushing and releasing the foot brake quickly to prevent skidding
- [ ] apply the handbrake to reduce the stopping distance

Answer

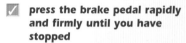 **press the brake pedal rapidly and firmly until you have stopped**

Keep pressure on the brake pedal until you have come to a stop. The anti-lock mechanism will activate automatically if it senses the wheels are about to lock.

Q. 4.35

Mark one answer

Vehicles fitted with anti-lock brakes

- [ ] are impossible to skid
- [ ] can be steered while you are braking
- [ ] accelerate much faster
- [ ] are not fitted with a handbrake

Answer

✓ **can be steered while you are braking**

Preventing the wheels from locking means that the vehicle's steering and stability can be maintained, leading to safer stopping. However, you must ensure that the engine does not stall, as this could disable the power steering. When stopping in an emergency, and braking harshly, depress the clutch pedal as you brake.

Q. 4.36

Mark two answers

Anti-lock brakes may not work as effectively if the road surface is

- dry
- loose
- wet
- good
- firm

Answers

- ☑ **loose**
- ☑ **wet**

Poor contact with the road surface could cause one or more of the tyres to lose grip on the road. This is more likely to happen when braking in poor weather conditions, when the road surface is uneven or has loose chippings.

Q. 4.37

Mark one answer

Anti-lock brakes are of most use when you are

- braking gently
- driving on worn tyres
- braking excessively
- driving normally

Answer

- ☑ **braking excessively**

Anti-lock brakes will not be required when braking normally. Looking well down the road and anticipating possible hazards could prevent you having to brake late and harshly.

Knowing that you have anti-lock brakes is not an excuse to drive in a careless or reckless way.

Q. 4.38

Mark one answer

Driving a vehicle fitted with anti-lock brakes allows you to

- brake harder because it is impossible to skid
- drive at higher speeds
- steer and brake at the same time
- pay less attention to the road ahead

Answer

- ☑ **steer and brake at the same time**

Anti-lock brakes will help you continue to steer when braking, but in poor weather conditions this will be less effective. You need to depress the clutch pedal to prevent the car stalling because the power steering system uses an engine-driven pump and will only operate when the engine is running.

questions  answers

Q. 4.39

Mark one answer

Anti-lock brakes can greatly assist with

- ▪ a higher cruising speed
- ▪ steering control when braking
- ▪ control when accelerating
- ▪ motorway driving

Answer

☑ steering control when braking

If the wheels of your vehicle lock they will not grip the road and you will lose steering control. In good conditions the anti-lock system will prevent the wheels locking and allow you to retain steering control.

Q. 4.40

Mark one answer

When would an anti-lock braking system start to work?

- ▪ After the parking brake has been applied
- ▪ When ever pressure on the brake pedal is applied
- ▪ Just as the wheels are about to lock
- ▪ When the normal braking system fails to operate

Answer

☑ Just as the wheels are about to lock

The anti-lock braking system has sensors that detect when the wheels are about to lock. It releases the brakes momentarily to allow the wheels to revolve and grip, then automatically reapplies them. This cycle is repeated several times a second to maximise braking performance.

Q. 4.41

Mark one answer

NI EXEMPT

You are driving a vehicle fitted with anti-lock brakes. You need to stop in an emergency. You should apply the footbrake

- ▪ slowly and gently
- ▪ slowly but firmly
- ▪ rapidly and gently
- ▪ rapidly and firmly

Answer

☑ rapidly and firmly

Look well ahead down the road as you drive and give yourself time and space to react safely to any hazards. You may have to stop in an emergency due to a misjudgement by another driver or a hazard arising suddenly such as a child running out into the road. In this case, if your vehicle has anti-lock brakes, you should apply the brakes immediately and keep them firmly applied until you stop.

Q. 4.42

Mark two answers

Your vehicle has anti-lock brakes, but they may not always prevent skidding. This is most likely to happen when driving

- ■ in foggy conditions
- ■ on surface water
- ■ on loose road surfaces
- ■ on dry tarmac
- ■ at night on unlit roads

Answers

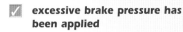 **on surface water**

☑ **on loose road surfaces**

In very wet weather water can build up between the tyre and the road surface. As a result your vehicle actually rides on a thin film of water and your tyres will not grip the road. Gravel or shingle surfaces also offer less grip and can present problems when braking. An anti-lock braking system may be ineffective in these conditions.

Q. 4.43

Mark one answer

Anti-lock brakes will take effect when

- ■ you do not brake quickly enough
- ■ excessive brake pressure has been applied
- ■ you have not seen a hazard ahead
- ■ speeding on slippery road surfaces

Answer

☑ **excessive brake pressure has been applied**

If your car is fitted with anti-lock brakes they will take effect when you use them harshly in an emergency. The system will only activate when it senses the wheels are about to lock.

Q. 4.44

Mark three answers

When driving in fog, which of the following are correct?

- ■ Use dipped headlights
- ■ Use headlights on full beam
- ■ Allow more time for your journey
- ■ Keep close to the car in front
- ■ Slow down
- ■ Use side lights only

Answers

☑ **Use dipped headlights**

☑ **Allow more time for your journey**

☑ **Slow down**

Don't venture out if your journey is not necessary. If you have to travel and someone is expecting you at the other end, let them know that you will be taking longer than usual for your journey. This will stop them worrying if you don't turn up on time and will also take the pressure off you, so you don't feel you have to rush.

questions   answers

Q. 4.45

Mark one answer

You are driving along a country road. You see this sign. AFTER dealing safely with the hazard you should always

Ford

■ check your tyre pressures

■ switch on your hazard warning lights

■ accelerate briskly

■ test your brakes

Answer

 test your brakes

Deep water can affect your brakes, so you should check that they're working properly before you build up speed again. Before you do this, remember to check your mirrors and consider what's behind you.

Q. 4.46

Mark one answer

You are driving in heavy rain. Your steering suddenly becomes very light. You should

■ steer towards the side of the road

■ apply gentle acceleration

■ brake firmly to reduce speed

■ ease off the accelerator

Answer

 ease off the accelerator

If the steering becomes light in these conditions it is probably due to a film of water that has built up between your tyres and the road surface. Easing off the accelerator should allow your tyres to displace the film of water and they should then regain their grip on the road.

Q. 4.47

Mark one answer

How can you tell when you are driving over black ice?

■ It is easier to brake

■ The noise from your tyres sounds louder

■ You see black ice on the road

■ Your steering feels light

Answer

☑ **Your steering feels light**

Sometimes you may not be able to see that the road is icy. Black ice makes a road look damp. The signs that you're travelling on black ice can be that

• the steering feels light

• the noise from your tyres suddenly goes quiet.

Q. 4.48

Mark one answer

The roads are icy. You should drive slowly

- ■ in the highest gear possible
- ■ in the lowest gear possible
- ■ with the handbrake partly on
- ■ with your left foot on the brake

Answer

✓ **in the highest gear possible**

Driving at a slow speed in a high gear will reduce the likelihood of wheel-spin and help your vehicle maintain the best possible grip.

Q. 4.49

Mark one answer

You are driving along a wet road. How can you tell if your vehicle is aquaplaning?

- ■ The engine will stall
- ■ The engine noise will increase
- ■ The steering will feel very heavy
- ■ The steering will feel very light

Answer

✓ **The steering will feel very light**

If you drive at speed in very wet conditions your steering may suddenly feel 'light'. This means that the tyres have lifted off the surface of the road and are skating on the surface of the water. This is known as aquaplaning. Reduce speed by easing off the accelerator, but don't brake until your steering returns to normal.

Q. 4.50

Mark two answers

How can you tell if you are driving on ice?

- ■ The tyres make a rumbling noise
- ■ The tyres make hardly any noise
- ■ The steering becomes heavier
- ■ The steering becomes lighter

Answers

✓ **The tyres make hardly any noise**

✓ **The steering becomes lighter**

Drive extremely carefully when the roads are icy. When travelling on ice, tyres make virtually no noise and the steering feels unresponsive.

In icy conditions, avoid harsh braking, acceleration and steering.

questions answers

Q. 4.51

Mark one answer

You are driving along a wet road. How can you tell if your vehicle's tyres are losing their grip on the surface?

- The engine will stall
- The steering will feel very heavy
- The engine noise will increase
- The steering will feel very light

Answer

☑ **The steering will feel very light**

If you drive at speed in very wet conditions your steering may suddenly feel lighter than usual. This means that the tyres have lifted off the surface of the road and are skating on the surface of the water. This is known as aquaplaning. Reduce speed but don't brake until your steering returns to a normal feel.

Q. 4.52

Mark one answer

You are travelling at 50 mph on a good, dry road. What is your shortest overall stopping distance?

- 36 metres (120 feet)
- 53 metres (175 feet)
- 75 metres (245 feet)
- 96 metres (315 feet)

Answer

☑ **53 metres (175 feet)**

Even in good conditions it will take you further than you think for your car to stop. Don't just learn the figures – understand how far the distance is.

Q. 4.53

Mark one answer

Your overall stopping distance will be much longer when driving

- in the rain
- in fog
- at night
- in strong winds

Answer

 in the rain

Extra care should be taken in wet weather as on wet roads your stopping distance could be double that in dry conditions.

Q. 4.54

Mark one answer

You have driven through a flood. What is the first thing you should do?

■ Stop and check the tyres

■ Stop and dry the brakes

■ Check your exhaust

■ Test your brakes

Answer

 Test your brakes

Before you test you brakes you must check for following traffic. If it is safe, gently apply the brakes to clear any water that may be covering the braking surfaces.

Q. 4.55

Mark one answer

You are on a good, dry road surface. Your vehicle has good brakes and tyres. What is the BRAKING distance at 50 mph?

■ 38 metres (125 feet)

■ 14 metres (46 feet)

■ 24 metres (79 feet)

■ 55 metres (180 feet)

Answer

 38 metres (125 feet)

The braking distance does not include the thinking distance or reaction time.

Q. 4.56

Mark one answer

You are on a good, dry, road surface and your vehicle has good brakes and tyres. What is the typical overall stopping distance at 40 mph?

■ 23 metres (75 feet)

■ 36 metres (120 feet)

■ 53 metres (175 feet)

■ 96 metres (315 feet)

Answer

☑ **36 metres (120 feet)**

Factors that affect how long it takes you to stop include

• how fast you're going

• whether you're travelling on the level, uphill or downhill

• the weather and road conditions

• the condition of tyres, brakes and suspension

• your reaction time.

Hazard awareness

This section looks at judgement and hazard perception.

The questions will ask you about

- **Anticipation**
  planning ahead to prevent last-second reactions.

- **Hazard awareness**
  recognising a hazard ahead and preparing yourself for it.

- **Attention**
  looking out for problems ahead when you're driving.

- **Speed and distance**
  being aware of the correct speed for the situation and leaving enough space to react.

- **Reaction time**
  being aware that you need time to react.

- **The effects of alcohol and drugs**
  understanding how these will affect your reaction time.

- **Tiredness**
  not driving if you're tired. You need to be alert at all times.

Q. 5.1

Mark one answer

You see this sign on the rear of a slow-moving lorry that you want to pass. It is travelling in the middle lane of a three lane motorway. You should

- cautiously approach the lorry then pass on either side
- follow the lorry until you can leave the motorway
- wait on the hard shoulder until the lorry has stopped
- approach with care and keep to the left of the lorry

Answer

☑ **approach with care and keep to the left of the lorry**

This sign is found on slow-moving or stationary works vehicles. If you wish to overtake, do so on the left, as indicated. Be aware that there might be workmen in the area.

Q. 5.2

Mark two answers

Where would you expect to see these markers?

- On a motorway sign
- At the entrance to a narrow bridge
- On a large goods vehicle
- On a builder's skip placed on the road

Answers

☑ **On a large goods vehicle**

☑ **On a builder's skip placed on the road**

These markers must be fitted to vehicles over 13 metres long, large goods vehicles, and rubbish skips placed in the road. They are reflective to make them easier to see in the dark.

questions answers

Q. 5.3

Mark one answer

What does this signal from a police officer mean to oncoming traffic?

▢ Go ahead

▢ Stop

▢ Turn left

▢ Turn right

Answer

✓ **Stop**

Police officers may need to direct traffic, for example, at a junction where the traffic lights have broken down. Check your copy of *The Highway Code* for the signals that they use.

Q. 5.4

Mark one answer

What is the main hazard shown in this picture?

▢ Vehicles turning right

▢ Vehicles doing U-turns

▢ The cyclist crossing the road

▢ Parked cars around the corner

Answer

✓ **The cyclist crossing the road**

Look at the picture carefully and try to imagine you're there. The cyclist in this picture appears to be trying to cross the road. You must be able to deal with the unexpected, especially when you're approaching a hazardous junction. Look well ahead to give yourself time to deal with any hazards.

questions answers

Q. 5.5
Mark one answer

Which road user has caused a hazard?

- The parked car (arrowed A)
- The pedestrian waiting to cross (arrowed B)
- The moving car (arrowed C)
- The car turning (arrowed D)

Answer

☑ **The parked car (arrowed A)**

The car arrowed A is parked within the area marked by zigzag lines at the pedestrian crossing. Parking here is illegal. It also

- blocks the view for pedestrians wishing to cross the road

- restricts the view of the crossing for approaching traffic.

Q. 5.6
Mark one answer

What should the driver of the car approaching the crossing do?

- Continue at the same speed
- Sound the horn
- Drive through quickly
- Slow down and get ready to stop

Answer

☑ **Slow down and get ready to stop**

Look well ahead to see if any hazards are developing. This will give you more time to deal with them in the correct way. The man in the picture is clearly intending to cross the road. You should be travelling at a speed that allows you to check your mirror, slow down and stop in good time. You shouldn't have to brake harshly.

questions   *answers*

Q. 5.7

Mark three answers

What THREE things should the driver of the grey car (arrowed) be especially aware of?

▣ Pedestrians stepping out between cars

▣ Other cars behind the grey car

▣ Doors opening on parked cars

▣ The bumpy road surface

▣ Cars leaving parking spaces

▣ Empty parking spaces

Answers

☑ **Pedestrians stepping out between cars**

☑ **Doors opening on parked cars**

☑ **Cars leaving parking spaces**

You need to be aware that other road users may not have seen you. Always be on the lookout for hazards that may develop suddenly and need you to take avoiding action.

Q. 5.8

Mark one answer

You think the driver of the vehicle in front has forgotten to cancel the right indicator. You should

▣ flash your lights to alert the driver

▣ sound your horn before overtaking

▣ overtake on the left if there is room

▣ stay behind and not overtake

Answer

☑ **stay behind and not overtake**

The driver may be unsure of the location of a junction and turn suddenly. Be cautious and don't attempt to overtake.

Q. 5.9

Mark one answer

What is the main hazard the driver of the red car (arrowed) should be most aware of?

▢ Glare from the sun may affect the driver's vision

▢ The black car may stop suddenly

▢ The bus may move out into the road

▢ Oncoming vehicles will assume the driver is turning right

Answer

 The bus may move out into the road

Try to anticipate the actions of the other road users around you. The driver of the red car should have made a mental note that the bus was at the bus stop. By doing this the driver would have been prepared for the bus pulling out.

As you approach a bus stop where a bus is stationary, look and see how many more passengers are waiting to board. If the last one has just got on, the bus is likely to move off.

You should give way to a bus driver who is signalling to move off from a bus stop, if you can do so safely.

Q. 5.10

Mark one answer

In heavy motorway traffic you are being followed closely by the vehicle behind. How can you lower the risk of an accident?

▢ Increase your distance from the vehicle in front

▢ Tap your foot on the brake pedal sharply

▢ Switch on your hazard lights

▢ Move onto the hard shoulder and stop

Answer

 Increase your distance from the vehicle in front

On a busy motorway, traffic may still travel at high speeds despite the vehicles being close together. Don't follow too close to the vehicle in front. If a driver behind seems to be 'pushing' you, increase your distance from the vehicle in front by slowing down gently. This will lessen the risk of an accident involving several vehicles.

questions answers

Q. 5.11

Mark one answer

You see this sign ahead. You should expect the road to

- [ ] go steeply uphill
- [ ] go steeply downhill
- [ ] bend sharply to the left
- [ ] bend sharply to the right

Answer

 bend sharply to the left

Adjust your speed in good time and select the correct gear for your speed. Going too fast into the bend could cause you to lose control.

Braking late and harshly while changing direction reduces your vehicle's grip on the road, and is likely to cause a skid.

Q. 5.12

Mark one answer

You are approaching this cyclist. You should

- [ ] overtake before the cyclist gets to the junction
- [ ] flash your headlights at the cyclist
- [ ] slow down and allow the cyclist to turn
- [ ] overtake the cyclist on the left-hand side

Answer

✓ **slow down and allow the cyclist to turn**

Keep well back and allow the cyclist room to take up the correct position for the turn. Don't get too close behind or try to squeeze past.

Q. 5.13

Mark one answer

Why must you take extra care when turning right at this junction?

☐ Road surface is poor

☐ Footpaths are narrow

☐ Road markings are faint

☐ There is reduced visibility

Answer

☑ **There is reduced visibility**

You may have to pull forward slowly until you can see up and down the road. Be aware that the traffic approaching the junction can't see you either. If you don't know that it's clear, don't go.

Q. 5.14

Mark one answer

This yellow sign on a vehicle indicates this is

☐ a vehicle broken down

☐ a school bus

☐ an ice cream van

☐ a private ambulance

Answer

☑ **a school bus**

Buses which carry children to and from school may stop at places other than scheduled bus stops. Be aware that they might pull over at any time to allow children to get on or off. This will normally be when traffic is heavy during rush hour.

questions answers

Q. 5.15

Mark one answer

When approaching this bridge you should give way to

- bicycles
- buses
- motorcycles
- cars

Answer

✓ **buses**

A double-deck bus or high-sided lorry will have to take up a position in the centre of the road so that it can clear the bridge. There is normally a sign to indicate this.

Look well down the road, through the bridge and be aware you may have to stop and give way to an oncoming large vehicle.

Q. 5.16

Mark one answer

What type of vehicle could you expect to meet in the middle of the road?

- Lorry
- Bicycle
- Car
- Motorcycle

Answer

✓ **Lorry**

The highest point of the bridge is in the centre so a large vehicle might have to move to the centre of the road to allow it enough room to pass under the bridge.

Q. 5.17

Mark one answer

At this blind junction you must stop

 behind the line, then edge forward to
see clearly

beyond the line at a point where you
can see clearly

only if there is traffic on the main road

only if you are turning to the right

Answer

 **behind the line, then edge
forward to see clearly**

The 'stop' sign has been put here because
there is a poor view into the main road. You
must stop because it will not be possible to
assess the situation on the move, however
slowly you are travelling.

Q. 5.18

Mark one answer

A driver pulls out of a side road in front of
you. You have to brake hard. You should

ignore the error and stay calm

flash your lights to show your
annoyance

sound your horn to show your
annoyance

overtake as soon as possible

Answer

 ignore the error and stay calm

Where there are a number of side roads, be
alert. Be especially careful if there are a lot
of parked vehicles because they can make
it more difficult for drivers emerging to see
you.

Try to be tolerant if a vehicle does emerge
and you have to brake quickly. Don't react
aggressively.

Q. 5.19

Mark one answer

An elderly person's driving ability could be
affected because they may be unable to

obtain car insurance

understand road signs

react very quickly

give signals correctly

Answer

react very quickly

Be tolerant of older drivers. Poor eyesight
and hearing could affect the speed with
which they react to a hazard and may
cause them to be hesitant.

questions   *answers*

Q. 5.20

Mark one answer

You have just passed these warning lights. What hazard would you expect to see next?

☐ A level crossing with no barrier

☐ An ambulance station

☐ A school crossing patrol

☐ An opening bridge

Answer

✓ **A school crossing patrol**

These lights warn that children may be crossing the road to a nearby school. Slow down so that you're ready to stop if necessary.

Q. 5.21

Mark two answers

Why should you be especially cautious when going past this bus?

☐ There is traffic approaching in the distance

☐ The driver may open the door

☐ It may suddenly move off

☐ People may cross the road in front of it

☐ There are bicycles parked on the pavement

Answers

✓ **It may suddenly move off**

✓ **People may cross the road in front of it**

A stationary bus at a bus stop can hide pedestrians just in front of it who might be about to cross the road. Only go past at a speed that will enable you to stop safely if you need to.

Q. 5.22

Mark one answer

In areas where there are 'traffic calming' measures you should

- drive at a reduced speed
- always drive at the speed limit
- position in the centre of the road
- only slow down if pedestrians are near

Answer

 drive at a reduced speed

Traffic calming measures such as road humps, chicanes and narrowings are intended to slow you down. Maintain a reduced speed until you reach the end of these features. They are there to protect pedestrians. Kill your speed!

Q. 5.23

Mark one answer

You are planning a long journey. Do you need to plan rest stops?

- Yes, you should plan to stop every half an hour
- Yes, regular stops help concentration
- No, you will be less tired if you get there as soon as possible
- No, only fuel stops will be needed

Answer

 Yes, regular stops help concentration

Try to plan your journey so that you can take rest stops. It's recommended that you take a break of at least 15 minutes after every two hours of driving. This should help to maintain your concentration.

Q. 5.24

Mark one answer

A driver does something that upsets you. You should

- try not to react
- let them know how you feel
- flash your headlights several times
- sound your horn

Answer

try not to react

There are occasions when other road users make a misjudgement or a mistake. If this happens try not to let it annoy you. Don't react by showing anger. Sounding your horn, flashing your headlights or shouting won't help the situation. Good anticipation will help to prevent these incidents becoming accidents.

questions   *answers*

Q. 5.25

Mark one answer

The red lights are flashing. What should you do when approaching this level crossing?

▪ Go through quickly

▪ Go through carefully

▪ Stop before the barrier

▪ Switch on hazard warning lights

Answer

☑ **Stop before the barrier**

At level crossings the red lights flash when the barrier is down or is about to come down. You must stop, even if the barriers are not yet down.

In this picture there's a junction on the left just before the crossing, you should keep this junction clear.

When you are able to cross don't

- go onto the crossing unless the road is clear on the other side

- follow other vehicles nose to tail over it

- stop on or just past the crossing.

Q. 5.26

Mark two answers

What are TWO main hazards you should be aware of when going along this street?

▪ Glare from the sun

▪ Car doors opening suddenly

▪ Lack of road markings

▪ The headlights on parked cars being switched on

▪ Large goods vehicles

▪ Children running out from between vehicles

Answers

☑ **Car doors opening suddenly**

☑ **Children running out from between vehicles**

On roads where there are many parked vehicles you should take extra care. You might not be able to see children between parked cars and they may run out into the road without looking.

People may open car doors without realising the hazard this can create. You will also need to look well down the road for oncoming traffic.

Q. 5.27

Mark one answer

What is the main hazard you should be aware of when following this cyclist?

- [ ] The cyclist may move into the left and dismount
- [ ] The cyclist may swerve out into the road
- [ ] The contents of the cyclist's carrier may fall onto the road
- [ ] The cyclist may wish to turn right at the end of the road

Answer

☑ **The cyclist may swerve out into the road**

When following a cyclist be aware that they also have to deal with the hazards around them. They may

- wobble or swerve to avoid a pothole in the road
- see a potential hazard and change direction suddenly.

Don't follow them too closely or rev your engine impatiently.

Q. 5.28

Mark two answers

When approaching this hazard why should you slow down?

- [ ] Because of the bend
- [ ] Because its hard to see to the right
- [ ] Because of approaching traffic
- [ ] Because of animals crossing
- [ ] Because of the level crossing

Answers

☑ **Because of the bend**

☑ **Because of the level crossing**

There are two hazards clearly signed in this picture. You should be preparing for the bend by slowing down and selecting the correct gear. You might also have to stop at the level crossing, so be alert and be prepared to stop if necessary.

questions   answers

Q. 5.29

Mark one answer

A driver's behaviour has upset you. It may help if you

- stop and take a break
- shout abusive language
- gesture to them with your hand
- follow their car, flashing the headlights

Answer

 stop and take a break

Tiredness may make you more irritable than you would be normally. You might react differently to situations because of it. If you feel yourself becoming tense, take a break.

Q. 5.30

Mark one answer

You are on a dual carriageway. Ahead you see a vehicle with an amber flashing light. What will this be?

- An ambulance
- A fire engine
- A doctor on call
- A disabled persons vehicle

Answer

 A disabled persons vehicle

An amber flashing light on a vehicle indicates that it is slow-moving.

Powered vehicles used by disabled people are limited to 8 mph. On dual carriageways they must display an amber flashing light.

Q. 5.31

Mark one answer

You are approaching crossroads. The traffic lights have failed. What should you do?

- Brake and stop only for large vehicles
- Brake sharply to a stop before looking
- Be prepared to brake sharply to a stop
- Be prepared to stop for any traffic.

Answer

 Be prepared to stop for any traffic.

When approaching a junction where the traffic lights have failed you should proceed with caution. Treat the situation as an unmarked junction and be prepared to stop.

Q. 5.32

Mark one answer

Why are destination markings painted on the road surface?

▓ To restrict the flow of traffic

▓ To warn you of oncoming traffic

▓ To enable you to change lanes early

▓ To prevent you changing lanes

Answer

 To enable you to change lanes early

The names of towns and cities may be painted on the road at busy junctions and complex road systems. Their purpose is to let you move into the correct lane in good time, allowing traffic to flow more freely.

Q. 5.33

Mark one answer

What should the driver of the red car (arrowed) do?

▓ Wave the pedestrians who are waiting to cross

▓ Wait for the pedestrian in the road to cross

▓ Quickly drive behind the pedestrian in the road

▓ Tell the pedestrian in the road she should not have crossed

Answer

 Wait for the pedestrian in the road to cross

Some people might take longer to cross the road. They may be elderly or have a disability.

Be patient and don't hurry them by showing your impatience. They might have poor eyesight or not be able to hear traffic approaching.

If pedestrians are standing at the side of the road, don't signal or wave them to cross. Other road users may not have seen your signal and this could lead the pedestrians into a hazardous situation.

questions

answers

Q. 5.34

Mark one answer

You are following a slower-moving vehicle on a narrow country road. There is a junction just ahead on the right. What should you do?

◼ Overtake after checking your mirrors and signalling

◼ Stay behind until you are past the junction

◼ Accelerate quickly to pass before the junction

◼ Slow down and prepare to overtake on the left

Answer

 Stay behind until you are past the junction

You should never overtake as you approach a junction. If a vehicle emerged from the junction while you were overtaking, a dangerous situation could develop very quickly.

Q. 5.35

Mark one answer

What should you do as you approach this overhead bridge?

◼ Move out to the centre of the road before going through

◼ Find another route, this is only for high vehicles

◼ Be prepared to give way to large vehicles in the middle of the road

◼ Move across to the right hand side before going through

Answer

 Be prepared to give way to large vehicles in the middle of the road

Oncoming large vehicles may need to move to the middle of the road so that they can pass safely under the bridge. There will not be enough room for you to continue and you should be ready to stop and wait.

Q. 5.36

Mark one answer

Why are mirrors often slightly curved (convex)?

- They give a wider field of vision
- They totally cover blind spots
- They make it easier to judge the speed of following traffic
- They make following traffic look bigger

Answer

☑ **They give a wider field of vision**

Although a convex mirror gives a wide view of the scene behind, you should be aware that it will not show you everything behind or to the side of the vehicle. Before you move off you will need to check over your shoulder to look for anything not visible in the mirrors.

Q. 5.37

Mark one answer

What does the solid white line at the side of the road indicate?

- Traffic lights ahead
- Edge of the carriageway
- Footpath on the left
- Cycle path

Answer

☑ **Edge of the carriageway**

This road marking gives you information which is especially useful in bad weather when visibility is restricted.

questions   answers

Q. 5.38

Mark one answer

You are driving towards this level crossing. What would be the first warning of an approaching train?

	Both half barriers down
	A steady amber light
	One half barrier down
	Twin flashing red lights

Answer

☑ **A steady amber light**

The steady amber light will be followed by twin flashing red lights that mean you must stop. An alarm will also sound to alert you to the fact that a train is approaching.

Q. 5.39

Mark two answers

You are driving along this motorway. It is raining. When following this lorry you should

	allow at least a two-second gap
	move left and drive on the hard shoulder
	allow at least a four-second gap
	be aware of spray reducing your vision
	move right and stay in the right-hand lane

Answers

☑ **allow at least a four-second gap**

☑ **be aware of spray reducing your vision**

The usual two-second time gap will increase to four seconds when the roads are wet. If you stay well back you will

• be able to see past the vehicle

• be out of the spray thrown up by the lorry's tyres

• give yourself more time to stop if the need arises

• increase your chances of being seen by the lorry driver.

questions   answers

Q. 5.40

Mark one answer

You are behind this cyclist. When the traffic lights change, what should you do?

☐ Try to move off before the cyclist

☐ Allow the cyclist time and room

☐ Turn right but give the cyclist room

☐ Tap your horn and drive through first

Answer

☑ **Allow the cyclist time and room**

Hold back and allow the cyclist to move off. In some towns, junctions have special areas marked across the front of the traffic lane. These allow cyclists to wait for the lights to change and move off ahead of other traffic.

Q. 5.41

Mark one answer

You are driving towards this left hand bend. What dangers should you be aware of?

☐ A vehicle overtaking you

☐ No white lines in the centre of the road

☐ No sign to warn you of the bend

☐ Pedestrians walking towards you

Answer

☑ **Pedestrians walking towards you**

Pedestrians walking on a road with no pavement should walk against the direction of the traffic.

You can't see around this bend: there may be hidden dangers. Always keep this in mind so you give yourself time to react if a hazard does arise.

questions

answers

Q. 5.42

Mark one answer

While driving, you see this sign ahead. You should

☐ stop at the sign

☐ slow, but continue around the bend

☐ slow to a crawl and continue

☐ stop and look for open farm gates

Answer

 slow, but continue around the bend

Drive around the bend at a steady speed in the correct gear. Be aware that you might have to stop for approaching trains.

Q. 5.43

Mark one answer

Why should the junction on the left be kept clear?

☐ To allow vehicles to enter and emerge

☐ To allow the bus to reverse

☐ To allow vehicles to make a 'U' turn

☐ To allow vehicles to park

Answer

 To allow vehicles to enter and emerge

You should always try to keep junctions clear. If you are in queuing traffic make sure that when you stop you leave enough space for traffic to flow in and out of the junction.

Q. 5.44

Mark one answer

When the traffic lights change to green the white car should

- ▪ wait for the cyclist to pull away
- ▪ move off quickly and turn in front of the cyclist
- ▪ move close up to the cyclist to beat the lights
- ▪ sound the horn to warn the cyclist

Answer

☑ **wait for the cyclist to pull away**

If you are waiting at traffic lights check all around you before you move away as cyclists often filter through waiting traffic. Allow the cyclist to move off safely.

Q. 5.45

Mark one answer

You intend to turn left at the traffic lights. Just before turning you should

- ▪ check your right mirror
- ▪ move close up to the white car
- ▪ straddle the lanes
- ▪ check for bicycles on your left

Answer

☑ **check for bicycles on your left**

Check your nearside for cyclists before moving away. This is especially important if you have been in a stationary queue of traffic and are about to move off, as cyclists often try to filter past on the nearside of stationary vehicles.

questions

answers

Q. 5.46

Mark one answer

You should reduce your speed when driving along this road because

■ there is a staggered junction ahead

■ there is a low bridge ahead

■ there is a change in the road surface

■ the road ahead narrows

Answer

☑ **there is a staggered junction ahead**

Traffic could be turning off to the left or right ahead of you.

Traffic turning left will be slowing down before the junction and any turning right may have to stop to allow oncoming traffic to clear. Be prepared for this as you might have to slow down or stop behind them.

Q. 5.47

Mark one answer

You are driving at 60 mph. As you approach this hazard you should

■ maintain your speed

■ reduce your speed

■ take the next right turn

■ take the next left turn

Answer

☑ **reduce your speed**

There could be stationary traffic ahead, waiting to turn right. Other traffic could be emerging and it may take time to gather speed.

questions   answers

Q. 5.48

Mark two answers

The traffic ahead of you in the left lane is slowing. You should

▨ be wary of cars on your right cutting in

▨ accelerate past the vehicles in the left lane

▨ pull up on the left hand verge

▨ move across and continue in the right hand lane

▨ slow down keeping a safe separation distance

Answers

☑ **be wary of cars on your right cutting in**

☑ **slow down keeping a safe separation distance**

Allow the traffic to merge into the nearside lane. Leave enough room so that your separation distance is not reduced drastically if a vehicle pulls in ahead of you.

Q. 5.49

Mark one answer

What might you expect to happen in this situation?

▨ Traffic will move into the right-hand lane

▨ Traffic speed will increase

▨ Traffic will move into the left-hand lane

▨ Traffic will not need to change position

Answer

☑ **Traffic will move into the left-hand lane**

Be courteous and allow the traffic to merge into the left-hand lane.

questions   answers

Q. 5.50

Mark one answer

You are driving on a road with several lanes. You see these signs above the lanes. What do they mean?

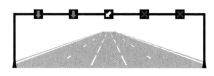

■ The two right lanes are open

■ The two left lanes are open

■ Traffic in the left lanes should stop

■ Traffic in the right lanes should stop

Answer

☑ **The two left lanes are open**

If you see a red cross above your lane it means that there is an obstruction ahead. You will have to move into one of the lanes which is showing the green light. If all the lanes are showing a red cross, then you must stop.

Q. 5.51

Mark two answers

As a provisional licence holder, you must not drive a motor car

■ at more than 50 mph

■ on your own

■ on the motorway

■ under the age of 18 years of age at night

■ with passengers in the rear seats

Answers

☑ **on your own**

☑ **on the motorway**

When you have passed your practical test you will be able to drive on a motorway. It is recommended that you have instruction on motorway driving before you venture out on your own. Ask your instructor about this.

Q. 5.52

Mark one answer

After passing your driving test, you suffer from ill health. This affects your driving. You MUST

■ inform your local police station

■ get on as best you can

■ not inform anyone as you hold a full licence

■ inform the licensing authority

Answer

☑ **inform the licensing authority**

The licensing authority won't automatically take away your licence without investigation. For advice, contact the Driver and Vehicle Licensing Agency (or DVNI in Northern Ireland).

Q. 5.53

Mark one answer

You are invited to a pub lunch. You know that you will have to drive in the evening. What is your best course of action?

- Avoid mixing your alcoholic drinks
- Not drink any alcohol at all
- Have some milk before drinking alcohol
- Eat a hot meal with your alcoholic drinks

Answer

☑ **Not drink any alcohol at all**

Alcohol will stay in the body for several hours and may make you unfit to drive later in the day. Drinking during the day will also affect your performance at work or study.

Q. 5.54

Mark one answer

You have been convicted of driving whilst unfit through drink or drugs. You will find this is likely to cause the cost of one of the following to rise considerably. Which one?

- Road fund licence
- Insurance premiums
- Vehicle test certificate
- Driving licence

Answer

☑ **Insurance premiums**

You have shown that you are a risk to yourself and others on the road. For this reason insurance companies may charge you a higher premium.

Q. 5.55

Mark one answer

What advice should you give to a driver who has had a few alcoholic drinks at a party?

- Have a strong cup of coffee and then drive home
- Drive home carefully and slowly
- Go home by public transport
- Wait a short while and then drive home

Answer

☑ **Go home by public transport**

Drinking black coffee or waiting a few hours won't make any difference. Alcohol takes time to leave the body.

A driver who has been drinking should go home by public transport or taxi. They might even be unfit to drive the following morning.

questions   answers

Q. 5.56

Mark one answer

You have been taking medicine for a few days which made you feel drowsy. Today you feel better but still need to take the medicine. You should only drive

- if your journey is necessary
- at night on quiet roads
- if someone goes with you
- after checking with your doctor

Answer

 after checking with your doctor

Take care – it's not worth taking risks. Always check with your doctor to be really sure. You may not feel drowsy now, but the medicine could have an effect on you later in the day.

Q. 5.57

Mark one answer

You are about to return home from holiday when you become ill. A doctor prescribes drugs which are likely to affect your driving. You should

- drive only if someone is with you
- avoid driving on motorways
- not drive yourself
- never drive at more than 30 mph

Answer

 not drive yourself

Find another way to get home even if this proves to be very inconvenient. You must not put other road users, your passengers or yourself at risk.

Q. 5.58

Mark two answers

During periods of illness your ability to drive may be impaired. You MUST

- see your doctor each time before you drive
- only take smaller doses of any medicines
- be medically fit to drive
- not drive after taking certain medicines
- take all your medicines with you when you drive

Answers

 be medically fit to drive

 not drive after taking certain medicines

Only drive if you are fit to do so.

Some medication can affect your concentration, your ability to stay awake and your judgement when dealing with hazards. Driving whilst taking such medication is highly dangerous.

Q. 5.59

Mark two answers

You feel drowsy when driving. You should

▪ stop and rest as soon as possible

▪ turn the heater up to keep you warm and comfortable

▪ make sure you have a good supply of fresh air

▪ continue with your journey but drive more slowly

▪ close the car windows to help you concentrate

Answers

✓ **stop and rest as soon as possible**

✓ **make sure you have a good supply of fresh air**

You will be putting other road users at risk if you continue to drive when drowsy. Pull over and stop in a safe place. If you are driving a long distance, think about finding some accommodation so you can get some sleep before continuing your journey.

Q. 5.60

Mark two answers

You are driving along a motorway and become tired. You should

▪ stop at the next service area and rest

▪ leave the motorway at the next exit and rest

▪ increase your speed and turn up the radio volume

▪ close all your windows and set heating to warm

▪ pull up on the hard shoulder and change drivers

Answers

✓ **stop at the next service area and rest**

✓ **leave the motorway at the next exit and rest**

If you have planned your journey properly, to include rest stops, you should arrive at your destination in good time.

Q. 5.61

Mark one answer

You are taking drugs that are likely to affect your driving. What should you do?

▪ Seek medical advice before driving

▪ Limit your driving to essential journeys

▪ Only drive if accompanied by a full licence-holder

▪ Drive only for short distances

Answer

✓ **Seek medical advice before driving**

Check with your doctor or pharmacist if you think that the drugs you're taking are likely to make you feel drowsy or impair your judgement.

questions

answers

Q. 5.62

Mark one answer

You are about to drive home. You feel very tired and have a severe headache. You should

- wait until you are fit and well before driving
- drive home, but take a tablet for headaches
- drive home if you can stay awake for the journey
- wait for a short time, then drive home slowly

Answer

✓ **wait until you are fit and well before driving**

All your concentration should be on your driving. Any pain you feel will distract you and you should avoid driving when drowsy. The safest course of action is to wait until you have rested and feel better.

Q. 5.63

Mark one answer

If you are feeling tired it is best to stop as soon as you can. Until then you should

- increase your speed to find a stopping place quickly
- ensure a supply of fresh air
- gently tap the steering wheel
- keep changing speed to improve concentration

Answer

✓ **ensure a supply of fresh air**

If you're travelling on a long journey, plan your route before you leave. This will help you to

- be decisive at intersections and junctions
- plan your rest stops
- know approximately how long the journey will take.

Make sure that the vehicle you're travelling in is well-ventilated. A warm, stuffy atmosphere can make you drowsy, which will impair your judgement and concentration.

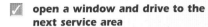

Q. 5.64

Mark one answer

If your motorway journey seems boring and you feel drowsy whilst driving you should

- ■ open a window and drive to the next service area
- ■ stop on the hard shoulder for a sleep
- ■ speed up to arrive at your destination sooner
- ■ slow down and let other drivers overtake

Answer

- ☑ **open a window and drive to the next service area**

Never stop on the hard shoulder to rest. If there is no service station for several miles, leave the motorway at the next exit and find somewhere safe to pull over.

Q. 5.65

Mark three answers

Driving long distances can be tiring. You can prevent this by

- ■ stopping every so often for a walk
- ■ opening a window for some fresh air
- ■ ensuring plenty of refreshment breaks
- ■ completing the journey without stopping
- ■ eating a large meal before driving

Answers

- ☑ **stopping every so often for a walk**
- ☑ **opening a window for some fresh air**
- ☑ **ensuring plenty of refreshment breaks**

Long-distance driving can be boring. This, coupled with a stuffy, warm vehicle, can make you feel tired. Make sure you take rest breaks to keep yourself awake and alert.

Q. 5.66

Mark one answer

You go to a social event and need to drive a short time after. What precaution should you take?

- ■ Avoid drinking alcohol on an empty stomach
- ■ Drink plenty of coffee after drinking alcohol
- ■ Avoid drinking alcohol completely
- ■ Drink plenty of milk before drinking alcohol

Answer

- ☑ **Avoid drinking alcohol completely**

This is always going to be the safest option. Just one drink could put you over the limit and dangerously impair your judgement and reactions.

questions answers

Q. 5.67

Mark one answer

You take some cough medicine given to you by a friend. What should you do before driving?

- Ask your friend if taking the medicine affected their driving
- Drink some strong coffee one hour before driving
- Check the label to see if the medicine will affect your driving
- Drive a short distance to see if the medicine is affecting your driving

Answer

☑ **Check the label to see if the medicine will affect your driving**

Never drive if you have taken drugs, without first checking what the side effects might be. They might affect your judgement and perception, and therefore endanger lives.

Q. 5.68

Mark one answer

You take the wrong route and find you are on a one-way street. You should

- reverse out of the road
- turn round in a side road
- continue to the end of the road
- reverse into a driveway

Answer

☑ **continue to the end of the road**

Never reverse or turn your vehicle around in a one-way street. This is highly dangerous. Carry on and find another route, checking the direction signs as you drive.

If you need to check a map, first stop in a safe place.

Q. 5.69

Mark three answers

Which THREE are likely to make you lose concentration while driving?

- Looking at road maps
- Listening to loud music
- Using your windscreen washers
- Looking in your wing mirror
- Using a mobile phone

Answers

☑ **Looking at road maps**

☑ **Listening to loud music**

☑ **Using a mobile phone**

Looking at road maps while driving is very dangerous. If you aren't sure of your route stop in a safe place and check the map. You must not allow anything to take your attention away from the road.

If you need to use a mobile phone, stop in a safe place before doing so.

Q. 5.70

Mark one answer

You are driving along this road. The driver on the left is reversing from a driveway. You should

☐ move to the opposite side of the road

☐ drive through as you have priority

☐ sound your horn and be prepared to stop

☐ speed up and drive through quickly

Answer

 sound your horn and be prepared to stop

White lights at the rear of a car show that it is about to reverse. Sound your horn to warn of your presence and reduce your speed as a precaution.

Q. 5.71

Mark one answer

You have been involved in an argument before starting your journey. This has made you feel angry. You should

☐ start to drive, but open a window

☐ drive slower than normal and turn your radio on

☐ have an alcoholic drink to help you relax before driving

☐ calm down before you start to drive

Answer

 calm down before you start to drive

If you are feeling upset or angry you should wait until you have calmed down before setting out on a journey.

questions

answers

Q. 5.72

Mark one answer

You start to feel tired while driving. What should you do?

 Increase your speed slightly

Decrease your speed slightly

Find a less busy route

Pull over at a safe place to rest

Answer

✓ **Pull over at a safe place to rest**

If you start to feel tired, stop at a safe place for a rest break.

Every year many fatal accidents are caused by drivers falling asleep at the wheel.

Q. 5.73

Mark one answer

You are driving on this dual carriageway. Why may you need to slow down?

There is a broken white line in the centre

There are solid white lines either side

There are roadworks ahead of you

There are no footpaths

Answer

✓ **There are roadworks ahead of you**

Look well ahead and read any road signs as you drive. They are there to inform you of what is ahead. In this case you may need to slow right down and change direction.

Make sure you can take whatever action is necessary in plenty of time. Check your mirrors so you know what is happening around you before you change speed or direction.

Q. 5.74

Mark one answer

You have just been overtaken by this motorcyclist who is cutting in sharply. You should

- sound the horn
- brake firmly
- keep a safe gap
- flash your lights

Answer

 keep a safe gap

If you need to, take your foot off the accelerator and drop back to allow a safe separation distance. Try not to react by braking sharply as you could lose control. If vehicles behind you are too close or unprepared, it could lead to an accident.

Q. 5.75

Mark one answer

You are about to drive home. You cannot find the glasses you need to wear. You should

- drive home slowly, keeping to quiet roads
- borrow a friend's glasses and use those
- drive home at night, so that the lights will help you
- find a way of getting home without driving

Answer

find a way of getting home without driving

Don't be tempted to drive if you've lost or forgotten your glasses. You must be able to see clearly when driving.

questions answers

Q. 5.76

Mark three answers

Which THREE result from drinking alcohol?

- Less control
- A false sense of confidence
- Faster reactions
- Poor judgement of speed
- Greater awareness of danger

Answers

- ☑ **Less control**
- ☑ **A false sense of confidence**
- ☑ **Poor judgement of speed**

You must understand the dangers of mixing alcohol with driving. Alcohol will severely reduce your ability to drive safely. Just one drink could put you over the limit. Don't risk people's lives – don't drink and drive.

Q. 5.77

Mark three answers

Which THREE of these are likely effects of drinking alcohol?

- Reduced co-ordination
- Increased confidence
- Poor judgement
- Increased concentration
- Faster reactions
- Colour blindness

Answers

- ☑ **Reduced co-ordination**
- ☑ **Increased confidence**
- ☑ **Poor judgement**

Alcohol can increase confidence to a point where a driver's behaviour might become 'out of character'. Someone who normally behaves sensibly suddenly takes risks and enjoys it. Never let yourself or your friends get into this situation.

Q. 5.78

Mark one answer

How does alcohol affect you?

- It speeds up your reactions
- It increases your awareness
- It improves your co-ordination
- It reduces your concentration

Answer

- ☑ **It reduces your concentration**

Concentration and good judgement are needed at all times to be a good, safe driver. Don't put yourself or others at risk by drinking and driving.

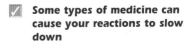
Q. 5.79

Mark one answer

Your doctor has given you a course of medicine. Why should you ask how it will affect you?

- Drugs make you a better driver by quickening your reactions
- You will have to let your insurance company know about the medicine
- Some types of medicine can cause your reactions to slow down
- The medicine you take may affect your hearing

Answer

✓ **Some types of medicine can cause your reactions to slow down**

Always check the label of any medication container. The contents might affect your driving. If you aren't sure, ask your doctor or pharmacist.

Q. 5.80

Mark two answers

You are not sure if your cough medicine will affect you. What TWO things could you do?

- Ask your doctor
- Check the medicine label
- Drive if you feel alright
- Ask a friend or relative for advice

Answers

✓ **Ask your doctor**

✓ **Check the medicine label**

If you're taking medicine or drugs prescribed by your doctor, check to ensure that they won't make you drowsy. If you forget to ask at the time of your visit to the surgery, check with your pharmacist.

Some over-the-counter medication can also cause drowsiness. Read the label and don't drive if you are affected.

Q. 5.81

Mark one answer

You are on a motorway. You feel tired. You should

- carry on but go slowly
- leave the motorway at the next exit
- complete your journey as quickly as possible
- stop on the hard shoulder

Answer

✓ **leave the motorway at the next exit**

If you do feel tired and there's no service station for many miles, leave the motorway at the next exit. Find a road off the motorway where you can pull up and stop safely.

questions  *answers*

Q. 5.82

Mark one answer

You find that you need glasses to read vehicle number plates at the required distance. When MUST you wear them?

- ☐ Only in bad weather conditions
- ☐ At all times when driving
- ☐ Only when you think it necessary
- ☐ Only in bad light or at night time

Answer

☑ **At all times when driving**

Have your eyesight tested before you start your practical training. Then, throughout your driving life, have checks periodically to ensure that your eyes haven't deteriorated.

Q. 5.83

Mark two answers

Which TWO things would help to keep you alert during a long journey?

- ☐ Finishing your journey as fast as you can
- ☐ Keeping off the motorways and using country roads
- ☐ Making sure that you get plenty of fresh air
- ☐ Making regular stops for refreshments

Answers

☑ **Making sure that you get plenty of fresh air**

☑ **Making regular stops for refreshments**

Make sure that the vehicle you're driving is well ventilated. A warm, stuffy atmosphere will make you feel drowsy. Open a window and turn down the heating.

Q. 5.84

Mark one answer

Which of the following types of glasses should NOT be worn when driving at night?

- ☐ Half-moon
- ☐ Round
- ☐ Bi-focal
- ☐ Tinted

Answer

☑ **Tinted**

If you are driving at night or in poor visibility, tinted lenses will reduce the efficiency of your vision, by reducing the amount of available light reaching your eyes.

questions

answers

Q. 5.85

Mark three answers

Drinking any amount of alcohol is likely to

- ■ slow down your reactions to hazards
- ■ increase the speed of your reactions
- ■ worsen your judgement of speed
- ■ improve your awareness of danger
- ■ give a false sense of confidence

Answers

- ☑ **slow down your reactions to hazards**
- ☑ **worsen your judgement of speed**
- ☑ **give a false sense of confidence**

If you are going to drive it's always the safest option not to drink at all. Don't be tempted – it's not worth it.

Q. 5.86

Mark three answers

What else can seriously affect your concentration, other than alcoholic drinks?

- ■ Drugs
- ■ Tiredness
- ■ Tinted windows
- ■ Contact lenses
- ■ Loud music

Answers

- ☑ **Drugs**
- ☑ **Tiredness**
- ☑ **Loud music**

Even a slight distraction can allow your concentration to drift. Maintain full concentration at all times so you stay in full control of your vehicle.

Q. 5.87

Mark one answer

As a driver you find that your eyesight has become very poor. Your optician says they cannot help you. The law says that you should tell

- ■ the licensing authority
- ■ your own doctor
- ■ the local police station
- ■ another optician

Answer

- ☑ **the licensing authority**

This will have a serious effect on your judgement and concentration. If you cannot meet the eyesight requirements you must tell DVLA (or DVNI in Northern Ireland).

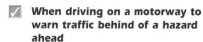

questions   *answers*

Q. 5.88

Mark one answer

For which of these may you use hazard warning lights?

- When driving on a motorway to warn traffic behind of a hazard ahead
- When you are double-parked on a two way road
- When your direction indicators are not working
- When warning oncoming traffic that you intend to stop

Answer

☑ **When driving on a motorway to warn traffic behind of a hazard ahead**

Hazard warning lights are an important safety feature. Use them when driving on a motorway to warn traffic behind you of danger ahead.

You should also use them if your vehicle has broken down and is causing an obstruction.

Q. 5.89

Mark one answer

When should you use hazard warning lights?

- When you are double-parked on a two way road
- When your direction indicators are not working
- When warning oncoming traffic that you intend to stop
- When your vehicle has broken down and is causing an obstruction

Answer

☑ **When your vehicle has broken down and is causing an obstruction**

Hazard warning lights are an important safety feature and should be used if you have broken down and are causing an obstruction. Don't use them as an excuse to park illegally such as when using a cash machine or post box.

You may also use them on motorways to warn traffic behind you of danger ahead.

Q. 5.90

Mark one answer

You want to turn left at this junction. The view of the main road is restricted. What should you do?

- Stay well back and wait to see if something comes
- Build up your speed so that you can emerge quickly
- Stop and apply the handbrake even if the road is clear
- Approach slowly and edge out until you can see more clearly

Answer

☑ **Approach slowly and edge out until you can see more clearly**

You should slow right down, and stop if necessary, at any junction where the view is restricted. Edge forward until you can see properly. Only then can you decide if it is safe to go.

Q. 5.91

Mark one answer

You are driving on a motorway. The traffic ahead is braking sharply because of an accident. How could you warn following traffic?

- Briefly use the hazard warning lights
- Switch on the hazard warning lights continuously
- Briefly use the rear fog lights
- Switch on the headlamps continuously

Answer

☑ **Briefly use the hazard warning lights**

The only time you are permitted to use your hazard warning lights while moving is if you are on a motorway or dual carriageway and you need to warn drivers behind you of a hazard or obstruction ahead. Only use them just long enough to ensure that your warning has been observed.

questions

answers

Q. 5.92

Mark one answer

When may you use hazard warning lights?

- [ ] To park alongside another car
- [ ] To park on double yellow lines
- [ ] When you are being towed
- [ ] When you have broken down

Answer

☑ **When you have broken down**

Hazard warning lights may be used to warn other road users when you

- have broken down and are causing an obstruction
- are on a motorway and want to warn the traffic behind you of a hazard ahead.

Don't use them when being towed.

Q. 5.93

Mark one answer

Hazard warning lights should be used when vehicles are

- [ ] broken down and causing an obstruction
- [ ] faulty and moving slowly
- [ ] being towed along a road
- [ ] reversing into a side road

Answer

☑ **broken down and causing an obstruction**

Don't use hazard lights as an excuse for illegal parking. If you do use them, don't forget to switch them off when you move away. There must be a warning light on the control panel to show when the hazard lights are in operation.

Q. 5.94

Mark one answer

When driving a car fitted with automatic transmission what would you use 'kick down' for?

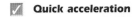 Cruise control

 Quick acceleration

 Slow braking

 Fuel economy

Answer

☑ **Quick acceleration**

'Kick down' selects a lower gear, enabling the vehicle to accelerate faster.

Vulnerable road users

This section looks at the risks when dealing with vulnerable road users.

The questions will ask you about

- **Pedestrians**

  being aware of their actions as they cross the road.

- **Children**

  being aware that they are particularly unpredictable on and around roads.

- **Elderly drivers**

  being aware that they may be slower to make decisions.

- **Disabled people**

  being aware that they might not be able to react to danger as quickly or easily as the able-bodied.

- **Cyclists**

  being aware that they may swerve to avoid obstructions and are often affected by adverse weather conditions.

- **Motorcyclists**

  being aware of their presence on the road.

- **Animals**

  being aware that animals can be unpredictable and may move slowly.

- **New drivers**

  being aware that they may be more hesitant, allowing for this and being patient. They lack experience and are therefore more vulnerable.

Q. 6.1

Mark one answer

Which sign means that there may be people walking along the road?

Answer

Always check the road signs. Triangular signs are warning signs and they'll keep you informed of hazards ahead and help you to anticipate any problems. There are a number of different signs showing pedestrians. Learn the meaning of each one.

Q. 6.2

Mark one answer

You are turning left at a junction. Pedestrians have started to cross the road. You should

☐ go on, giving them plenty of room

☐ stop and wave at them to cross

☐ blow your horn and proceed

☐ give way to them

Answer

☑ **give way to them**

If you're turning into a side road, pedestrians already crossing the road have priority and you should give way to them. Don't

- wave them across the road
- sound your horn
- flash your lights
- give any other misleading signal – other road users may misinterpret your signal and you might lead the pedestrian into a dangerous situation.

If a pedestrian is slow or indecisive be patient and wait. Don't hurry them across by revving your engine.

questions   answers

Q. 6.3

Mark one answer

You are turning left from a main road into a side road. People are already crossing the road into which you are turning. You should

■ continue, as it is your right of way

■ signal to them to continue crossing

■ wait and allow them to cross

■ sound your horn to warn them of your presence

Answer

☑ **wait and allow them to cross**

Always check the road you're turning into. Approaching at the correct speed will allow you enough time to observe and react.

Give way to any pedestrians already crossing the road.

Q. 6.4

Mark one answer

You are at a road junction, turning into a minor road. There are pedestrians crossing the minor road. You should

■ stop and wave the pedestrians across

■ sound your horn to let the pedestrians know that you are there

■ give way to the pedestrians who are already crossing

■ carry on; the pedestrians should give way to you

Answer

☑ **give way to the pedestrians who are already crossing**

Always look into the road you're turning into. If there are pedestrians crossing, give way to them, but don't wave or signal to them to cross.

Signal your intention to turn as you approach.

Q. 6.5

Mark one answer

You are turning left into a side road. What hazards should you be especially aware of?

■ One way street

■ Pedestrians

■ Traffic congestion

■ Parked vehicles

Answer

✓ **Pedestrians**

Make sure that you have reduced your speed and are in the correct gear for the turn. Look into the road before you turn and always give way to any pedestrians who are crossing.

Q. 6.6

Mark one answer

You intend to turn right into a side road. Just before turning you should check for motorcyclists who might be

■ overtaking on your left

■ following you closely

■ emerging from the side road

■ overtaking on your right

Answer

✓ **overtaking on your right**

Never attempt to change direction to the right without first checking your right-hand mirror. A motorcyclist might not have seen your signal and could be hidden by the car behind you. This action should become a matter of routine.

Q. 6.7

Mark one answer

A toucan crossing is different from other crossings because

■ moped riders can use it

■ it is controlled by a traffic warden

■ it is controlled by two flashing lights

■ cyclists can use it

Answer

✓ **cyclists can use it**

Toucan crossings are shared by pedestrians and cyclists and they are shown the green light together. Cyclists are permitted to cycle across.

The signals are push-button operated and there is no flashing amber phase.

questions *answers*

Q. 6.8

Mark two answers

At toucan crossings

- there is no flashing amber light
- cyclists are not permitted
- there is a continuously flashing amber beacon
- pedestrians and cyclists may cross
- you only stop if someone is waiting to cross

Answers

✓ **there is no flashing amber light**

✓ **pedestrians and cyclists may cross**

There are some crossings where cycle routes lead the cyclists to cross at the same place as pedestrians. These are called toucan crossings. Always look out for cyclists, as they're likely to be approaching faster than pedestrians.

Q. 6.9

Mark one answer

What does this sign tell you?

- No cycling
- Cycle route ahead
- Route for cycles only
- End of cycle route

Answer

✓ **Cycle route ahead**

With people's concern today for the environment, cycle routes are being created in our towns and cities. These are usually defined by road markings and signs.

Respect the presence of cyclists on the road and give them plenty of room if you need to pass.

Q. 6.10

Mark one answer

How will a school crossing patrol signal you to stop?

- By pointing to children on the opposite pavement
- By displaying a red light
- By displaying a stop sign
- By giving you an arm signal

Answer

✓ **By displaying a stop sign**

If a school crossing patrol steps out into the road with a stop sign you must stop. Don't

- wave anyone across the road
- get impatient or rev your engine.

Q. 6.11

Mark one answer

Where would you see this sign?

- In the window of a car taking children to school
- At the side of the road
- At playground areas
- On the rear of a school bus or coach

Answer

 On the rear of a school bus or coach

Vehicles that are used to carry children to and from school will be travelling at busy times of the day. If you're following a vehicle with this sign be prepared for it to make frequent stops. It might pick up or set down passengers in places other than normal bus stops.

Q. 6.12

Mark one answer

Which sign tells you that pedestrians may be walking in the road as there is no pavement?

Answer

Give pedestrians who are walking at the side of the road plenty of room when you pass them. They may turn around when they hear your engine and accidentally step into the road.

questions

answers

Q. 6.13

Mark one answer

What does this sign mean?

No route for pedestrians and cyclists

A route for pedestrians only

A route for cyclists only

A route for pedestrians and cyclists

Answer

☑ **A route for pedestrians and cyclists**

This sign shows a shared route for pedestrians and cyclists: when it ends, the cyclists will be rejoining the main road.

Q. 6.14

Mark one answer

You see a pedestrian with a white stick and red band. This means that the person is

physically disabled

deaf only

blind only

deaf and blind

Answer

☑ **deaf and blind**

If someone is deaf as well as blind, they may be carrying a white stick with a red reflective band.

You can't see if a pedestrian is deaf. Don't assume everyone can hear you approaching.

questions answers

Q. 6.15

Mark one answer

What action would you take when elderly people are crossing the road?

- Wave them across so they know that you have seen them
- Be patient and allow them to cross in their own time
- Rev the engine to let them know that you are waiting
- Tap the horn in case they are hard of hearing

Answer

☑ **Be patient and allow them to cross in their own time**

Be aware that elderly people might take a long time to cross the road. They might also be hard of hearing and not hear you approaching.

Don't hurry elderly people across the road by getting too close to them or revving your engine.

Q. 6.16

Mark one answer

You see two elderly pedestrians about to cross the road ahead. You should

- expect them to wait for you to pass
- speed up to get past them quickly
- stop and wave them across the road
- be careful, they may misjudge your speed

Answer

☑ **be careful, they may misjudge your speed**

Elderly people may have impaired

- hearing
- vision
- concentration
- judgement.

They may also walk slowly and so could take a long time to cross the road.

questions *answers*

Q. 6.17

Mark one answer

What does this sign mean?

- Contra-flow pedal cycle lane
- With-flow pedal cycle lane
- Pedal cycles and buses only
- No pedal cycles or buses

Answer

☑ **With-flow pedal cycle lane**

The picture of a cycle will also usually be painted on the road, sometimes with a different colour surface. Leave these clear for cyclists and don't pass too closely when you overtake.

Q. 6.18

Mark one answer

You are coming up to a roundabout. A cyclist is signalling to turn right. What should you do?

- Overtake on the right
- Give a horn warning
- Signal the cyclist to move across
- Give the cyclist plenty of room

Answer

☑ **Give the cyclist plenty of room**

If you're following a cyclist who's signalling to turn right at a roundabout leave plenty of room. Give them space and time to get into the correct lane.

Q. 6.19

Mark one answer

You are approaching this roundabout and see the cyclist signal right. Why is the cyclist keeping to the left?

- ☐ It is a quicker route for the cyclist
- ☐ The cyclist is going to turn left instead
- ☐ The cyclist thinks The Highway Code does not apply to bicycles
- ☐ The cyclist is slower and more vulnerable

Answer

☑ **The cyclist is slower and more vulnerable**

Cycling in today's heavy traffic can be hazardous. Some cyclists may not feel happy about crossing the path of traffic to take up a position in an outside lane. Be aware of this and understand that, although in the left-hand lane, the cyclist might be turning right.

Q. 6.20

Mark one answer

When you are overtaking a cyclist you should leave as much room as you would give to a car. What is the main reason for this?

- ☐ The cyclist might change lanes
- ☐ The cyclist might get off the bike
- ☐ The cyclist might swerve
- ☐ The cyclist might have to make a right turn

Answer

☑ **The cyclist might swerve**

Look at the road ahead if you intend to overtake a cyclist. Check if the cyclist is likely to need to change direction for a parked vehicle or an uneven road surface. When you have a safe place to overtake leave as much room as you would for a car. Don't cut in sharply or pass too closely.

questions   answers

Q. 6.21

Mark two answers

Which TWO should you allow extra room when overtaking?

- Motorcycles
- Tractors
- Bicycles
- Road-sweeping vehicles

Answers

- ☑ **Motorcycles**
- ☑ **Bicycles**

Don't pass riders too closely as this may cause them to lose balance. Always leave as much room as you would for a car, and don't cut in.

Q. 6.22

Mark one answer

Why should you look particularly for motorcyclists and cyclists at junctions?

- They may want to turn into the side road
- They may slow down to let you turn
- They are harder to see
- They might not see you turn

Answer

- ☑ **They are harder to see**

Cyclists and motorcyclists are smaller than other vehicles and so are more difficult to see. They can easily become hidden from your view by cars parked near a junction.

Q. 6.23

Mark one answer

You are waiting to come out of a side road. Why should you watch carefully for motorcycles?

- Motorcycles are usually faster than cars
- Police patrols often use motorcycles
- Motorcycles are small and hard to see
- Motorcycles have right of way

Answer

- ☑ **Motorcycles are small and hard to see**

If you're waiting to emerge from a side road watch out for motorcycles: they're small and can be difficult to see. Be especially careful if there are parked vehicles restricting your view, there might be a motorcycle approaching.

IF YOU DON'T KNOW, DON'T GO.

Q. 6.24

Mark one answer

In daylight, an approaching motorcyclist is using a dipped headlight. Why?

- So that the rider can be seen more easily
- To stop the battery overcharging
- To improve the rider's vision
- The rider is inviting you to proceed

Answer

☑ **So that the rider can be seen more easily**

A motorcycle can be lost from sight behind another vehicle. The use of the headlight helps to make it more conspicuous and therefore more easily seen.

Q. 6.25

Mark one answer

Motorcyclists should wear bright clothing mainly because

- they must do so by law
- it helps keep them cool in summer
- the colours are popular
- drivers often do not see them

Answer

☑ **drivers often do not see them**

Motorcycles are small vehicles and can be difficult to see. If the rider wears bright clothing it can make it easier for other road users to see them approaching, especially at junctions.

Q. 6.26

Mark one answer

There is a slow-moving motorcyclist ahead of you. You are unsure what the rider is going to do. You should

- pass on the left
- pass on the right
- stay behind
- move closer

Answer

☑ **stay behind**

If a motorcyclist is travelling slowly it may be that they are looking for a turning or entrance. Be patient and stay behind them in case they need to make a sudden change of direction.

VULNERABLE ROAD USERS

questions   *answers*

Q. 6.27

Mark one answer

Motorcyclists will often look round over their right shoulder just before turning right. This is because

- ☐ they need to listen for following traffic
- ☐ motorcycles do not have mirrors
- ☐ looking around helps them balance as they turn
- ☐ they need to check for traffic in their blind area

Answer

- ☑ **they need to check for traffic in their blind area**

If you see a motorcyclist take a quick glance over their shoulder, this could mean they are about to change direction. Recognising a clue like this helps you to be prepared and take appropriate action, making you safer on the road.

Q. 6.28

Mark three answers

At road junctions which of the following are most vulnerable?

- ☐ Cyclists
- ☐ Motorcyclists
- ☐ Pedestrians
- ☐ Car drivers
- ☐ Lorry drivers

Answers

- ☑ **Cyclists**
- ☑ **Motorcyclists**
- ☑ **Pedestrians**

Pedestrians and riders on two wheels can be harder to see than other road users. Make sure you keep a look-out for them, especially at junctions. Good effective observation, coupled with appropriate action, can save lives.

Q. 6.29

Mark one answer

Motorcyclists are particularly vulnerable

- ☐ when moving off
- ☐ on dual carriageways
- ☐ when approaching junctions
- ☐ on motorways

Answer

- ☑ **when approaching junctions**

Another road user failing to see a motorcyclist is a major cause of collisions at junctions. Wherever streams of traffic join or cross there's the potential for this type of accident to occur.

Q. 6.30

Mark one answer

An injured motorcyclist is lying unconscious in the road. You should

■ remove the safety helmet

■ seek medical assistance

■ move the person off the road

■ remove the leather jacket

Answer

☑ **seek medical assistance**

If someone has been injured, the sooner proper medical attention is given the better. Either send someone to phone for help or go yourself.

Only move an injured person if there is a risk of further danger. Never remove an injured motorcyclist's safety helmet.

Q. 6.31

Mark one answer

You notice horse riders in front. What should you do FIRST?

■ Pull out to the middle of the road

■ Be prepared to slow down

■ Accelerate around them

■ Signal right

Answer

☑ **Be prepared to slow down**

Be particularly careful when approaching horse riders – slow down and be prepared to stop. Always pass wide and slowly and look out for signals given by horse riders.

Horses are unpredictable: always treat them as potential hazards and take great care when passing them.

Q. 6.32

Mark two answers

You are approaching a roundabout. There are horses just ahead of you. You should

■ be prepared to stop

■ treat them like any other vehicle

■ give them plenty of room

■ accelerate past as quickly as possible

■ sound your horn as a warning

Answers

☑ **be prepared to stop**

☑ **give them plenty of room**

Horse riders often keep to the outside of the roundabout even if they are turning right. Give them plenty of room and remember that they may have to cross lanes of traffic.

questions *answers*

Q. 6.33

Mark three answers

Which THREE should you do when passing sheep on a road?

- Allow plenty of room
- Go very slowly
- Pass quickly but quietly
- Be ready to stop
- Briefly sound your horn

Answers

- ☑ **Allow plenty of room**
- ☑ **Go very slowly**
- ☑ **Be ready to stop**

Slow down and be ready to stop if you see animals in the road ahead. Animals are easily frightened by

- noise
- vehicles passing too close to them.

Stop if signalled to do so by the person in charge.

Q. 6.34

Mark one answer

At night you see a pedestrian wearing reflective clothing and carrying a bright red light. What does this mean?

- You are approaching roadworks
- You are approaching an organised walk
- You are approaching a slow-moving vehicle
- You are approaching an accident black spot

Answer

- ☑ **You are approaching an organised walk**

The people involved in the walk should be keeping to the left, but this can't be assumed. Pass slowly, ensuring that you have the time to do so safely. Be aware that the pedestrians have their backs to you and might not know that you're there.

Q. 6.35

Mark one answer

As you approach a pelican crossing the lights change to green. Elderly people are halfway across. You should

- wave them to cross as quickly as they can
- rev your engine to make them hurry
- flash your lights in case they have not heard you
- wait because they will take longer to cross

Answer

- ☑ **wait because they will take longer to cross**

Even if the lights turn to green, wait for them to clear the crossing. Allow them to cross the road in their own time, and don't try to hurry them by revving your engine.

Q. 6.36

Mark one answer

There are flashing amber lights under a school warning sign. What action should you take?

 Reduce speed until you are clear of the area

 Keep up your speed and sound the horn

 Increase your speed to clear the area quickly

 Wait at the lights until they change to green

Answer

 Reduce speed until you are clear of the area

The flashing amber lights are switched on to warn you that children may be crossing near a school. Slow down and take extra care as you may have to stop.

Q. 6.37

Mark one answer

Which of the following types of crossing can detect when people are on them?

 Pelican

 Toucan

 Zebra

 Puffin

Answer

 Puffin

'Puffin' is an acronym for Pedestrian User Friendly Intelligent crossing. Sensors detect when people are crossing and will hold the waiting traffic on a red signal until the pedestrians are clear.

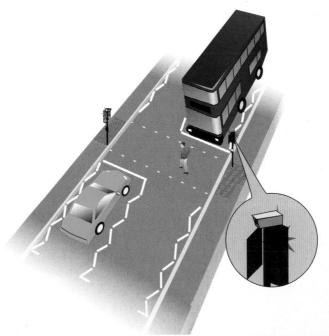

questions   answers

Q. 6.38

Mark one answer

You are approaching this crossing. You should

■ prepare to slow down and stop

■ stop and wave the pedestrians across

■ speed up and pass by quickly

■ drive on unless the pedestrians step out

Answer

☑ **prepare to slow down and stop**

Be courteous and prepare to stop. Do not wave people across as this could be dangerous if another vehicle is approaching the crossing.

Q. 6.39

Mark one answer

You see a pedestrian with a dog. The dog has a bright orange lead and collar. This especially warns you that the pedestrian is

■ elderly

■ dog training

■ colour blind

■ deaf

Answer

 deaf

Take extra care as the pedestrian may not be aware of vehicles approaching.

Q. 6.40

Mark one answer

These road markings must be kept clear to allow

☐ school children to be dropped off

☐ for teachers to park

☐ school children to be picked up

☐ a clear view of the crossing area

Answer

☑ **a clear view of the crossing area**

The markings are there to show that the area must be kept clear to allow an unrestricted view for

• approaching drivers and riders

• children wanting to cross the road.

Q. 6.41

Mark one answer

You must not stop on these road markings because you may obstruct

☐ childrens view of the crossing area

☐ teachers access to the school

☐ delivery vehicles access to the school

☐ emergency vehicles access to the school

Answer

☑ **childrens view of the crossing area**

These markings are found on the road outside schools. DO NOT stop (even to set down or pick up children) or park on them. The markings are to make sure that drivers, riders and children have a clear view.

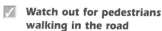

questions *answers*

Q. 6.42

Mark one answer

The left hand pavement is closed due to street repairs. What should you do?

- Watch out for pedestrians walking in the road
- Use your right hand mirror more often
- Speed up to get past the road works quicker
- Position close to the left hand kerb

Answer

 **Watch out for pedestrians walking in the road**

Where street repairs have closed off pavements, proceed carefully and slowly as pedestrians might have to walk in the road.

Q. 6.43

Mark one answer

Where would you see this sign?

- Near a school crossing
- At a playground entrance
- On a school bus
- At a 'pedestrians only' area

Answer

✓ **On a school bus**

Watch out for children crossing the road from the other side of the bus.

Q. 6.44

Mark one answer

You are following a motorcyclist on an uneven road. You should

- allow less room so you can be seen in their mirrors
- overtake immediately
- allow extra room in case they swerve to avoid pot-holes
- allow the same room as normal because road surfaces do not affect motorcyclists

Answer

✓ **allow extra room in case they swerve to avoid pot-holes**

Potholes and bumps in the road can unbalance a motorcyclist. For this reason the rider might swerve to avoid an uneven road surface. Watch out at places where this is likely to occur.

Q. 6.45

Mark one answer

You are following two cyclists. They approach a roundabout in the left-hand lane. In which direction should you expect the cyclists to go?

- Left
- Right
- Any direction
- Straight ahead

Answer

☑ **Any direction**

Cyclists approaching a roundabout in the left-hand lane may be turning right but may not have been able to get into the correct lane due to the heavy traffic. They may also feel safer keeping to the left all the way round the roundabout. Be aware of them and give them plenty of room.

Q. 6.46

Mark one answer

You are travelling behind a moped. You want to turn left just ahead. You should

- overtake the moped before the junction
- pull alongside the moped and stay level until just before the junction
- sound your horn as a warning and pull in front of the moped
- stay behind until the moped has passed the junction

Answer

☑ **stay behind until the moped has passed the junction**

Passing the moped and turning into the junction could mean that you cut across the front of the rider. This might force them to slow down, stop or even lose control. Slow down and stay behind the moped until it has passed the junction and you can then turn safely.

Q. 6.47

Mark three answers

Which THREE of the following are hazards motorcyclists present in queues of traffic?

- Cutting in just in front of you
- Riding in single file
- Passing very close to you
- Riding with their headlight on dipped beam
- Filtering between the lanes

Answers

☑ **Cutting in just in front of you**

☑ **Passing very close to you**

☑ **Filtering between the lanes**

Where there's more than one lane of queuing traffic, motorcyclists may use the opportunity to make progress by riding between the lanes. Be aware that they may be passing on either side. Check your mirrors before you move off.

questions   *answers*

Q. 6.48

Mark one answer

You see a horse rider as you approach a roundabout. They are signalling right but keeping well to the left. You should

- proceed as normal
- keep close to them
- cut in front of them
- stay well back

Answer

 stay well back

Allow the riders to enter and exit the roundabout in their own time. The riders may feel safer keeping to the left all the way around the roundabout. Don't drive up close behind or alongside them, as this could disturb the horses.

Q. 6.49

Mark one answer

How would you react to drivers who appear to be inexperienced?

- Sound your horn to warn them of your presence
- Be patient and prepare for them to react more slowly
- Flash your headlights to indicate that it is safe for them to proceed
- Overtake them as soon as possible

Answer

 Be patient and prepare for them to react more slowly

Learners might not have confidence when they first start to drive. Allow them plenty of room and don't react adversely to their hesitation. We all learn from experience, but new drivers will have had less practice in dealing with all the situations that might occur.

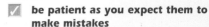

Q. 6.50

Mark one answer

You are following a learner driver who stalls at a junction. You should

■ be patient as you expect them to make mistakes

■ stay very close behind and flash your headlights

■ start to rev your engine if they take too long to restart

■ immediately steer around them and drive on

Answer

☑ **be patient as you expect them to make mistakes**

Learning is a process of practice and experience. Try to understand this and tolerate others who are at the beginning of this process.

Q. 6.51

Mark one answer

You are on a country road. What should you expect to see coming towards you on YOUR side of the road?

■ Motorcycles

■ Bicycles

■ Pedestrians

■ Horse riders

Answer

☑ **Pedestrians**

On a quiet country road always be aware that there may be a hazard just around the next bend, such as a slow-moving vehicle or pedestrians. Pedestrians are advised to walk on the right-hand side of the road if there is no pavement, so they may be walking towards you on your side of the road.

questions *answers*

Q. 6.52

Mark one answer

You are turning left into a side road. Pedestrians are crossing the road near the junction. You must

☐ wave them on

☐ sound your horn

☐ switch on your hazard lights

☐ wait for them to cross

Answer

 wait for them to cross

Check that it's clear before you turn into a junction. If there are pedestrians crossing, let them cross in their own time.

Q. 6.53

Mark one answer

You are following a car driven by an elderly driver. You should

☐ expect the driver to drive badly

☐ flash your lights and overtake

☐ be aware that the driver's reactions may not be as fast as yours

☐ stay very close behind but be careful

Answer

☑ **be aware that the driver's reactions may not be as fast as yours**

You must show consideration to other road users. The reactions of older drivers may be slower and they might need more time to deal with a situation. Be tolerant and don't lose patience or show your annoyance.

Q. 6.54

Mark one answer

You are following a cyclist. You wish to turn left just ahead. You should

■ overtake the cyclist before the junction

■ pull alongside the cyclist and stay level until after the junction

■ hold back until the cyclist has passed the junction

■ go around the cyclist on the junction

Answer

 hold back until the cyclist has passed the junction

Make allowances for cyclists. Allow them plenty of room. Don't try to overtake and then turn left as you would have to cut in across the path of the cyclist. Be patient and stay behind them until they have passed the junction.

Q. 6.55

Mark one answer

A horse rider is in the left-hand lane approaching a roundabout. You should expect the rider to

■ go in any direction

■ turn right

■ turn left

■ go ahead

Answer

☑ **go in any direction**

Horses and their riders will move more slowly than other road users. They might not have time to cut across heavy traffic to take up positions in the offside lane. For this reason a horse and rider may approach a roundabout in the left-hand lane, even though they're turning right.

Q. 6.56

Mark one answer

You have just passed your test. How can you decrease your risk of accidents on the motorway?

- ▨ By keeping up with the car in front
- ▨ By never going over 40 mph
- ▨ By staying only in the left hand lane
- ▨ By taking further training

Answer

☑ **By taking further training**

You're more likely to have an accident in the first year after taking your test. Lack of experience means that you might not react to hazards as quickly as a more experienced person. Further training will help you to become safer on the roads.

Q. 6.57

Mark one answer

Powered vehicles used by disabled people are small and hard to see. How do they give early warning when on a dual carriageway?

- ▨ They will have a flashing red light
- ▨ They will have a flashing green light
- ▨ They will have a flashing blue light
- ▨ They will have a flashing amber light.

Answer

☑ **They will have a flashing amber light.**

Powered vehicles used by disabled people are small, low, hard to see and travel very slowly. On a dual carriageway they will have a flashing amber light to warn other road users.

Q. 6.58

Mark one answer

You should never attempt to overtake a cyclist

- ▨ just before you turn left
- ▨ on a left hand bend
- ▨ on a one-way street
- ▨ on a dual carriageway

Answer

☑ **just before you turn left**

If you want to turn left and there's a cyclist in front of you, hold back. Wait until the cyclist has passed the junction and then turn left behind them.

Q. 6.59

Mark one answer

Ahead of you there is a moving vehicle with a flashing amber beacon. This means it is

 slow moving

 broken down

 a doctor's car

 a school crossing patrol

Answer

 slow moving

As you approach the vehicle, assess the situation. Due to its slow progress you will need to judge whether it is safe to overtake.

Q. 6.60

Mark one answer

You want to reverse into a side road. You are not sure that the area behind your car is clear. What should you do?

 Look through the rear window only

 Get out and check

 Check the mirrors only

 Carry on, assuming it is clear

Answer

 Get out and check

If you cannot be sure whether there is anything behind you, it is always safest to check before reversing. There may be a small child or a low obstruction close behind your car. The shape and size of your vehicle can restrict visibility.

Q. 6.61

Mark one answer

You are about to reverse into a side road. A pedestrian wishes to cross behind you. You should

 wave to the pedestrian to stop

 give way to the pedestrian

 wave to the pedestrian to cross

 reverse before the pedestrian starts to cross

Answer

 give way to the pedestrian

If you need to reverse into a side road try to find a place that's free from traffic and pedestrians.

Look all around before and during the manoeuvre. Always stop and give way to any pedestrians who wish to cross behind you. Don't

• wave them across the road

• sound the horn

• flash your lights

• give any other misleading signal – other road users may not have seen your signal and you might lead the pedestrian into a dangerous situation.

questions   *answers*

Q. 6.62

Mark one answer

Who is especially in danger of not being seen as you reverse your car?

- Motorcyclists
- Car drivers
- Cyclists
- Children

Answer

☑ **Children**

As you look through the rear of your vehicle you may not be able to see a small child. Be aware of this before you reverse. If there are children about, get out and check if it is clear before reversing.

Q. 6.63

Mark one answer

You are reversing around a corner when you notice a pedestrian walking behind you. What should you do?

- Slow down and wave the pedestrian across
- Continue reversing and steer round the pedestrian
- Stop and give way
- Continue reversing and sound your horn

Answer

☑ **Stop and give way**

Wait until the pedestrian has passed, then look around again before you start to reverse. Don't forget that you may not be able to see a small child directly behind your vehicle. Be aware of the possibility of hidden dangers.

Q. 6.64

Mark one answer

You want to turn right from a junction but your view is restricted by parked vehicles. What should you do?

- Move out quickly, but be prepared to stop
- Sound your horn and pull out if there is no reply
- Stop, then move slowly forward until you have a clear view
- Stop, get out and look along the main road to check

Answer

☑ **Stop, then move slowly forward until you have a clear view**

If you want to turn right from a junction and your view is restricted, STOP. Ease forward until you can see – there might be something approaching.

IF YOU DON'T KNOW, DON'T GO.

Q. 6.65

Mark one answer

You are at the front of a queue of traffic waiting to turn right into a side road. Why is it important to check your right mirror just before turning?

■ To look for pedestrians about to cross

■ To check for overtaking vehicles

■ To make sure the side road is clear

■ To check for emerging traffic

Answer

☑ **To check for overtaking vehicles**

There could be a motorcyclist riding along the outside of the queue. Always check your mirror before turning as situations behind you can change in the time you have been waiting to turn.

Q. 6.66

Mark one answer

What must a driver do at a pelican crossing when the amber light is flashing?

■ Signal the pedestrian to cross

■ Always wait for the green light before proceeding

■ Give way to any pedestrians on the crossing

■ Wait for the red-and-amber light before proceeding

Answer

☑ **Give way to any pedestrians on the crossing**

The flashing amber light allows pedestrians already on the crossing to get to the other side before a green light shows to the traffic. Be aware that some pedestrians, such as elderly people and young children, need longer to cross. Let them do this at their own pace.

Q. 6.67

Mark two answers

You have stopped at a pelican crossing. A disabled person is crossing slowly in front of you. The lights have now changed to green. You should

■ allow the person to cross

■ drive in front of the person

■ drive behind the person

■ sound your horn

■ be patient

■ edge forward slowly

Answers

☑ **allow the person to cross**

☑ **be patient**

At a pelican crossing the green light means you may proceed as long as the crossing is clear. If someone hasn't finished crossing, be patient and wait for them.

questions *answers*

Q. 6.68

Mark one answer

You are driving past parked cars. You notice a wheel of a bicycle sticking out between them. What should you do?

- Accelerate past quickly and sound your horn

- Slow down and wave the cyclist across

- Brake sharply and flash your headlights

- Slow down and be prepared to stop for a cyclist

Answer

 Slow down and be prepared to stop for a cyclist

Scan the road as you drive. Try to anticipate hazards by being aware of the places where they are likely to occur. You'll then be able to react in good time, if necessary.

Q. 6.69

Mark one answer

You are driving past a line of parked cars. You notice a ball bouncing out into the road ahead. What should you do?

- Continue driving at the same speed and sound your horn

- Continue driving at the same speed and flash your headlights

- Slow down and be prepared to stop for children

- Stop and wave the children across to fetch their ball

Answer

 Slow down and be prepared to stop for children

Beware of children playing in the street and running out into the road. If a ball bounces out from the pavement, slow down and stop. Don't encourage anyone to retrieve it. Other road users may not see your signal and you might lead a child into a dangerous situation.

Q. 6.70

Mark one answer

You want to turn right from a main road into a side road. Just before turning you should

- cancel your right-turn signal
- select first gear
- check for traffic overtaking on your right
- stop and set the handbrake

Answer

☑ **check for traffic overtaking on your right**

Motorcyclists often overtake queues of vehicles. Make one last check in your mirror and your blind spot to avoid turning across their path.

Q. 6.71

Mark one answer

You are driving in slow-moving queues of traffic. Just before changing lane you should

- sound the horn
- look for motorcyclists filtering through the traffic
- give a 'slowing down' arm signal
- change down to first gear

Answer

☑ **look for motorcyclists filtering through the traffic**

In this situation motorcyclists could be passing you on either side. Always check before you change lanes or change direction.

Q. 6.72

Mark one answer

You are driving in town. There is a bus at the bus stop on the other side of the road. Why should you be careful?

- The bus may have broken down
- Pedestrians may come from behind the bus
- The bus may move off suddenly
- The bus may remain stationary

Answer

☑ **Pedestrians may come from behind the bus**

If you see a bus ahead watch out for pedestrians. They may not be able to see you if they're crossing behind the bus.

questions   *answers*

Q. 6.73

Mark one answer

How should you overtake horse riders?

- [ ] Drive up close and overtake as soon as possible
- [ ] Speed is not important but allow plenty of room
- [ ] Use your horn just once to warn them
- [ ] Drive slowly and leave plenty of room

Answer

☑ **Drive slowly and leave plenty of room**

If you're driving on a country road then take extra care. Be ready for

- farm animals
- horses
- pedestrians
- farm vehicles.

Always be prepared to slow down or stop.

Q. 6.74

Mark one answer

A friend wants to teach you to drive a car. They must

- [ ] be over 21 and have held a full licence for at least two years
- [ ] be over 18 and hold an advanced driver's certificate
- [ ] be over 18 and have fully comprehensive insurance
- [ ] be over 21 and have held a full licence for at least three years

Answer

☑ **be over 21 and have held a full licence for at least three years**

Teaching someone to drive is a responsible task. Before learning to drive you're advised to find a qualified Approved Driving Instructor (ADI) to teach you. This will ensure that you're taught the correct procedures from the start.

Q. 6.75

Mark one answer

You are dazzled at night by a vehicle behind you. You should

- [ ] set your mirror to anti dazzle
- [ ] set your mirror to dazzle the other driver
- [ ] brake sharply to a stop
- [ ] switch your rear lights on and off

Answer

☑ **set your mirror to anti dazzle**

The interior mirror of most vehicles can be set to the anti dazzle position. You will still be able to see the lights of the traffic behind you, but the dazzle will be greatly reduced.

Q. 6.76

Mark one answer

You have a collision whilst your car is moving. What is the first thing you must do?

- Stop only if there are injured people
- Call the emergency services
- Stop at the scene of the accident
- Call your insurance company

Answer

☑ **Stop at the scene of the accident**

If you are involved in an accident which causes damage or injury to any other person, vehicle, animal or property, by law you MUST STOP. Give your name, the vehicle owner's name and address, and the vehicle's registration number to anyone who has reasonable grounds for requiring them.

Q. 6.77

Mark one answer

Yellow zig zag lines on the road outside schools mean

- sound your horn to alert other road users
- stop to allow children to cross
- you must not wait or park on these lines
- you must not drive over these lines

Answer

☑ **you must not wait or park on these lines**

You must not stop where there are yellow zig zag markings, not even to pick up or drop off children. A vehicle parked on the zig zag lines would obstruct children's view of the road and other drivers' view of the pavement.

questions   *answers*

Q. 6.78

Mark one answer

What do these road markings outside a
school mean?

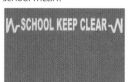

- You may park here if you are a teacher
- Sound your horn before parking
- When parking use your hazard warning
  lights
- You must not wait or park your vehicle
  here

Answer

☑ **You must not wait or park your
vehicle here**

Parking here would block people's view of
the school entrance. This could endanger
the lives of children on their way to and
from school.

Q. 6.79

Mark one answer

You are driving on a main road. You intend
to turn right into a side road. Just before
turning you should

- adjust your interior mirror
- flash your headlamps
- steer over to the left
- check for traffic overtaking on
  your right

Answer

☑ **check for traffic overtaking on
your right**

A last check in the offside mirror and blind
spot will allow you sight of any cyclist or
motorcyclist overtaking as you wait to turn.

Q. 6.80

Mark one answer

Why should you allow extra room when
overtaking a motorcyclist on a windy day?

- The rider may turn off suddenly to get
  out of the wind
- The rider may be blown in front
  of you
- The rider may stop suddenly
- The rider may be travelling faster than
  normal

Answer

☑ **The rider may be blown across in
front of you**

If you're driving in high winds, be aware
that the conditions might force a
motorcyclist or cyclist to swerve or wobble.
Take this into consideration if you're
following or wish to overtake a two-wheeled
vehicle.

Q. 6.81

Mark one answer

Which age group of drivers is most likely to be involved in a road accident?

■ 36 to 45-year-olds

■ 55-year-olds and over

■ 46 to 55-year-olds

■ 17 to 25-year-olds

Answer

☑ **17 to 25-year-olds**

Statistics show that if you're a driver between the ages of 17 and 25 you're more likely to be involved in a road accident than any other age group. There are several reasons contributing to this, but in most cases accidents are due to driver error.

Q. 6.82

Mark one answer

You are driving towards a zebra crossing. Waiting to cross is a person in a wheelchair. You should

■ continue on your way

■ wave to the person to cross

■ wave to the person to wait

■ be prepared to stop

Answer

☑ **be prepared to stop**

You should slow down and be prepared to stop as you would with an able-bodied person. Don't wave them across as other traffic may not stop.

Q. 6.83

Mark one answer

Where in particular should you look out for motorcyclists?

■ In a filling station

■ At a road junction

■ Near a service area

■ When entering a car park

Answer

☑ **At a road junction**

Always look out for motorcyclists, and cyclists, particularly at junctions. They are smaller and usually more difficult to see than other vehicles.

questions   *answers*

Q. 6.84

Mark one answer

Where should you take particular care to look out for motorcyclists and cyclists?

◼ On dual carriageways

◼ At junctions

◼ At zebra crossings

◼ On one-way streets

Answer

☑ **At junctions**

Motorcyclists and cyclists are often more difficult to see on the road. This is especially the case at junctions. You may not be able to see a motorcyclist approaching a junction if your view is blocked by other traffic. A motorcycle may be travelling as fast as a car, sometimes faster. Make sure that you judge speeds correctly before you emerge.

Q. 6.85

Mark one answer

The road outside this school is marked with yellow zigzag lines. What do these lines mean?

◼ You may park on the lines when dropping off schoolchildren

◼ You may park on the lines when picking schoolchildren up

◼ You must not wait or park your vehicle here at all

◼ You must stay with your vehicle if you park here

Answer

☑ **You must not wait or park your vehicle here at all**

Parking here would block the view of the school entrance and would endanger the lives of children on their way to and from school.

Other types of vehicle

This section looks at the risks when dealing with different types of vehicle.

The questions will ask you about

- **Motorcycles**

  these often filter through traffic and may need as much room as a car.

- **Lorries**

  these are usually larger than other vehicles and need more room on the road.

- **Buses**

  these are larger than cars and vans and may make frequent stops.

- **Trams**

  these move very quietly and can't deviate from their route.

Q. 7.1

Mark one answer

The road is wet. Why might a motorcyclist steer round drain covers on a bend?

 To avoid puncturing the tyres on the edge of the drain covers

■ To prevent the motorcycle sliding on the metal drain covers

■ To help judge the bend using the drain covers as marker points

■ To avoid splashing pedestrians on the pavement

Answer

 To prevent the motorcycle sliding on the metal drain covers

The actions of other drivers or riders may be due to the size or characteristics of their vehicle. If you understand this it will help you to anticipate their actions.

Motorcyclists will be checking the road ahead for uneven or slippery surfaces, especially in wet weather. They may need to move across their lane to avoid road surface hazards such as potholes and drain covers.

Q. 7.2

Mark one answer

You are about to overtake a slow-moving motorcyclist. Which one of these signs would make you take special care?

■  ■

■ ■

Answer

In windy weather, watch out for motorcyclists and also cyclists as they can be blown sideways into your path. When you pass them, leave plenty of room and check their position in your mirror before pulling back in.

questions   *answers*

Q. 7.3

Mark one answer

You are waiting to emerge left from a minor road. A large vehicle is approaching from the right. You have time to turn, but you should wait. Why?

- The large vehicle can easily hide an overtaking vehicle
- The large vehicle can turn suddenly
- The large vehicle is difficult to steer in a straight line
- The large vehicle can easily hide vehicles from the left

Answer

✓ **The large vehicle can easily hide an overtaking vehicle**

Large vehicles can hide other vehicles that are overtaking, especially motorcycles which may be filtering past queuing traffic. You need to be aware of the possibility of hidden vehicles and not assume that it is safe to emerge.

Q. 7.4

Mark one answer

You are following a long vehicle. It approaches a crossroads and signals left, but moves out to the right. You should

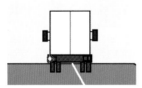

- get closer in order to pass it quickly
- stay well back and give it room
- assume the signal is wrong and it is really turning right
- overtake as it starts to slow down

Answer

✓ **stay well back and give it room**

A lorry may swing out to the right as it approaches a left turn. This is to allow the rear wheels to clear the kerb as it turns. Don't try to filter through if you see a gap on the nearside.

questions   *answers*

Q. 7.5

Mark one answer

You are following a long vehicle approaching a crossroads. The driver signals right but moves close to the left-hand kerb. What should you do?

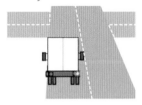

- Warn the driver of the wrong signal
- Wait behind the long vehicle
- Report the driver to the police
- Overtake on the right-hand side

Answer

☑ **Wait behind the long vehicle**

When a long vehicle is going to turn right it may need to keep close to the left-hand kerb. This is to prevent the rear end of the trailer cutting the corner. You need to be aware of how long vehicles behave in such situations. Don't overtake the lorry because it could turn as you're alongside. Stay behind and wait for it to turn.

Q. 7.6

Mark one answer

You are approaching a mini-roundabout. The long vehicle in front is signalling left but positioned over to the right. You should

- sound your horn
- overtake on the left
- follow the same course as the lorry
- keep well back

Answer

☑ **keep well back**

At mini-roundabouts there isn't much room for a long vehicle to manoeuvre. It will have to swing out wide so that it can complete the turn safely. Keep well back and don't try to move up alongside it.

questions   answers

Q. 7.7

Mark one answer

Before overtaking a large vehicle you should keep well back. Why is this?

- To give acceleration space to overtake quickly on blind bends
- To get the best view of the road ahead
- To leave a gap in case the vehicle stops and rolls back
- To offer other drivers a safe gap if they want to overtake you

Answer

☑ **To get the best view of the road ahead**

When following a large vehicle keep well back. If you're too close you won't be able to see the road ahead and the driver of the long vehicle might not be able to see you in their mirrors.

Q. 7.8

Mark one answer

Why is passing a lorry more risky than passing a car?

- Lorries are longer than cars
- Lorries may suddenly pull up
- The brakes of lorries are not as good
- Lorries climb hills more slowly

Answer

☑ **Lorries are longer than cars**

Hazards to watch for include

- oncoming traffic
- junctions
- bends or dips, which could restrict your view
- any signs or road markings prohibiting overtaking.

Never begin to overtake unless you can see that it's safe to complete the manoeuvre.

Q. 7.9

Mark two answers

You are travelling behind a bus that pulls up at a bus stop. What should you do?

- Accelerate past the bus sounding your horn
- Watch carefully for pedestrians
- Be ready to give way to the bus
- Pull in closely behind the bus

Answers

☑ **Watch carefully for pedestrians**

☑ **Be ready to give way to the bus**

There might be pedestrians crossing from in front of the bus. Look out for them if you intend to pass. Consider staying back and waiting.

How many people are waiting to get on the bus? Check the queue if you can. The bus might move off straight away if there is no one waiting to get on.

If a bus is signalling to pull out, give it priority as long as it is safe to do so.

Q. 7.10

Mark one answer

When you approach a bus signalling to move off from a bus stop you should

▪ get past before it moves

▪ allow it to pull away, if it is safe to do so

▪ flash your headllights as you approach

▪ signal left and wave the bus on

Answer

☑ **allow it to pull away, if it is safe to do so**

Give way to buses whenever you can do so safely, especially when they signal to pull away from bus stops. Look out for people who've got off the bus and may try to cross the road. Don't

- try to accelerate past before it moves away

- flash your lights – other road users may be misled by this signal.

Q. 7.11

Mark one answer

Which of these vehicles is LEAST likely to be affected by crosswinds?

▪ Cyclists

▪ Motorcyclists

▪ High-sided vehicles

▪ Cars

Answer

☑ **Cars**

Although cars are the least likely vehicle to be affected, crosswinds can take anyone by surprise, especially

- after overtaking a large vehicle

- when passing gaps between hedges or buildings

- on exposed sections of road.

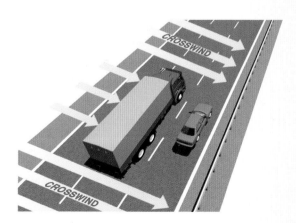

questions   *answers*

Q. 7.12

Mark one answer

You are following a large lorry on a wet road. Spray makes it difficult to see. You should

◾ drop back until you can see better

◾ put your headlights on full beam

◾ keep close to the lorry, away from the spray

◾ speed up and overtake quickly

Answer

☑ **drop back until you can see better**

Large vehicles may throw up a lot of spray when the roads are wet. This will make it difficult for you to see ahead. Dropping back further will

• move you out of the spray and allow you to see further

• increase your separation distance. It takes longer to stop when the roads are wet and you need to allow more room.

Don't

• follow the vehicle in front too closely

• overtake, unless you can see and are sure that the way ahead is clear.

Q. 7.13

Mark one answer

Some two way roads are divided into three lanes. Why are these particularly dangerous?

◾ Traffic in both directions can use the middle lane to overtake

◾ Traffic can travel faster in poor weather conditions

◾ Traffic can overtake on the left

◾ Traffic uses the middle lane for emergencies only

Answer

☑ **Traffic in both directions can use the middle lane to overtake**

If you intend to overtake you must consider that approaching traffic could be planning the same manoeuvre. When you have considered the situation and have decided it is safe, indicate your intentions early. This will show the approaching traffic that you intend to pull out.

questions   answers

Q. 7.14

Mark one answer

What should you do as you approach this lorry?

☐ Slow down and be prepared to wait

☐ Make the lorry wait for you

☐ Flash your lights at the lorry

☐ Move to the right hand side of the road

Answer

☑ **Slow down and be prepared to wait**

When turning, long vehicles need much more room on the road than other vehicles. At junctions they may take up the whole of the road space, so be patient and allow them the room they need.

Q. 7.15

Mark one answer

You are following a large articulated vehicle. It is going to turn left into a narrow road. What action should you take?

☐ Move out and overtake on the right

☐ Pass on the left as the vehicle moves out

☐ Be prepared to stop behind

☐ Overtake quickly before the lorry moves out

Answer

☑ **Be prepared to stop behind**

Lorries are larger and longer than other vehicles and this can affect their position when approaching junctions. When turning left they may move out to the right so that they don't cut in and mount the kerb with the rear wheels.

questions *answers*

Q. 7.16

Mark one answer

You keep well back while waiting to overtake a large vehicle. A car fills the gap. You should

- ☐ sound your horn
- ☐ drop back further
- ☐ flash your headlights
- ☐ start to overtake

Answer

 drop back further

It's very frustrating when your separation distance is shortened by another vehicle. React positively, stay calm and drop further back.

Q. 7.17

Mark one answer

At a junction you see this signal. It means

- ☐ cars must stop
- ☐ trams must stop
- ☐ both trams and cars must stop
- ☐ both trams and cars can continue

Answer

 trams must stop

The white light shows that trams must stop, but the green light shows that other vehicles may go if the way is clear.

You may not live in an area where there are trams but you should still learn the signs. You never know when you may go to a town with trams.

Q. 7.18

Mark one answer

You are following a large vehicle approaching crossroads. The driver signals to turn left. What should you do?

- ☐ Overtake if you can leave plenty of room
- ☐ Overtake only if there are no oncoming vehicles
- ☐ Do not overtake until the vehicle begins to turn.
- ☐ Do not overtake when at or approaching a junction.

Answer

☑ **Do not overtake when at or approaching a junction.**

Hold back and wait until the vehicle has turned before proceeding. Do not overtake because the vehicle turning left could hide a vehicle emerging from the same junction.

questions   answers

Q. 7.19

Mark one answer

You are following a long lorry. The driver signals to turn left into a narrow road. What should you do?

- [ ] Overtake on the left before the lorry reaches the junction
- [ ] Overtake on the right as soon as the lorry slows down
- [ ] Do not overtake unless you can see there is no oncoming traffic
- [ ] Do not overtake, stay well back and be prepared to stop.

Answer

☑ **Do not overtake, stay well back and be prepared to stop.**

When turning into narrow roads articulated and long vehicles will need more room. Initially they will need to swing out in the opposite direction to which they intend to turn. They could mask another vehicle turning out of the same junction. DON'T be tempted to overtake them or pass on the inside.

Q. 7.20

Mark one answer

You wish to overtake a long, slow moving vehicle on a busy road. You should

- [ ] follow it closely and keep moving out to see the road ahead
- [ ] flash your headlights for the oncoming traffic to give way
- [ ] stay behind until the driver waves you past
- [ ] keep well back until you can see that it is clear

Answer

☑ **keep well back until you can see that it is clear**

If you wish to overtake a long vehicle, stay well back so that you can see the road ahead. DON'T

- get up close to the vehicle – this will restrict your view of the road ahead
- get impatient – overtaking on a busy road calls for sound judgement
- take a gamble – only overtake when you can see that you can safely complete the manoeuvre.

Q. 7.21

Mark one answer

It is very windy. You are behind a motorcyclist who is overtaking a high-sided vehicle. What should you do?

- [ ] Overtake the motorcyclist immediately
- [ ] Keep well back
- [ ] Stay level with the motorcyclist
- [ ] Keep close to the motorcyclist

Answer

☑ **Keep well back**

Motorcyclists are affected more by windy weather than other vehicles. In windy conditions, high-sided vehicles cause air turbulence. You should keep well back as the motorcyclist could be blown off course.

questions   answers

Q. 7.22

Mark one answer

It is very windy. You are about to overtake a motorcyclist. You should

- ■ overtake slowly
- ■ allow extra room
- ■ sound your horn
- ■ keep close as you pass

Answer

☑ **allow extra room**

Crosswinds can blow a motorcyclist or cyclist across the lane. Passing too close could also cause a draught, unbalancing the rider.

Q. 7.23

Mark one answer

You are towing a caravan. Which is the safest type of rear view mirror to use?

- ■ Interior wide-angle-view mirror
- ■ Extended-arm side mirrors
- ■ Ordinary door mirrors
- ■ Ordinary interior mirror

Answer

☑ **Extended-arm side mirrors**

Towing a large trailer or caravan can greatly reduce your view of the road. You need to use the correct equipment to make sure you can see clearly behind and down both sides of the caravan or trailer.

Q. 7.24

Mark one answer

You are driving downhill. There is a car parked on the other side of the road. Large, slow lorries are coming towards you. You should

- ■ keep going because you have the right of way
- ■ slow down and give way
- ■ speed up and get past quickly
- ■ pull over on the right behind the parked car

Answer

☑ **slow down and give way**

Large vehicles need several gear changes to build up speed and this takes time, especially on an uphill gradient. You should keep this in mind and give way so that they can maintain momentum up the hill.

Q. 7.25

Mark two answers

You are driving in town. Ahead of you a bus is at a bus stop. Which TWO of the following should you do?

◾ Be prepared to give way if the bus suddenly moves off

◾ Continue at the same speed but sound your horn as a warning

◾ Watch carefully for the sudden appearance of pedestrians

◾ Pass the bus as quickly as you possibly can

Answers

☑ **Be prepared to give way if the bus suddenly moves off**

☑ **Watch carefully for the sudden appearance of pedestrians**

As you approach, look out for any signal the driver might make. If you pass the vehicle watch out for pedestrians attempting to cross the road from the other side of the bus. They will be hidden from view until the last moment.

Q. 7.26

Mark two answers

You are driving in heavy traffic on a wet road. Spray makes it difficult to be seen. You should use your

◾ full beam headlights

◾ rear fog lights if visibility is less than 100 metres (328 feet)

◾ rear fog lights if visibility is more than 100 metres (328 feet)

◾ dipped headlights

◾ side lights only

Answers

☑ **rear fog lights if visibility is less than 100 metres (328 feet)**

☑ **dipped headlights**

You must ensure that you can be seen by others on the road. Use your dipped headlights during the day if the visibility is bad. If you use your rear fog lights, don't forget to turn them off when the visibility improves.

OTHER TYPES OF VEHICLE

questions   *answers*

Q. 7.27
Mark one answer

You are driving along this road. What should you be prepared to do?

■ Sound your horn and continue
■ Slow down and give way
■ Report the driver to the police
■ Squeeze through the gap

Answer

 Slow down and give way

Sometimes large vehicles may need more space than other road users. If a vehicle needs more time and space to turn be prepared to stop and wait.

Q. 7.28
Mark one answer

You are on a wet motorway with surface spray. You should use

■ hazard flashers
■ dipped headlights
■ rear fog lights
■ sidelights

Answer

✓ **dipped headlights**

When surface spray reduces visibility switch on your dipped headlights. This will help other road users to see you.

Q. 7.29

Mark one answer

As a driver why should you be more careful where trams operate?

- ▇ Because they do not have a horn
- ▇ Because they do not stop for cars
- ▇ Because they do not have lights
- ▇ Because they cannot steer to avoid you

Answer

☑ **Because they cannot steer to avoid you**

You should take extra care when you first encounter trams. You will have to get used to dealing with a different traffic system.

Be aware that they can accelerate and travel very quickly and that they cannot change direction to avoid obstructions.

Vehicle handling

This section looks at the handling of your vehicle in different conditions.

The questions will ask you about

- **Weather conditions**

  being aware of how wet or icy roads will affect the handling of your vehicle.

- **Road conditions**

  being aware of how the road surface may affect your vehicle.

- **Time of day**

  being aware of hazards when driving at night.

- **Speed**

  being aware that it's more difficult to control your vehicle at high speeds.

- **Traffic calming**

  being aware of measures used to slow down traffic where there are pedestrians.

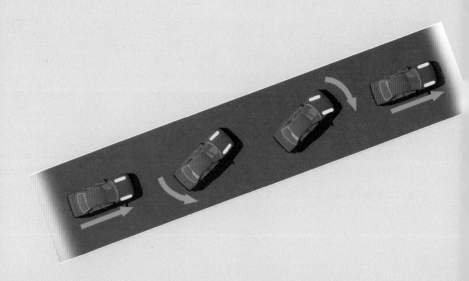

Q. 8.1

Mark one answer

You are following a vehicle at a safe distance on a wet road. Another driver overtakes you and pulls into the gap you have left. What should you do?

■ Flash your headlights as a warning

■ Try to overtake safely as soon as you can

■ Drop back to regain a safe distance

■ Stay close to the other vehicle until it moves on

Answer

☑ **Drop back to regain a safe distance**

Wet weather will affect the time it takes for you to stop and can affect your control.

Your speed should allow you to stop safely and in good time. If another vehicle pulls into the gap you've left, ease back until you've regained your stopping distance.

Q. 8.2

Mark three answers

In which THREE of these situations may you overtake another vehicle on the left?

■ When you are in a one-way street

■ When approaching a motorway slip road where you will be turning off

■ When the vehicle in front is signalling to turn right

■ When a slower vehicle is travelling in the right-hand lane of a dual carriageway

■ In slow-moving traffic queues when traffic in the right-hand lane is moving more slowly

Answers

☑ **When you are in a one-way street**

☑ **When the vehicle in front is signalling to turn right**

☑ **In slow-moving traffic queues when traffic in the right-hand lane is moving more slowly**

At certain times of the day traffic might be heavy. If traffic is moving slowly in queues and vehicles in the right-hand lane are moving more slowly, you may overtake on the left. Don't keep changing lanes to try and beat the queue.

Q. 8.3

Mark one answer

You are travelling in very heavy rain. Your overall stopping distance is likely to be

■ doubled

■ halved

■ up to ten times greater

■ no different

Answer

☑ **doubled**

As well as visibility being reduced, the road will be extremely wet. This will reduce the grip the tyres have on the road and increase the distance it takes to stop. Double your separation distance.

questions   answers

Q. 8.4

Mark two answers

Which TWO of the following are correct?
When overtaking at night you should

- ▪ wait until a bend so that you can see the oncoming headlights
- ▪ sound your horn twice before moving out
- ▪ be careful because you can see less
- ▪ beware of bends in the road ahead
- ▪ put headlights on full beam

Answers

- ☑ **be careful because you can see less**
- ☑ **beware of bends in the road ahead**

Only overtake the vehicle in front if it's really necessary. At night the risks are increased due to the poor visibility. Don't overtake if there's a possibility of

- road junctions
- bends ahead
- the brow of a bridge or hill, except on a dual carriageway
- pedestrian crossings
- double white lines ahead
- vehicles changing direction
- any other potential hazard.

Q. 8.5

Mark one answer

When may you wait in a box junction?

- ▪ When you are stationary in a queue of traffic
- ▪ When approaching a pelican crossing
- ▪ When approaching a zebra crossing
- ▪ When oncoming traffic prevents you turning right

Answer

- ☑ **When oncoming traffic prevents you turning right**

The purpose of this road marking is to keep the junction clear by preventing traffic from stopping in the path of crossing traffic.

You must not enter a box junction unless your exit is clear. The only exception to this is if you want to turn right but you have to wait because of oncoming traffic or other vehicles waiting to turn right.

Q. 8.6

Mark one answer

Which of these plates normally appear with this road sign?

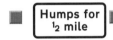

Answer

Humps for
½ mile

Road humps are used to slow down the traffic. They are found in places where there are often pedestrians, such as

- in shopping areas
- near schools
- in residential areas.

Watch out for people close to the kerb or crossing the road.

Q. 8.7

Mark three answers

Areas reserved for trams may have

- metal studs around them
- white line markings
- zig zag markings
- a different coloured surface
- yellow hatch markings
- a different surface texture

Answers

- ☑ **white line markings**
- ☑ **a different coloured surface**
- ☑ **a different surface texture**

Trams can run on roads used by other vehicles and pedestrians. The part of the road used by the trams is known as the reserved area and this should be kept clear. It has a coloured surface and is usually edged with white road markings. It might also have different surface texture.

Q. 8.8

Mark one answer

Traffic calming measures are used to

- stop road rage
- help overtaking
- slow traffic down
- help parking

Answer

 slow traffic down

Traffic calming measures are used to make the roads safer for vulnerable road users, such as cyclists, pedestrians and children. These can be designed as chicanes, road humps or other obstacles that encourage drivers and riders to slow down.

questions   *answers*

Q. 8.9

Mark one answer

Why should you always reduce your speed when travelling in fog?

⬛ Because the brakes do not work as well

⬛ Because you could be dazzled by other people's fog lights

⬛ Because the engine is colder

⬛ Because it is more difficult to see events ahead

Answer

 Because it is more difficult to see events ahead

You won't be able to see as far ahead in fog as you can on a clear day. You will need to reduce your speed so that, if a hazard looms out of the fog, you have the time and space to take avoiding action.

Travelling in fog is hazardous. If you can, try and delay your journey until it has cleared.

Q. 8.10

Mark one answer

You are on a motorway in fog. The left-hand edge of the motorway can be identified by reflective studs. What colour are they?

⬛ Green

⬛ Amber

⬛ Red

⬛ White

Answer

✓ **Red**

Be especially careful if you're on a motorway in fog. Reflective studs are used to help you in poor visibility. Different colours are used so that you'll know which lane you are in. These are

• red on the left-hand side of the road

• white between lanes

• amber on the right-hand edge of the carriageway

• green between the carriageway and slip roads.

questions   answers

Q. 8.11

Mark two answers

A rumble device is designed to

■ give directions

■ prevent cattle escaping

■ alert you to low tyre pressure

■ alert you to a hazard

■ encourage you to reduce speed

Answers

☑ **alert you to a hazard**

☑ **encourage you to reduce speed**

A rumble device usually consists of raised markings or strips across the road. It gives an audible, visual and tactile warning of a hazard. These strips are found in places where traffic has constantly ignored warning or restriction signs. They are there for a good reason. Slow down and be ready to deal with a hazard.

Q. 8.12

Mark one answer

You are on a narrow road at night. A slower-moving vehicle ahead has been signalling right for some time. What should you do?

■ Overtake on the left

■ Flash your headlights before overtaking

■ Signal right and sound your horn

■ Wait for the signal to be cancelled before overtaking

Answer

☑ **Wait for the signal to be cancelled before overtaking**

If the vehicle in front has been indicating right for some time, but has made no attempt to turn, wait for the signal to be cancelled. The other driver may have misjudged the distance to the road junction or there might be a hidden hazard.

questions   *answers*

Q. 8.13

Mark one answer

Why should you test your brakes after this hazard?

- ▓ Because you will be on a slippery road
- ▓ Because your brakes will be soaking wet
- ▓ Because you will have gone down a long hill
- ▓ Because you will have just crossed a long bridge

Answer

☑ **Because your brakes will be soaking wet**

A ford is a crossing over a stream that's shallow enough to go through. When you've gone through a ford or a deep puddle the water can affect your brakes. If they don't work properly it will help to dry them. To do this, apply a light brake pressure while moving slowly.

Don't travel at normal speeds until you are sure your brakes are working properly again.

Q. 8.14

Mark one answer

You have to make a journey in foggy conditions. You should

- ▓ follow other vehicles' tail lights closely
- ▓ avoid using dipped headlights
- ▓ leave plenty of time for your journey
- ▓ keep two seconds behind other vehicles

Answer

☑ **leave plenty of time for your journey**

If you're planning to make a journey when it's foggy, listen to the weather reports on the radio or television. Don't travel if visibility is very poor or your trip isn't necessary.

If you do travel, leave plenty of time for your journey. If someone is expecting you at the other end, let them know that you'll be taking longer than normal to arrive.

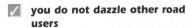

Q. 8.15

Mark one answer

You are overtaking a car at night. You must be sure that

■ you flash your headlights before overtaking

■ you select a higher gear

■ you have switched your lights to full beam before overtaking

■ you do not dazzle other road users

Answer

☑ **you do not dazzle other road users**

To prevent your lights from dazzling the driver of the car in front, wait until you've overtaken before switching to full beam.

Q. 8.16

Mark one answer

You see a vehicle coming towards you on a single track road. You should

■ go back to the main road

■ do an emergency stop

■ stop at a passing place

■ put on your hazard warning lights

Answer

☑ **stop at a passing place**

You must take extra care when on single track roads. You may not be able to see around bends due to high hedges or fences. Proceed with caution and expect to meet oncoming vehicles around the next bend. If you do, pull into or opposite a passing place.

Q. 8.17

Mark one answer

You are on a road which has speed humps. A driver in front is travelling slower than you. You should

■ sound your horn

■ overtake as soon as you can

■ flash your headlights

■ slow down and stay behind

Answer

☑ **slow down and stay behind**

Be patient and stay behind the car in front. Normally, you should not overtake other vehicles in traffic-calmed areas because if you overtake here your speed may exceed that which is safe along that road, defeating the purpose of the traffic calming measures.

questions   *answers*

Q. 8.18

Mark one answer

You are following other vehicles in fog with your lights on. How else can you reduce the chances of being involved in an accident?

- ◼ Keep close to the vehicle in front
- ◼ Use your main beam instead of dipped headlights
- ◼ Keep together with the faster vehicles
- ◼ Reduce your speed and increase the gap

Answer

☑ **Reduce your speed and increase the gap**

When you're travelling in fog, always ensure that you have your dipped headlights and/or fog lights on so that you can be seen by other road users.

Keep at a sensible speed and don't follow the vehicle in front too closely. If the road is wet and slippery you'll need to allow twice the normal stopping distance.

Q. 8.19

Mark one answer

You see these markings on the road. Why are they there?

- ◼ To show a safe distance between vehicles
- ◼ To keep the area clear of traffic
- ◼ To make you aware of your speed
- ◼ To warn you to change direction

Answer

☑ **To make you aware of your speed**

These lines may be painted on the road on the approach to a roundabout, village or a particular hazard. The lines are raised and painted yellow and their purpose is to make you aware of your speed. Reduce your speed in good time so that you avoid having to brake harshly over the last few metres before reaching the junction.

Q. 8.20

Mark one answer

When MUST you use dipped headlights during the day?

- ◼ All the time
- ◼ Along narrow streets
- ◼ In poor visibility
- ◼ When parking

Answer

☑ **In poor visibility**

You MUST use dipped headlights and/or fog lights in fog when visibility is 100 metres (328 feet) or less.

You should use dipped headlights, but NOT fog lights, when visibility is reduced, such as in heavy rain.

Q. 8.21

Mark two answers

What are TWO main reasons why coasting downhill is wrong?

- Fuel consumption will be higher
- The vehicle will pick up speed
- It puts more wear and tear on the tyres
- You have less braking and steering control
- It damages the engine

Answers

☑ **The vehicle will pick up speed**

☑ **You have less braking and steering control**

Coasting is when you allow the vehicle to freewheel in neutral or with the clutch pedal depressed. Doing this gives you less control over the vehicle. It's especially important not to let your vehicle coast when approaching hazards such as junctions and bends and when travelling downhill.

Q. 8.22

Mark two answers

Hills can affect the performance of your vehicle. Which TWO apply when driving up steep hills?

- Higher gears will pull better
- You will slow down sooner
- Overtaking will be easier
- The engine will work harder
- The steering will feel heavier

Answers

☑ **You will slow down sooner**

☑ **The engine will work harder**

The engine will need more power to pull the vehicle up the hill. When approaching a steep hill you should select a lower gear to help maintain your speed. You should do this without hesitation, so that you don't lose too much speed before engaging the lower gear.

Q. 8.23

Mark one answer

Why is coasting wrong?

- It will cause the car to skid
- It will make the engine stall
- The engine will run faster
- There is no engine braking

Answer

☑ **There is no engine braking**

Try to look ahead and read the road. Plan your approach to junctions and select the correct gear in good time. This will give you the control you need to deal with any hazards that occur.

You'll coast a little every time you change gear. This can't be avoided, but it should be kept to a minimum.

questions 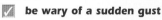 *answers*

Q. 8.24

Mark one answer

You are driving on the motorway in windy conditions. When passing high-sided vehicles you should

- ▪ increase your speed
- ▪ be wary of a sudden gust
- ▪ drive alongside very closely
- ▪ expect normal conditions

Answer

 be wary of a sudden gust

The draught caused by other vehicles could be strong enough to push you out of your lane. Keep both hands on the steering wheel to maintain full control.

Q. 8.25

Mark one answer

To correct a rear-wheel skid you should

- ▪ not steer at all
- ▪ steer away from it
- ▪ steer into it
- ▪ apply your handbrake

Answer

☑ **steer into it**

Prevention is better than cure, so it's important that you take every precaution to avoid a skid from starting.

If you feel the rear wheels of your vehicle beginning to skid, try to steer in the same direction to recover control. Don't brake suddenly – this will only make the situation worse.

Q. 8.26

Mark two answers

You have to make a journey in fog. What are the TWO most important things you should do before you set out?

- ▪ Top up the radiator with antifreeze
- ▪ Make sure that you have a warning triangle in the vehicle
- ▪ Check that your lights are working
- ▪ Check the battery
- ▪ Make sure that the windows are clean

Answers

☑ **Check that your lights are working**

☑ **Make sure that the windows are clean**

Don't drive in fog unless you really have to. Adjust your driving to the conditions. You should always be able to pull up within the distance you can see clearly ahead.

questions

Q. 8.27

Mark one answer

You are driving in fog. Why should you keep well back from the vehicle in front?

- ▪ In case it changes direction suddenly
- ▪ In case its fog lights dazzle you
- ▪ In case it stops suddenly
- ▪ In case its brake lights dazzle you

Q. 8.28

Mark one answer

You should switch your rear fog lights on when visibility drops below

- ▪ your overall stopping distance
- ▪ ten car lengths
- ▪ 200 metres (656 feet)
- ▪ 100 metres (328 feet)

Q. 8.29

Mark one answer

Whilst driving, the fog clears and you can see more clearly. You must remember to

- ▪ switch off the fog lights
- ▪ reduce your speed
- ▪ switch off the demister
- ▪ close any open windows

answers

Answer

☑ In case it stops suddenly

If you're following another road user in fog stay well back. The driver in front won't be able to see hazards until they're close and might brake suddenly. Another reason why it is important to maintain a good separation distance in fog is that the road surface is likely to be wet and slippery.

Answer

☑ 100 metres (328 feet)

If visibility falls below 100 metres in fog, switching on your rear fog lights will help following road users to see you. Don't forget to turn them off once visibility improves: their brightness might be mistaken for brake lights and they could dazzle other drivers.

Answer

☑ switch off the fog lights

Bright rear fog lights might be mistaken for brake lights and could be misleading for the traffic behind.

questions *answers*

Q. 8.30

Mark one answer

You have to park on the road in fog. You should

- ☑ leave sidelights on
- ☐ leave dipped headlights and fog lights on
- ☐ leave dipped headlights on
- ☐ leave main beam headlights on

Answer

☑ **leave sidelights on**

If you have to park your vehicle in foggy conditions it's important that it can be seen by other road users.

Try to find a place to park off the road. If this isn't possible leave it facing in the same direction as the traffic. Make sure that your lights are clean and that you leave your sidelights on.

Q. 8.31

Mark one answer

On a foggy day you unavoidably have to park your car on the road. You should

- ☐ leave your headlights on
- ☐ leave your fog lights on
- ☑ leave your sidelights on
- ☐ leave your hazard lights on

Answer

☑ **leave your sidelights on**

Ensure that your vehicle can be seen by other traffic. If possible, park your car off the road in a car park or driveway to avoid the extra risk to other road users.

Q. 8.32

Mark one answer

You are travelling at night. You are dazzled by headlights coming towards you. You should

- ☐ pull down your sun visor
- ☑ slow down or stop
- ☐ switch on your main beam headlights
- ☐ put your hand over your eyes

Answer

☑ **slow down or stop**

If you're driving at night there will be extra hazards to deal with. Visibility may be very limited and the lights of oncoming vehicles can often dazzle you. If this happens don't

- close your eyes
- swerve
- flash your headlights. This will only distract the other driver too.

Q. 8.33

Mark four answers

Which of the following may apply when dealing with this hazard?

- ■ It could be more difficult in winter
- ■ Use a low gear and drive slowly
- ■ Use a high gear to prevent wheelspin
- ■ Test your brakes afterwards
- ■ Always switch on fog lamps
- ■ There may be a depth gauge .

Answers

- ☑ **It could be more difficult in winter**
- ☑ **Use a low gear and drive slowly**
- ☑ **Test your brakes afterwards**
- ☑ **There may be a depth gauge**

During the winter the stream is likely to flood. It is also possible that in extremely cold weather it could ice over. Assess the situation carefully before you drive through. If you drive a vehicle with low suspension you may have to find a different route.

Q. 8.34

Mark one answer

Front fog lights may be used ONLY if

- ■ visibility is seriously reduced
- ■ they are fitted above the bumper
- ■ they are not as bright as the headlights
- ■ an audible warning device is used

Answer

- ☑ **visibility is seriously reduced**

Your vehicle should have a warning light on the dashboard which illuminates when the fog lights are being used. You need to be familiar with the layout of your dashboard so you are aware if they have been switched on in error, or you have forgotten to switch them off.

Q. 8.35

Mark one answer

Front fog lights may be used ONLY if

- ■ your headlights are not working
- ■ they are operated with rear fog lights
- ■ they were fitted by the vehicle manufacturer
- ■ visibility is seriously reduced

Answer

- ☑ **visibility is seriously reduced**

It is illegal to use fog lights unless visibility is seriously reduced generally when you cannot see for more than 100 metres (328 feet). Check that they have been switched off when conditions improve.

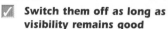

questions   answers

Q. 8.36

Mark one answer

You are driving with your front fog lights
switched on. Earlier fog has now cleared.
What should you do?

N 512 CTW

☐ Leave them on if other drivers have
their lights on

☐ Switch them off as long as visibility
remains good

☐ Flash them to warn oncoming traffic
that it is foggy

☐ Drive with them on instead of your
headlights

Answer

☑ **Switch them off as long as
visibility remains good**

Switch off your fog lights if the weather
improves, but be prepared to use them
again if visibility reduces to less than
100 metres (328 feet).

Q. 8.37

Mark one answer

Front fog lights should be used ONLY when

☐ travelling in very light rain

☐ visibility is seriously reduced

☐ daylight is fading

☐ driving after midnight

Answer

☑ **visibility is seriously reduced**

Fog lights will help others see you, but
remember, they must only be used if
visibility is seriously reduced to less than
100 metres (328 feet).

Q. 8.38

Mark two answers

NI EXEMPT

Why is it dangerous to leave rear fog lights on when they are not needed?

- ◼ Brake lights are less clear
- ◼ Following drivers can be dazzled
- ◼ Electrical systems could be overloaded
- ◼ Direction indicators may not work properly
- ◼ The battery could fail

Answers

- ☑ **Brake lights are less clear**
- ☑ **Following drivers can be dazzled**

If your rear fog lights are left on when it isn't foggy, the glare they cause makes it difficult for road users behind to know whether you are braking or you have forgotten to turn off your rear fog lights. This can be a particular problem on wet roads and on motorways.

If you leave your rear fog lights on at night, road users behind you are likely to be dazzled and this could put them at risk.

Q. 8.39

Mark two answers

NI EXEMPT

You are driving on a clear dry night with your rear fog lights switched on. This may

- ◼ reduce glare from the road surface
- ◼ make other drivers think you are braking
- ◼ give a better view of the road ahead
- ◼ dazzle following drivers
- ◼ help your indicators to be seen more clearly

Answers

- ☑ **make other drivers think you are braking**
- ☑ **dazzle following drivers**

A warning light will show on the dashboard to indicate when your rear fog lights are on. You should know the meaning of all the lights on your dashboard and check them before you move off and as you drive.

Q. 8.40

Mark one answer

You have just driven out of fog. Visibility is now good. You MUST

- ◼ switch off all your fog lights
- ◼ keep your rear fog lights on
- ◼ keep your front fog lights on
- ◼ leave fog lights on in case fog returns

Answer

- ☑ **switch off all your fog lights**

You must turn off your fog lights if visibility is over 100 metres (328 feet). However, be prepared for the fact that the fog may be patchy.

questions

answers

Q. 8.41

Mark three answers

NI EXEMPT

You forget to switch off your rear fog lights when the fog has cleared. This may

- dazzle other road users
- reduce battery life
- cause brake lights to be less clear
- be breaking the law
- seriously affect engine power

Answers

- ✓ **dazzle other road users**
- ✓ **cause brake lights to be less clear**
- ✓ **be breaking the law**

Don't forget to switch off your fog lights when the weather improves. You could be prosecuted for driving with them on in good visibility. The high intensity of the rear fog lights can look like brakes lights, and on a high speed road this can cause other road users to brake unnecessarily.

Q. 8.42

Mark one answer

NI EXEMPT

You have been driving in thick fog which has now cleared. You must switch OFF your rear fog lights because

- they use a lot of power from the battery
- they make your brake lights less clear
- they will cause dazzle in your rear view mirrors
- they may not be properly adjusted

Answer

- ✓ **they make your brake lights less clear**

It is essential that the traffic behind is given a clear warning when you brake. In good visibility, your rear fog lights can make it hard for others to see your brake lights. Make sure you switch off your fog lights when the visibility improves.

Q. 8.43

Mark one answer

Front fog lights should be used

- when visibility is reduced to 100 metres (328 feet)
- as a warning to oncoming traffic
- when driving during the hours of darkness
- in any conditions and at any time

Answer

- ✓ **when visibility is reduced to 100 metres (328 feet)**

When visibility is seriously reduced, switch on your fog lights if you have them fitted. It is essential not only that you can see ahead, but also that other road users are able to see you.

questions   *answers*

Q. 8.44

Mark one answer

Using rear fog lights in clear daylight will

◼ be useful when towing a trailer

◼ give extra protection

◼ dazzle other drivers

◼ make following drivers keep back

Answer

 dazzle other drivers

Rear fog lights shine brighter than normal rear lights so that they show up in reduced visibility. When the weather is clear they could dazzle the driver behind, so switch them off.

Q. 8.45

Mark one answer

Using front fog lights in clear daylight will

◼ flatten the battery

◼ dazzle other drivers

◼ improve your visibility

◼ increase your awareness

Answer

 dazzle other drivers

Fog lights can be brighter than normal dipped headlights. If the weather has improved turn them off to avoid dazzling other road users.

Q. 8.46

Mark one answer

You may use front fog lights with headlights ONLY when visibility is reduced to less than

◼ 100 metres (328 feet)

◼ 200 metres (656 feet)

◼ 300 metres (984 feet)

◼ 400 metres (1312 feet)

Answer

 100 metres (328 feet)

It is an offence to use fog lights if the visibility is better than 100 metres (328 feet). Switch front fog lights off if the fog clears to avoid dazzling other road users, but be aware that the fog may be patchy.

questions   *answers*

Q. 8.47

Mark one answer

You may drive with front fog lights switched-on

☐ when visibility is less than 100 metres (328 feet)

☐ at any time to be noticed

☐ instead of headlights on high speed roads

☐ when dazzled by the lights of oncoming vehicles

Answer

✓ **when visibility is less than 100 metres (328 feet)**

Only use front fog lights if the distance you are able to see is less than 100 metres (328 feet). Turn off your fog lights as the weather improves.

Q. 8.48

Mark one answer

Chains can be fitted to your wheels to help prevent

☐ damage to the road surface

☐ wear to the tyres

☐ skidding in deep snow

☐ the brakes locking

Answer

✓ **skidding in deep snow**

Snow chains can be fitted to your tyres during snowy conditions. They can help you to move off from rest or to keep moving in deep snow. You will still need to adjust your driving according to the road conditions at the time.

Q. 8.49

Mark one answer

Pressing the clutch pedal down or rolling in neutral for too long while driving will

☐ use more fuel

☐ cause the engine to overheat

☐ reduce your control

☐ improve tyre wear

Answer

✓ **reduce your control**

Holding the clutch down or staying in neutral for too long will cause your vehicle to freewheel. This is known as 'coasting' and it is dangerous as it reduces your control of the vehicle.

Q. 8.50

Mark one answer

How can you use the engine of your vehicle to control your speed?

- By changing to a lower gear
- By selecting reverse gear
- By changing to a higher gear
- By selecting neutral

Answer

☑ **By changing to a lower gear**

You should brake and slow down before selecting a lower gear. The gear can then be used to keep the speed low and help you control the vehicle. This is particularly helpful on long downhill stretches, where brake fade can occur if the brakes overheat.

Q. 8.51

Mark one answer

You are driving down a steep hill. Why could keeping the clutch down or selecting neutral for too long be dangerous?

- Fuel consumption will be higher
- Your vehicle will pick up speed
- It will damage the engine
- It will wear tyres out more quickly

Answer

☑ **Your vehicle will pick up speed**

Driving in neutral or with the clutch down for long periods is known as 'coasting'. There will be no engine braking and your vehicle will pick up speed on downhill slopes. Coasting can be very dangerous because it reduces steering and braking control.

Q. 8.52

Mark one answer

Why could keeping the clutch down or selecting neutral for long periods of time be dangerous?

- Fuel spillage will occur
- Engine damage may be caused
- You will have less steering and braking control
- It will wear tyres out more quickly

Answer

☑ **You will have less steering and braking control**

Letting your vehicle roll or coast in neutral reduces your control over steering and braking. This can be dangerous on downhill slopes where your vehicle could pick up speed very quickly.

questions *answers*

Q. 8.53

Mark one answer

You are driving on an icy road. What distance should you drive from the car in front?

■ four times the normal distance

■ six times the normal distance

■ eight times the normal distance

■ ten times the normal distance

Answer

 ten times the normal distance

Don't travel in icy or snowy weather unless your journey is necessary.

Drive extremely carefully when roads are or may be icy. Stopping distances can be ten times greater than on dry roads.

Q. 8.54

Mark one answer

You are on a well-lit motorway at night. You must

■ use only your sidelights

■ always use your headlights

■ always use rear fog lights

■ use headlights only in bad weather

Answer

 always use your headlights

If you're driving on a motorway at night or or in poor visibility, you must always use your headlights, even if the road is well-lit. The other road users in front must be able to see you in their mirrors.

Q. 8.55

Mark one answer

You are on a motorway at night with other vehicles just ahead of you. Which lights should you have on?

■ Front fog lights

■ Main beam headlights

■ Sidelights only

■ Dipped headlights

Answer

☑ **Dipped headlights**

If you're driving behind other traffic at night on the motorway

• leave a two-second time gap

• dip your headlights.

Full beam will dazzle the driver ahead. Your headlights' beam should fall short of the vehicle in front.

Q. 8.56

Mark three answers

Which THREE of the following will affect your stopping distance?

- How fast you are going
- The tyres on your vehicle
- The time of day
- The weather
- The street lighting

Answers

- ☑ **How fast you are going**
- ☑ **The tyres on your vehicle**
- ☑ **The weather**

There are several factors that can affect the distance it takes to stop your vehicle.

Adjust your driving to take account of how the weather conditions could affect your tyres' grip on the road.

Q. 8.57

Mark one answer

You are on a motorway at night. You MUST have your headlights switched on unless

- there are vehicles close in front of you
- you are travelling below 50 mph
- the motorway is lit
- your vehicle is broken down on the hard shoulder

Answer

- ☑ **your vehicle is broken down on the hard shoulder**

Always use your headlights at night on a motorway unless you have stopped on the hard shoulder.

If you break down and have to stop on the hard shoulder, switch off the headlights but leave the sidelights on so that other road users can see your vehicle.

Q. 8.58

Mark one answer

You will feel the effects of engine braking when you

- only use the handbrake
- only use neutral
- change to a lower gear
- change to a higher gear

Answer

- ☑ **change to a lower gear**

When going downhill, prolonged use of the brakes can cause them to overheat and lose their effectiveness. Changing to a lower gear will assist your braking.

questions  answers

Q. 8.59

Mark one answer

Daytime visibility is poor but not seriously reduced. You should switch on

- headlights and fog lights
- front fog lights
- dipped headlights
- rear fog lights

Answer

✓ **dipped headlights**

Only use your fog lights when visibility is seriously reduced. Use dipped headlights in poor conditions.

Q. 8.60

Mark one answer

Why are vehicles fitted with rear fog lights?

- To be seen when driving at high speed
- To use if broken down in a dangerous position
- To make them more visible in thick fog
- To warn drivers following closely to drop back

Answer

 To make them more visible in thick fog

Rear fog lights make it easier to spot a vehicle ahead in foggy conditions.

Avoid the temptation to use other vehicles' lights as a guide, though, as they will give you a false sense of security.

Q. 8.61

Mark one answer

While you are driving in fog, it becomes necessary to use front fog lights. You should

- only turn them on in heavy traffic conditions
- remember not to use them on motorways
- only use them on dual carriageways
- remember to switch them off as visibility improves

Answer

✓ **remember to switch them off as visibility improves**

It is an offence to have your fog lights on in conditions other than seriously reduced visibility, ie. less than 100 metres (328 feet).

questions   answers

Q. 8.62

Mark one answer

When snow is falling heavily you should

- only drive with your hazard lights on
- not drive unless you have a mobile phone
- only drive when your journey is short
- not drive unless it is essential

Answer

 not drive unless it is essential

Consider if the increased risk is worth it. If the weather conditions are bad and your journey isn't essential, then stay at home.

Q. 8.63

Mark one answer

You are driving down a long steep hill. You suddenly notice your brakes are not working as well as normal. What is the usual cause of this?

- The brakes overheating
- Air in the brake fluid
- Oil on the brakes
- Badly adjusted brakes

Answer

 The brakes overheating

This is more likely to happen on vehicles fitted with drum brakes but can apply to disc brakes as well. Using a lower gear will assist the braking and help you to keep control of your vehicle.

Motorway rules

This section looks at motorway rules.

The questions will ask you about

- **Speed limits**

  being aware of the speed restrictions on the motorway.

- **Lane discipline**

  keeping to the left unless overtaking.

- **Stopping**

  knowing when and where you can stop on the motorway.

- **Lighting**

  being aware of the importance of being seen.

- **Parking**

  not parking on the motorway except in an emergency.

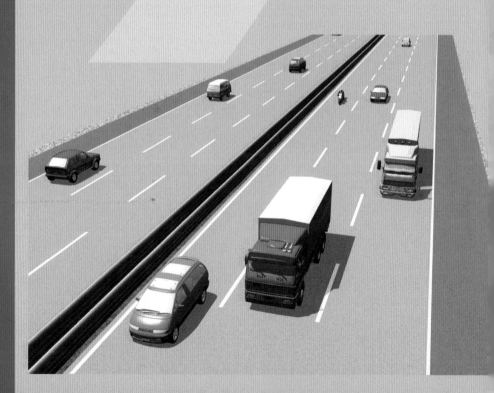

Q. 9.1

Mark four answers

Which FOUR of these must NOT use motorways?

- Learner car drivers
- Motorcycles over 50cc
- Double deck buses
- Farm tractors
- Horse riders
- Cyclists

Answers

- ☑ **Learner car drivers**
- ☑ **Farm tractors**
- ☑ **Horse riders**
- ☑ **Cyclists**

In addition, motorways MUST NOT be used by

- pedestrians
- motorcycles under 50 cc
- certain slow-moving vehicles, without permission
- invalid carriages weighing less than 254 kg (560 lbs).

Q. 9.2

Mark four answers

Which FOUR of these must NOT use motorways?

- Learner car drivers
- Motorcycles over 50cc
- Double-decker buses
- Farm tractors
- Learner motorcyclists
- Cyclists

Answers

- ☑ **Learner car drivers**
- ☑ **Farm tractors**
- ☑ **Learner motorcyclists**
- ☑ **Cyclists**

Learner car drivers and motorcyclists are not allowed on the motorway until they have passed their practical test.

Motorways have rules that you need to know before you venture out for the first time. When you've passed your practical test it's a good idea to have some lessons on motorways. Check with your instructor about this.

Q. 9.3

Mark one answer

Immediately after joining a motorway you should normally

- try to overtake
- re-adjust your mirrors
- position your vehicle in the centre lane
- keep in the left lane

Answer

- ☑ **keep in the left lane**

Stay in the left-hand lane long enough to get used to the higher speeds of motorway traffic.

questions

answers

Q. 9.4

Mark one answer

When joining a motorway you must always

- use the hard shoulder
- stop at the end of the acceleration lane
- come to a stop before joining the motorway
- give way to traffic already on the motorway

Answer

✓ **give way to traffic already on the motorway**

You must give way to traffic already on the motorway. Don't try to force your way into the traffic stream.

You should join the motorway where there's a suitable gap in the left-hand lane. The traffic may be travelling at high speed so you should adjust your speed to fit in with the vehicles on the motorway.

Q. 9.5

Mark one answer

What is the national speed limit for cars and motorcycles in the centre lane of a three-lane motorway?

- 40 mph
- 50 mph
- 60 mph
- 70 mph

Answer

✓ **70 mph**

Unless otherwise indicated the speed limit for the motorway applies to all the lanes.

Be on the lookout for any indication of speed limit changes due to roadworks or traffic flow control.

Q. 9.6

Mark one answer

What is the national speed limit on motorways for cars and motorcycles?

- 30 mph
- 50 mph
- 60 mph
- 70 mph

Answer

✓ **70 mph**

Travelling at the national speed limit doesn't allow you to hog the right-hand lane. Always use the left-hand lane whenever possible. When leaving the motorway, always adjust your speed in good time to deal with

- bends or curves on the slip road
- traffic queuing at roundabouts.

questions answers

Q. 9.7

Mark one answer

The left-hand lane on a three-lane motorway is for use by

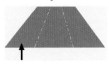

■ any vehicle

■ large vehicles only

■ emergency vehicles only

■ slow vehicles only

Answer

 any vehicle

On a motorway all traffic should use the left-hand lane unless overtaking. Use the centre or right-hand lanes if you need to overtake.

Make sure that you move back to the left-hand lane when you've finished overtaking. Don't stay in the middle or right-hand lane if the left-hand lane is free.

Q. 9.8

Mark one answer

What is the right hand lane used for on a three lane motorway?

■ Emergency vehicles only

■ Overtaking

■ Vehicles towing trailers

■ Coaches only

Answer

 Overtaking

You should keep to the left and only use the right-hand lane if you're passing slower-moving traffic.

Q. 9.9

Mark one answer

Which of these IS NOT allowed to travel in the right-hand lane of a three-lane motorway?

■ A small delivery van

■ A motorcycle

■ A vehicle towing a trailer

■ A motorcycle and side-car

Answer

 A vehicle towing a trailer

A vehicle with a trailer is restricted to 60 mph. For this reason it isn't allowed in the right-hand lane as it might hold up the faster-moving traffic that wishes to overtake in that lane.

questions *answers*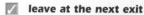

Q. 9.10

Mark two answers

You are travelling on a motorway. You decide you need a rest. You should

- ▨ stop on the hard shoulder
- ▨ go to a service area
- ▨ park on the slip road
- ▨ park on the central reservation
- ▨ leave at the next exit

Answers

- ✓ **go to a service area**
- ✓ **leave at the next exit**

You must not stop on the motorway or hard shoulder except in an emergency, in a traffic queue or when signalled to do so by a police officer or traffic signals. You should plan your journey so that you have regular rest stops.

Q. 9.11

Mark one answer

NI EXEMPT

You break down on a motorway. You need to call for help. Why may it be better to use an emergency roadside telephone rather than a mobile phone?

- ▨ It connects you to a local garage
- ▨ Using a mobile phone will distract other drivers
- ▨ It allows easy location by the emergency services
- ▨ Mobile phones do not work on motorways

Answer

- ✓ **It allows easy location by the emergency services**

On a motorway it is best to use a roadside emergency telephone so that the emergency services are able to locate you easily. The nearest telephone is indicated by an arrow on the marker posts at the edge of the hard shoulder.

If you do use a mobile phone, the emergency services will want to know your exact location. Before you call, find out the number on the nearest marker post. This number will tell the emergency services your exact location.

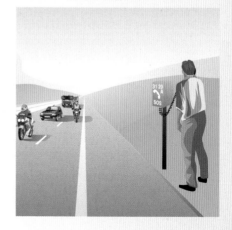

Q. 9.12

Mark one answer

What should you use the hard shoulder of a motorway for?

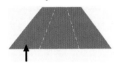

- ▓ Stopping in an emergency
- ▓ Leaving the motorway
- ▓ Stopping when you are tired
- ▓ Joining the motorway

Answer

☑ **Stopping in an emergency**

Don't use the hard shoulder for stopping unless it is an emergency. If you want to stop for any other reason go to the next exit or service station.

Q. 9.13

Mark one answer

After a breakdown you need to rejoin the main carriageway of a motorway from the hard shoulder. You should

- ▓ move out onto the carriageway then build up your speed
- ▓ move out onto the carriageway using your hazard lights
- ▓ gain speed on the hard shoulder before moving out onto the carriageway
- ▓ wait on the hard shoulder until someone flashes their headlights at you

Answer

☑ **gain speed on the hard shoulder before moving out onto the carriageway**

Wait for a safe gap in the traffic before you move out. Indicate your intention and use the hard shoulder to gain speed but don't force your way into the traffic.

questions   *answers*

Q. 9.14

Mark one answer

A crawler lane on a motorway is found

■ on a steep gradient

■ before a service area

■ before a junction

■ along the hard shoulder

Answer

 on a steep gradient

Slow-moving, large vehicles might slow down the progress of other traffic. On a steep gradient this extra lane is provided for these slow-moving vehicles to allow the faster-moving traffic to flow more easily.

Q. 9.15

Mark one answer

You are driving on a motorway. There are red flashing lights above every lane. You must

■ pull onto the hard shoulder

■ slow down and watch for further signals

■ leave at the next exit

■ stop and wait

Answer

 stop and wait

Red flashing lights above every lane mean you must not go on any further. You'll also see a red cross illuminated. Stop and wait. Don't

* change lanes

* continue

* pull onto the hard shoulder (unless in an emergency).

Q. 9.16

Mark one answer

You are driving in the right hand lane on a motorway. You see these overhead signs. This means

■ move to the left and reduce your speed to 50 mph

■ there are roadworks 50 metres (55 yards) ahead

■ use the hard shoulder until you have passed the hazard

■ leave the motorway at the next exit

Answer

☑ **move to the left and reduce your speed to 50 mph**

You must obey this sign. There might not be any visible signs of a problem ahead. However, there might be queuing traffic or another hazard which you cannot yet see.

Q. 9.17

Mark one answer

What do these motorway signs show?

■ They are countdown markers to a bridge

■ They are distance markers to the next telephone

■ They are countdown markers to the next exit

■ They warn of a police control ahead

Answer

☑ **They are countdown markers to the next exit**

The exit from a motorway is indicated by countdown markers. These are positioned 90 metres (100 yards) apart, the first being 270 metres (300 yards) from the start of the slip road. Move into the left-hand lane well before you reach the start of the slip road.

questions   *answers*

Q. 9.18

Mark one answer

On a motorway the amber reflective studs can be found between

- the hard shoulder and the carriageway
- the acceleration lane and the carriageway
- the central reservation and the carriageway
- each pair of the lanes

Answer

 the central reservation and the carriageway

On motorways reflective studs are fitted into the road to help you

- in the dark
- in conditions of poor visibility.

Amber-coloured studs are on the right-hand edge of the main carriageway, next to the central reservation.

Q. 9.19

Mark one answer

What colour are the reflective studs between the lanes on a motorway?

- Green
- Amber
- White
- Red

Answer

 White

White studs are put between the lanes on motorways. The light from your headlights is reflected back and this is especially useful in bad weather, when visibility is restricted.

Q. 9.20

Mark one answer

What colour are the reflective studs between a motorway and its slip road?

- Amber
- White
- Green
- Red

Answer

 Green

The studs between the carriageway and the hard shoulder are normally red. These change to green where there is a slip road. They will help you identify slip roads when visibility is poor or when it is dark.

Q. 9.21

Mark one answer

You are allowed to stop on a motorway when you

- ■ need to walk and get fresh air
- ■ wish to pick up hitch hikers
- ■ are told to do so by flashing red lights
- ■ need to use a mobile telephone

Answer

☑ **are told to do so by flashing red lights**

You must stop if there are red lights flashing above every lane on the motorway. However, if any of the other lanes show a green arrow you may move into that lane and continue if it is safe to do so.

Q. 9.22

Mark one answer

You have broken down on a motorway. To find the nearest emergency telephone you should always walk

- ■ with the traffic flow
- ■ facing oncoming traffic
- ■ in the direction shown on the marker posts
- ■ in the direction of the nearest exit

Answer

☑ **in the direction shown on the marker posts**

Along the hard shoulder there are marker posts at 100-metre intervals. These will direct you to the nearest emergency telephone.

Q. 9.23

Mark one answer

You are travelling along the left lane of a three lane motorway. Traffic is joining from a slip road. You should

- ■ race the other vehicles
- ■ move to another lane
- ■ maintain a steady speed
- ■ switch on your hazard flashers

Answer

☑ **move to another lane**

You should move to another lane if it is safe to do so. This can greatly assist the flow of traffic joining the motorway, especially at peak times.

questions

answers

Q. 9.24
Mark one answer

You are joining a motorway. Why is it important to make full use of the slip road?

- Because there is space available to turn round if you need to
- To allow you direct access to the overtaking lanes
- To build up a speed similar to traffic on the motorway
- Because you can continue on the hard shoulder

Answer

☑ **To build up a speed similar to traffic on the motorway**

Try to join the motorway without affecting the progress of the traffic already travelling on it. Always give way to traffic already on the motorway. At busy times you may have to slow down to merge into slow-moving traffic.

Q. 9.25
Mark one answer

How should you use the emergency telephone on a motorway?

- Stay close to the carriageway
- Face the oncoming traffic
- Keep your back to the traffic
- Stand on the hard shoulder

Answer

☑ **Face the oncoming traffic**

Traffic is passing you at speed. If the draught from a large lorry catches you by surprise it could blow you off balance and even onto the carriageway. By facing the oncoming traffic you can see approaching lorries and so be prepared for their draught. You are also in a position to see other hazards approaching.

Q. 9.26
Mark one answer

You are on a motorway. What colour are the reflective studs on the left of the carriageway?

- Green
- Red
- White
- Amber

Answer

☑ **Red**

Red studs are placed between the edge of the carriageway and the hard shoulder. Where slip roads leave or join the motorway the studs are green.

Q. 9.27

Mark one answer

On a three-lane motorway which lane should you normally use?

- Left
- Right
- Centre
- Either the right or centre

Answer

 Left

On a three-lane motorway you should travel in the left-hand lane unless you're overtaking. This applies regardless of the speed you're travelling at.

Q. 9.28

Mark one answer

A basic rule when on motorways is

- use the lane that has least traffic
- keep to the left lane unless overtaking
- overtake on the side that is clearest
- try to keep above 50 mph to prevent congestion

Answer

keep to the left lane unless overtaking

You should normally travel in the left-hand lane unless you are overtaking a slower-moving vehicle. Once you are passed that vehicle move back into the left-hand lane as soon as it's safe to do so. Don't cut across in front of the vehicle that you're overtaking.

Q. 9.29

Mark one answer

When going through a contraflow system on a motorway you should

- ensure that you do not exceed 30 mph
- keep a good distance from the vehicle ahead
- switch lanes to keep the traffic flowing
- stay close to the vehicle ahead to reduce queues

Answer

keep a good distance from the vehicle ahead

There's likely to be a speed restriction in force. Keep to this. Don't

- switch lanes
- get too close to traffic in front of you.

Be aware there will be no permanent barrier between you and the oncoming traffic.

questions   *answers*

Q. 9.30

Mark one answer

You are on a three-lane motorway. There are red reflective studs on your left and white ones to your right. Where are you?

▪ In the right-hand lane

▪ In the middle lane

▪ On the hard shoulder

▪ In the left-hand lane

Answer

☑ **In the left-hand lane**

The colours of the reflective studs on the motorway and their locations are

- red – between the hard shoulder and the carriageway

- white – lane markings

- amber – between the edge of the carriageway and the central reservation

- green – along slip road exits and entrances

- bright green/yellow – roadworks and contraflow systems.

Q. 9.31

Mark three answers

When may you stop on a motorway?

▪ If you have to read a map

▪ When you are tired and need a rest

▪ If red lights show above every lane

▪ When told to by the police

▪ If your mobile phone rings

▪ In an emergency or a breakdown

Answers

☑ **If red lights show above every lane**

☑ **When told to by the police**

☑ **In an emergency or a breakdown**

You may only stop on the carriageway of a motorway

- when told to do so by the police

- when flashing red lights show above every lane

- in a traffic jam

- in an emergency or breakdown.

Q. 9.32

Mark one answer

You are approaching roadworks on a motorway. What should you do?

▪ Speed up to clear the area quickly

▪ Always use the hard shoulder

▪ Obey all speed limits

▪ Stay very close to the vehicle in front

Answer

☑ **Obey all speed limits**

Accidents can often happen at roadworks. Be aware of the speed limits and reduce your speed in good time.

questions answers

Q. 9.33

Mark one answer

On motorways you should never overtake on the left UNLESS

- you can see well ahead that the hard shoulder is clear
- the traffic in the right-hand lane is signalling right
- you warn drivers behind by signalling left
- there is a queue of slow moving traffic to your right that is moving slower than you are

Answer

 ✓ **there is a queue of slow moving traffic to your right that is moving slower than you are**

Only overtake on the left if traffic is moving slowly in queues and the traffic on your right is moving more slowly than the traffic in your lane.

Q. 9.34

Mark one answer

You are towing a trailer on a motorway. What is your maximum speed limit?

- 40 mph
- 50 mph
- 60 mph
- 70 mph

Answer

✓ **60 mph**

Don't forget that you're towing a trailer. If you're towing a small, light trailer it won't reduce your vehicle's performance by very much. However, strong winds or buffeting from large vehicles might cause the trailer to snake from side to side. Be aware of your speed and don't exceed the lower limit imposed.

Q. 9.35

Mark one answer

The left-hand lane of a motorway should be used for

- breakdowns and emergencies only
- overtaking slower traffic in the other lanes
- slow vehicles only
- normal driving

Answer

✓ **normal driving**

You should keep to the left-hand lane whenever possible. Only use the other lanes for overtaking or when directed by signals. Using other lanes when the left-hand lane is empty can frustrate drivers behind you.

questions   *answers*

Q. 9.36

Mark one answer

You are driving on a motorway. You have to slow down quickly due to a hazard. You should

- ▨ switch on your hazard lights
- ▨ switch on your headlights
- ▨ sound your horn
- ▨ flash your headlights

Answer

 switch on your hazard lights

Using your hazard lights will give the traffic behind you an extra warning of the hazard ahead, in addition to your brake lights. Only use them for long enough to ensure that your warning has been seen.

Q. 9.37

Mark one answer

You get a puncture on the motorway. You manage to get your vehicle onto the hard shoulder. You should

- ▨ change the wheel yourself immediately
- ▨ use the emergency telephone and call for assistance
- ▨ try to wave down another vehicle for help
- ▨ only change the wheel if you have a passenger to help you

Answer

 use the emergency telephone and call for assistance

Due to the danger from passing traffic you should park as far to the left as you can and leave the vehicle by the nearside door.

Do not attempt even simple repairs. Instead walk to an emergency telephone on your side of the road and phone for assistance. While waiting for assistance to arrive wait near your car, keeping well away from the carriageway and hard shoulder.

Q. 9.38

Mark one answer

You are driving on a motorway. By mistake, you go past the exit that you wanted to take. You should

- ▨ carefully reverse on the hard shoulder
- ▨ carry on to the next exit
- ▨ carefully reverse in the left-hand lane
- ▨ make a U-turn at the next gap in the central reservation

Answer

▨ **carry on to the next exit**

It is against the law to reverse, cross the central reservation or drive against the traffic flow on a motorway.

If you have missed your exit ask yourself if your concentration is fading. It could be that you need to take a rest break before completing your journey.

questions   answers

Q. 9.39

Mark one answer

NI EXEMPT

Your vehicle breaks down on the hard shoulder of a motorway. You decide to use your mobile phone to call for help. You should

- ▪ stand at the rear of the vehicle while making the call
- ▪ try to repair the vehicle yourself
- ▪ get out of the vehicle by the right hand door
- ▪ check your location from the marker posts on the left

Answer

 check your location from the marker posts on the left

The emergency services need to know your exact location so they can reach you as quickly as possible. Look for a number on the nearest marker post beside the hard shoulder. Give this number when you call the emergency services as it will help them to locate you. Be ready to describe where you are, for example, by reference to the last junction or service station you passed.

Q. 9.40

Mark one answer

You are driving a car on a motorway. Unless signs show otherwise you must NOT exceed

- ▪ 50 mph
- ▪ 60 mph
- ▪ 70 mph
- ▪ 80 mph

Answer

☑ **70 mph**

The national speed limit for a car or motorcycle on the motorway is 70 mph. Lower speed limits may be in force, for example in roadworks, so look out for the signs. Variable speed limits operate in some areas to control very busy stretches of motorway. The speed limit may change depending on the volume of traffic.

Q. 9.41

Mark one answer

NI EXEMPT

You are on a three lane motorway towing a trailer. You may use the right hand lane when

- ▪ there are lane closures
- ▪ there is slow moving traffic
- ▪ you can maintain a high speed
- ▪ large vehicles are in the left and centre lanes

Answer

☑ **there are lane closures**

If you are towing a caravan or trailer you must not use the right-hand lane on a motorway with three or more lanes, except in certain circumstances, such as lane closures.

questions   answers

Q. 9.42

Mark one answer

You are on a motorway. There is a contra flow system ahead. What would you expect to find?

- Temporary traffic lights
- Lower speed limits
- Wider lanes than normal
- Speed humps

Answer

☑ **Lower speed limits**

When approaching a contraflow system reduce speed in good time and obey all speed limits. You may be travelling in a narrower lane than normal with no permanent barrier between you and the oncoming traffic. Be aware that the hard shoulder may be used for traffic and the road ahead could be obstructed by slow-moving or broken down vehicles.

Q. 9.43

Mark one answer

You are driving at 70 mph on a three-lane motorway. There is no traffic ahead. Which lane should you use?

- Any lane
- Middle lane
- Right lane
- Left lane

Answer

☑ **Left lane**

If the left-hand lane is free you should use it regardless of the speed you're travelling.

Q. 9.44

Mark one answer

Your vehicle has broken down on a motorway. You are not able to stop on the hard shoulder. What should you do?

- Switch on your hazard warning lights
- Stop following traffic and ask for help
- Attempt to repair your vehicle quickly
- Stand behind your vehicle to warn others

Answer

☑ **Switch on your hazard warning lights**

If you can't get your vehicle onto the hard shoulder, use your hazard warning lights to warn others. Leave your vehicle only when you can safely get clear of the carriageway.

Do not

- try to repair the vehicle
- attempt to place any warning device on the carriageway.

Q. 9.45

Mark one answer

Why is it particularly important to carry out a check on your vehicle before making a long motorway journey?

- ■ You will have to do more harsh braking on motorways
- ■ Motorway service stations do not deal with breakdowns
- ■ The road surface will wear down the tyres faster
- ■ Continuous high speeds may increase the risk of your vehicle breaking down

Answer

☑ **Continuous high speeds may increase the risk of your vehicle breaking down**

Before you start your journey make sure that your vehicle can cope with the demands of high-speed driving. Check your vehicle's

- oil
- water
- tyres.

Plan rest stops if you're going to be travelling a long way.

Q. 9.46

Mark one answer

For what reason may you use the right-hand lane of a motorway?

- ■ For keeping out of the way of lorries
- ■ For driving at more than 70 mph
- ■ For turning right
- ■ For overtaking other vehicles

Answer

☑ **For overtaking other vehicles**

The right-hand lane of the motorway is for overtaking.

Sometimes you may be directed into a right-hand lane as a result of roadworks or an accident. This will be indicated by signs or police directing the traffic.

questions   *answers*

Q. 9.47

Mark one answer

On a motorway you may ONLY stop on the hard shoulder

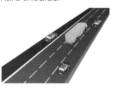

	in an emergency
	if you feel tired and need to rest
	if you accidentally go past the exit that you wanted to take
	to pick up a hitchhiker

Answer

☑ **in an emergency**

DON'T stop on the hard shoulder to

- have a rest or a picnic
- pick up hitchhikers
- answer a mobile phone
- check a road map

Never reverse along the hard shoulder if you accidentally go past the exit you wanted.

Q. 9.48

Mark one answer

You are driving on a motorway. The car ahead shows its hazard lights for a short time. This tells you that

	the driver wants you to overtake
	the other car is going to change lanes
	traffic ahead is slowing or stopping suddenly
	there is a police speed check ahead

Answer

☑ **traffic ahead is slowing or stopping suddenly**

If the vehicle in front shows its hazard lights there may be an accident or queuing traffic ahead. Look well ahead, not just at the car in front, to help you get an earlier warning of any hazards.

Q. 9.49

Mark one answer

The emergency telephones on a motorway are connected to the

	ambulance service
	police control
	fire brigade
	breakdown service

Answer

☑ **police control**

The controller will ask you

- the make and colour of your vehicle
- whether you are a member of an emergency breakdown service
- the number shown on the emergency telephone casing
- whether you are travelling alone.

Q. 9.50

Mark one answer

You are intending to leave the motorway at the next exit. Before you reach the exit you should normally position your vehicle

- in the middle lane
- in the left-hand lane
- on the hard shoulder
- in any lane

Answer

☑ **in the left-hand lane**

You'll see the first advance direction sign one mile from the exit. If you're travelling at 60 mph in the right-hand lane you'll only have about 50 seconds before you reach the countdown markers. There will be another sign at the half-mile point. Move in to the left-hand lane in good time. Don't cut across traffic at the last moment and don't risk missing your exit.

Q. 9.51

Mark one answer

As a provisional licence holder you should not drive a car

- over 30 mph
- at night
- on the motorway
- with passengers in rear seats

Answer

☑ **on the motorway**

When you've passed your practical test ask your instructor to take you for a lesson on the motorway. You'll need to get used to the speed of traffic and how to deal with multiple lanes.

Rules of the road

This section looks at rules of the road.

The questions will ask you about

- **Speed limits**

  being aware of the speed limits for different types of vehicle.

- **Lane discipline**

  being sure you select the correct lane for the direction you wish to take.

- **Parking**

  choosing a sensible place to park.

- **Lighting**

  making sure your vehicle doesn't become a hazard.

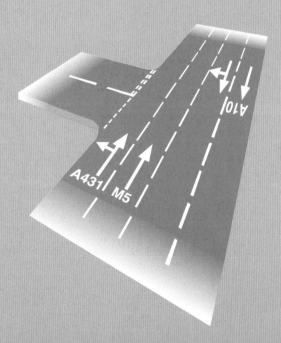

questions   *answers*

Q. 10.1

Mark one answer

What is the meaning of this sign?

▪ Local speed limit applies

▪ No waiting on the carriageway

▪ National speed limit applies

▪ No entry to vehicular traffic

Answer

☑ **National speed limit applies**

This sign doesn't tell you the speed limit in figures. You should know the speed limit for the type of road that you're on. Study your copy of *The Highway Code*.

Q. 10.2

Mark one answer

What is the national speed limit on a single carriageway road for cars and motorcycles?

▪ 70 mph

▪ 60 mph

▪ 50 mph

▪ 30 mph

Answer

☑ **60 mph**

Exceeding the speed limit is dangerous and can result in you receiving penalty points on your licence. It isn't worth it. You should know the speed limit for the road that you're on by observing the road signs. Different speed limits apply if you are towing a trailer.

Q. 10.3

Mark one answer

What is the national speed limit for cars and motorcycles on a dual carriageway?

▪ 30 mph

▪ 50 mph

▪ 60 mph

▪ 70 mph

Answer

☑ **70 mph**

Ensure that you know the speed limit for the road that you're on. The speed limit on a dual carriageway or motorway is 70 mph for cars and motorcycles, unless there are signs to indicate otherwise. The speed limits for different types of vehicles are listed in *The Highway Code*.

questions . *answers*

Q. 10.4

Mark one answer

There are no speed limit signs on the road. How is a 30 mph limit indicated?

- By hazard warning lines
- By street lighting
- By pedestrian islands
- By double or single yellow lines

Answer

✅ **By street lighting**

There is usually a 30 mph speed limit where street lights are not more than 185 metres (600 feet) apart.

Q. 10.5

Mark one answer

Where you see street lights but no speed limit signs the limit is usually

- 30 mph
- 40 mph
- 50 mph
- 60 mph

Answer

✅ **30 mph**

A 30 mph limit usually applies where there are street lights but no speed limit signs.

Q. 10.6

Mark one answer

What does this sign mean?

- Minimum speed 30 mph
- End of maximum speed
- End of minimum speed
- Maximum speed 30 mph

Answer

✅ **End of minimum speed**

A red slash through this sign indicates that the restriction has ended. In this case the restriction was a minimum speed limit of 30 mph.

questions

answers

Q. 10.7

Mark one answer

There is a tractor ahead of you. You wish to overtake but you are NOT sure if it is safe to do so. You should

- follow another overtaking vehicle through
- sound your horn to the slow vehicle to pull over
- speed through but flash your lights to oncoming traffic
- not overtake if you are in doubt

Answer

☑ **not overtake if you are in doubt**

Never overtake if you're not sure if it's safe to do so.

Can you see far enough down the road to ensure that you can complete the manoeuvre safely?

If the answer is no, don't go.

Q. 10.8

Mark three answers

Which three of the following are most likely to take an unusual course at roundabouts?

- Horse riders
- Milk floats
- Delivery vans
- Long vehicles
- Estate cars
- Cyclists

Answers

☑ **Horse riders**

☑ **Long vehicles**

☑ **Cyclists**

Long vehicles might have to take a slightly different position when approaching the roundabout or going around it. This is to stop the rear of the vehicle cutting in and mounting the kerb.

Horse riders and cyclists might stay in the left-hand lane although they are turning right. Be aware of this and allow them room.

questions

answers

Q. 10.9

Mark four answers

In which FOUR places must you NOT park or wait?

- On a dual carriageway
- At a bus stop
- On the slope of a hill
- Opposite a traffic island
- In front of someone else's drive
- On the brow of a hill

Answers

- ☑ **At a bus stop**
- ☑ **Opposite a traffic island**
- ☑ **In front of someone else's drive**
- ☑ **On the brow of a hill**

Care and thought should be taken when parking. DON'T park

- on a footpath, pavement or cycle track
- near a school entrance
- on the approach to a zebra crossing (except in an authorised parking place)
- opposite another parked vehicle.

Q. 10.10

Mark two answers

In which TWO places must you NOT park?

- Near a school entrance
- Near a police station
- In a side road
- At a bus stop
- In a one-way street

Answers

- ☑ **Near a school entrance**
- ☑ **At a bus stop**

It may be tempting to park where you shouldn't while you run a quick errand. Careless parking is a selfish act and could endanger other road users.

Q. 10.11

Mark one answer

On a clearway you must not stop

- at any time
- when it is busy
- in the rush hour
- during daylight hours

Answer

- ☑ **at any time**

Clearways are in place so that traffic can flow without the obstruction of parked vehicles. Just one parked vehicle will cause an obstruction for all other traffic.

Do not stop where a clearway is in force, not even to pick up or set down passengers.

questions

Q. 10.12

Mark one answer

What is the meaning of this sign?

- No entry
- Waiting restrictions
- National speed limit
- School crossing patrol

Q. 10.13

Mark one answer

You can park on the right-hand side of a road at night

- in a one-way street
- with your sidelights on
- more than 10 metres (32 feet) from a junction
- under a lamp-post

answers

Answer

☑ **Waiting restrictions**

This sign indicates that there are waiting restrictions. It is normally accompanied by details of when restrictions are in force.

Details of most signs which are in common use are shown in *The Highway Code* and a more comprehensive selection is available in *Know Your Traffic Signs*.

Answer

☑ **in a one-way street**

Red rear reflectors show up when headlights shine on them. These are useful when you are parked at night but will only reflect if you park in the same direction as the traffic flow. Normally you should park on the left, but if you're in a one-way street you may also park on the right-hand side.

questions   *answers*

Q. 10.14

Mark one answer

On a three-lane dual carriageway the right-hand lane can be used for

- overtaking only, never turning right
- overtaking or turning right
- fast-moving traffic only
- turning right only, never overtaking

Answer

☑ **overtaking or turning right**

You should normally use the left-hand lane on any dual carriageway unless you are overtaking or turning right.

When overtaking on a dual carriageway, look for vehicles ahead that are turning right. They're likely to be slowing or stopped. You need to see them in good time so that you can take appropriate action.

Q. 10.15

Mark one answer

You are approaching a busy junction. There are several lanes with road markings. At the last moment you realise that you are in the wrong lane. You should

- continue in that lane
- force your way across
- stop until the area has cleared
- use clear arm signals to cut across

Answer

☑ **continue in that lane**

There are times where road markings can be obscured by queuing traffic, or you might be unsure which lane you need to be in.

If you realise that you're in the wrong lane, don't cut across lanes or bully other drivers to let you in. Follow the lane you're in and find somewhere safe to turn around if you need to.

Q. 10.16

Mark one answer

Where may you overtake on a one-way street?

- Only on the left-hand side
- Overtaking is not allowed
- Only on the right-hand side
- Either on the right or the left

Answer

☑ **Either on the right or the left**

You can overtake other traffic on either side when travelling in a one-way street. Make full use of your mirrors and ensure that it's clear all around before you attempt to overtake. Look for signs and road markings and use the most suitable lane for your destination.

Q. 10.17

Mark one answer

When going straight ahead at a roundabout you should

- indicate left before leaving the roundabout
- not indicate at any time
- indicate right when approaching the roundabout
- indicate left when approaching the roundabout

Answer

☑ **indicate left before leaving the roundabout**

When you want to go straight on at a roundabout, don't signal as you approach it, but indicate left just after you pass the exit before the one you wish to take.

Q. 10.18

Mark one answer

Which vehicle might have to use a different course to normal at roundabouts?

- Sports car
- Van
- Estate car
- Long vehicle

Answer

☑ **Long vehicle**

A long vehicle may have to straddle lanes either on or approaching a roundabout so that the rear wheels don't cut in over the kerb.

If you're following a long vehicle, stay well back and give it plenty of room.

Q. 10.19

Mark one answer

You are going straight ahead at a roundabout. How should you signal?

- Signal right on the approach and then left to leave the roundabout
- Signal left as you leave the roundabout
- Signal left on the approach to the roundabout and keep the signal on until you leave
- Signal left just after you pass the exit before the one you will take

Answer

☑ **Signal left just after you pass the exit before the one you will take**

To go straight ahead at a roundabout you should normally approach in the left-hand lane without signalling. Where there are road markings, use the lane indicated.

Ensure that you signal correctly when you are travelling around the roundabout. Other road users need to know your intentions.

questions *answers*

Q. 10.20

Mark one answer

You may only enter a box junction when

- there are less than two vehicles in front of you
- the traffic lights show green
- your exit road is clear
- you need to turn left

Answer

 your exit road is clear

Box junctions are marked on the road to prevent the road becoming blocked. Don't enter the box unless your exit road is clear. You may only wait in the box if your exit road is clear but oncoming traffic is preventing you from completing the turn.

Q. 10.21

Mark one answer

You may wait in a yellow box junction when

- oncoming traffic is preventing you from turning right
- you are in a queue of traffic turning left
- you are in a queue of traffic to go ahead
- you are on a roundabout

Answer

☑ **oncoming traffic is preventing you from turning right**

The purpose of this road marking is to keep the junction clear of queuing traffic. You may only wait in the marked area when you're turning right and your exit lane is clear but you can't complete the turn because of oncoming traffic.

questions

answers

Q. 10.22

Mark three answers

You MUST stop when signalled to do so by which THREE of these?

- A police officer
- A pedestrian
- A school crossing patrol
- A bus driver
- A red traffic light

Q. 10.23

Mark one answer

You will see these markers when approaching

- the end of a motorway
- a concealed level crossing
- a concealed speed limit sign
- the end of a dual carriageway

Q. 10.24

Mark one answer

Someone is waiting to cross at a zebra crossing. They are standing on the pavement. You should normally

- go on quickly before they step onto the crossing
- stop before you reach the zigzag lines and let them cross
- stop, let them cross, wait patiently
- ignore them as they are still on the pavement

questions  *answers*

Q. 10.25

Mark one answer

At toucan crossings, apart from pedestrians you should be aware of

▣ emergency vehicles emerging

▣ buses pulling out

▣ trams crossing in front

▣ cyclists riding across

Answer

 cyclists riding across

The use of cycles is being encouraged and more toucan crossings are being installed. These crossings enable pedestrians and cyclists to cross the path of other traffic. Watch out as cyclists will approach the crossing faster than pedestrians.

Q. 10.26

Mark two answers

Who can use a toucan crossing?

▣ Trains

▣ Cyclists

▣ Buses

▣ Pedestrians

▣ Trams

Answers

 Cyclists

▣ **Pedestrians**

Toucan crossings are similar to pelican crossings but there is no flashing amber phase. Cyclists share the crossing with pedestrians and are allowed to cycle across when the green cycle symbol is shown.

Q. 10.27

Mark one answer

At a pelican crossing, what does a flashing amber light mean?

▣ You must not move off until the lights stop flashing

▣ You must give way to pedestrians still on the crossing

▣ You can move off, even if pedestrians are still on the crossing

▣ You must stop because the lights are about to change to red

Answer

▣ **You must give way to pedestrians still on the crossing**

If there is no-one on the crossing when the amber light is flashing, you may proceed over the crossing. You don't need to wait for the green light to show.

Q. 10.28

Mark one answer

You are waiting at a pelican crossing. The red light changes to flashing amber. This means you must

☐ wait for pedestrians on the crossing to clear

☐ move off immediately without any hesitation

☐ wait for the green light before moving off

☐ get ready and go when the continuous amber light shows

Answer

☑ **wait for pedestrians on the crossing to clear**

This light allows time for the pedestrians already on the crossing to get to the other side in their own time, without being rushed. Don't rev your engine or start to move off while they are still crossing.

Q. 10.29

Mark one answer

You are travelling on a well lit road at night in a built up area. By using dipped headlights you will be able to

☐ see further along the road

☐ go at a much faster speed

☐ switch to main beam quickly

☐ be easily seen by others

Answer

☑ **be easily seen by others**

You may be difficult to see when you're travelling at night, even on a well lit road. If you use dipped headlights rather than sidelights other road users will see you more easily.

Q. 10.30

Mark one answer

When can you park on the left opposite these road markings?

☐ If the line nearest to you is broken

☐ When there are no yellow lines

☐ To pick up or set down passengers

☐ During daylight hours only

Answer

☑ **To pick up or set down passengers**

You must not park or stop on a road marked with double white lines (even where one of the lines is broken) except to pick up or set down passengers.

questions   *answers*

Q. 10.31

Mark one answer

You are intending to turn right at a crossroads. An oncoming driver is also turning right. It will normally be safer to

- keep the other vehicle to your RIGHT and turn behind it (offside to offside)
- keep the other vehicle to your LEFT and turn in front of it (nearside to nearside)
- carry on and turn at the next junction instead
- hold back and wait for the other driver to turn first

Answer

 keep the other vehicle to your RIGHT and turn behind it (offside to offside)

At some junctions the layout may make it difficult to turn offside to offside. If this is the case, be prepared to pass nearside to nearside, but take extra care as your view ahead will be obscured by the vehicle turning in front of you.

Q. 10.32

Mark one answer

You are on a road that has no traffic signs. There are street lights. What is the speed limit?

- 20 mph
- 30 mph
- 40 mph
- 60 mph

Answer

✓ **30 mph**

If you aren't sure of the speed limit a good indication is the presence of street lights. If there is street lighting the speed limit will be 30 mph unless otherwise indicated.

Q. 10.33

Mark three answers

You are going along a street with parked vehicles on the left-hand side. For which THREE reasons should you keep your speed down?

- So that oncoming traffic can see you more clearly
- You may set off car alarms
- Vehicles may be pulling out
- Drivers' doors may open
- Children may run out from between the vehicles

Answers

✓ **Vehicles may be pulling out**

✓ **Drivers' doors may open**

✓ **Children may run out from between the vehicles**

Travel slowly and carefully where there are parked vehicles in a built-up area.

Beware of

- vehicles pulling out, especially bicycles and other motorcycles
- pedestrians, especially children, who may run out from between cars
- drivers opening their doors.

questions answers

Q. 10.34
Mark one answer

You meet an obstruction on your side of the road. You should

- ■ carry on, you have priority
- ■ give way to oncoming traffic
- ■ wave oncoming vehicles through
- ■ accelerate to get past first

Answer

☑ **give way to oncoming traffic**

Take care if you have to pass a parked vehicle on your side of the road. Give way to oncoming traffic if there isn't enough room for you both to continue safely.

Q. 10.35
Mark two answers

You are on a two-lane dual carriageway. For which TWO of the following would you use the right-hand lane?

- ■ Turning right
- ■ Normal progress
- ■ Staying at the minimum allowed speed
- ■ Constant high speed
- ■ Overtaking slower traffic
- ■ Mending punctures

Answers

☑ **Turning right**

☑ **Overtaking slower traffic**

Normally you should travel in the left-hand lane and only use the right-hand lane for overtaking or turning right. Move back into the left lane as soon as it's safe but don't cut in across the path of the vehicle you've just passed.

Q. 10.36
Mark one answer

Who has priority at an unmarked crossroads?

- ■ The larger vehicle
- ■ No one has priority
- ■ The faster vehicle
- ■ The smaller vehicle

Answer

☑ **No one has priority**

Practise good observation in all directions before you emerge or make a turn. Proceed only when you're sure it's safe to do so.

questions

answers

Q. 10.37

Mark one answer

NI EXEMPT

What is the nearest you may park to a junction?

■ 10 metres (32 feet)

■ 12 metres (39 feet)

■ 15 metres (49 feet)

■ 20 metres (66 feet)

Answer

☑ **10 metres (32 feet)**

Don't park within 10 metres (32 feet) of a junction (unless in an authorised parking place). This is to allow drivers emerging from, or turning into, the junction a clear view of the road they are joining. It also allows them to see hazards such as pedestrians or cyclists at the junction.

Q. 10.38

Mark three answers

NI EXEMPT

In which THREE places must you NOT park?

■ Near the brow of a hill

■ At or near a bus stop

■ Where there is no pavement

■ Within 10 metres (32 feet) of a junction

■ On a 40 mph road

Answers

☑ **Near the brow of a hill**

☑ **At or near a bus stop**

☑ **Within 10 metres (32 feet) of a junction**

Other traffic will have to pull out to pass you. They may have to use the other side of the road and if you park near the brow of a hill they may not be able to see oncoming traffic.

It's important not to park at or near a bus stop as this could inconvenience passengers and may put them at risk as they get on or off the bus.

Parking near a junction could restrict the view for emerging vehicles.

Q. 10.39

Mark one answer

You are waiting at a level crossing. A train has passed but the lights keep flashing. You must

■ carry on waiting

■ phone the signal operator

■ edge over the stop line and look for trains

■ park and investigate

Answer

☑ **carry on waiting**

If the lights at a level crossing continue to flash after a train has passed, wait as there might be another train coming. Time seems to pass slowly when you're held up in a queue. Be patient and wait until the lights stop flashing.

questions

answers

Q. 10.40

Mark one answer

You park overnight on a road with a 40 mph speed limit. You should park

- facing the traffic
- with parking lights on
- with dipped headlights on
- near a street light

Answer

☑ with parking lights on

You must use parking lights when parking at night on a road or lay-by with a speed limit greater than 30 mph. You must also park in the direction of the traffic flow.

Q. 10.41

Mark one answer

The dual carriageway you are turning right onto has a very narrow central reserve. What should you do?

- Proceed to the central reserve and wait
- Wait until the road is clear in both directions
- Stop in the first lane so that other vehicles give way
- Emerge slightly to show your intentions

Answer

☑ Wait until the road is clear in both directions

When the central reservation is narrow you should treat a dual carriageway as one road and wait until the road is clear in both directions before emerging to turn right. If you try to treat it as two separate roads and wait in the middle, you are likely to cause an obstruction and possibly an accident.

Q. 10.42

Mark one answer

At a crossroads there are no signs or road markings. Two vehicles approach. Which has priority?

- Neither of the vehicles
- The vehicle travelling the fastest
- Oncoming vehicles turning right
- Vehicles approaching from the right

Answer

☑ Neither of the vehicles

At a crossroads where there are no 'give way' signs or road markings be very careful. No vehicle has priority, even if the sizes of the roads are different.

questions   answers

Q. 10.43

Mark one answer

What does this sign tell you?

- That it is a no-through road
- End of traffic calming zone
- Free parking zone ends
- No waiting zone ends

Answer

☑ **No waiting zone ends**

The blue and red circular sign on its own means that waiting restrictions are in force. This sign shows that you are leaving the controlled zone and waiting restrictions no longer apply.

Q. 10.44

Mark one answer

You are entering an area of roadworks. There is a temporary speed limit displayed. You should

- not exceed the speed limit
- obey the limit only during rush hour
- ignore the displayed limit
- obey the limit except at night

Answer

☑ **not exceed the speed limit**

Where there are extra hazards such as roadworks, it's often necessary to slow traffic down by imposing a temporary speed limit. These speed limits aren't advisory – they must be adhered to.

Q. 10.45

Mark one answer

You may drive over a footpath

- to overtake slow-moving traffic
- when the pavement is very wide
- if no pedestrians are near
- to get into a property

Answer

☑ **to get into a property**

It is against the law to drive on or over a footpath, except to gain access to a property. If you need to cross a pavement, watch for pedestrians in both directions.

Q. 10.46

Mark one answer

A single carriageway road has this sign. What is the maximum permitted speed for a car towing a trailer?

- ■ 30 mph
- ■ 40 mph
- ■ 50 mph
- ■ 60 mph

Answer

 50 mph

When towing trailers, speed limits are also lower on dual carriageways and motorways. On these roads vehicles towing a trailer are restricted to 60 mph.

These speed limits also apply to vehicles towing a caravan or horse box.

Q. 10.47

Mark one answer

You are towing a small caravan on a dual carriageway. You must not exceed

- ■ 50 mph
- ■ 40 mph
- ■ 70 mph
- ■ 60 mph

Answer

 60 mph

The speed limit is reduced for vehicles towing caravans and trailers to lessen the risk of the outfit becoming unstable. Due to the increased weight and size of the vehicle and caravan combination, you should plan well ahead. Be extra-careful in windy weather, as strong winds could cause a caravan or large trailer to snake from side to side.

questions

answers

Q. 10.48

Mark one answer

You want to park and you see this sign. On the days and times shown you should

- park in a bay and not pay
- park on yellow lines and pay
- park on yellow lines and not pay
- park in a bay and pay

Answer

✓ **park in a bay and pay**

Parking restrictions can apply in a variety of places and situations. Make sure you know where these are by reading *The Highway Code*.

Controlled parking areas will be indicated by signs and road markings. Look at these carefully to find out where and when the restrictions apply.

Parking in the wrong place could cause an obstruction and you could be fined.

Q. 10.49

Mark three answers

As a car driver which THREE lanes are you NOT normally allowed to use?

- Crawler lane
- Bus lane
- Overtaking lane
- Acceleration lane
- Cycle lane
- Tram lane

Answers

✓ **Bus lane**

✓ **Cycle lane**

✓ **Tram lane**

Look out for signs or road markings that tell you which lane to use. Some lanes can only be used by certain road users.

Bus lanes help the traffic to flow at certain times. Some bus lanes operate 24 hours a day while others only operate at certain times. Outside these hours other drivers may use them but check the times before you do so.

Cycle lanes are there to help protect vulnerable road users.

Q. 10.50

Mark one answer

Answer

☑ **you must not drive in that lane**

You are driving along a road that has a cycle lane. The lane is marked by a solid white line. This means that during its period of operation

Leave the lane free for cyclists. At other times, when the lane is not in operation, you should still be aware that there may be cyclists about. Give them room and don't pass too closely.

- ■ the lane may be used for parking your car
- ■ you may drive in that lane at any time
- ■ the lane may be used when necessary
- ■ you must not drive in that lane

Q. 10.51

Mark one answer

Answer

☑ **during its period of operation**

A cycle lane is marked by a solid white line. You must not drive or park in it

The cycle lanes are there for a reason. Keep them free and allow cyclists to use them.

- ■ at any time
- ■ during the rush hour
- ■ if a cyclist is using it
- ■ during its period of operation

It is illegal to drive or park in a cycle lane, marked by a solid white line, during its hours of operation. Parking in a cycle lane will obstruct cyclists and they may move into the path of traffic on the main carriageway as they ride around the obstruction. This could be hazardous for both the cyclist and other road users.

Q. 10.52

Mark one answer

Answer

☑ **keep well to the left of the road**

While driving, you intend to turn left into a minor road. On the approach you should

Don't swing out into the centre of the road in order to make the turn. This could endanger oncoming traffic and may cause other road users to misunderstand your intentions.

- ■ keep just left of the middle of the road
- ■ keep in the middle of the road
- ■ swing out wide just before turning
- ■ keep well to the left of the road

questions   *answers*

Q. 10.53

Mark one answer

You are waiting at a level crossing. The red warning lights continue to flash after a train has passed by. What should you do?

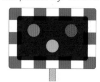

- Get out and investigate
- Telephone the signal operator
- Continue to wait
- Drive across carefully

Answer

☑ **Continue to wait**

At a level crossing flashing red lights mean you must stop. If the train passes but the lights keep flashing, wait. There may be another train coming.

Q. 10.54

Mark one answer

You are driving over a level crossing. The warning lights come on and a bell rings. What should you do?

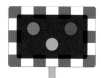

- Get everyone out of the vehicle immediately
- Stop and reverse back to clear the crossing
- Keep going and clear the crossing
- Stop immediately and use your hazard warning lights

Answer

☑ **Keep going and clear the crossing**

Keep going – don't stop on the crossing.

If the amber warning lights come on as you're approaching the crossing, you must stop unless it is unsafe to do so. Red flashing lights together with an audible signal mean you must stop.

questions *answers*

Q. 10.55

Mark one answer

You are on a busy main road and find that you are travelling in the wrong direction. What should you do?

☐ Turn into a side road on the right and reverse into the main road

☐ Make a U-turn in the main road

☐ Make a 'three-point' turn in the main road

☐ Turn round in a side road

Answer

 Turn round in a side road

Don't

- turn in a busy street
- reverse into a main road.

Find a quiet side road. Choose a place where you won't obstruct an entrance or exit. Look out for pedestrians and cyclists as well as other traffic.

Q. 10.56

Mark one answer

You may remove your seat belt when carrying out a manoeuvre that involves

☐ reversing

☐ a hill start

☐ an emergency stop

☐ driving slowly

Answer

☑ **reversing**

Don't forget to put your seat belt back on when you've finished reversing.

Q. 10.57

Mark one answer

You must not reverse

☐ for longer than necessary

☐ for more than a car's length

☐ into a side road

☐ in a built-up area

Answer

☑ **for longer than necessary**

You may decide to turn your vehicle around by reversing into an opening or side road. When you reverse, always look behind and all around and watch for pedestrians.

Don't reverse from a side road into a main road.

You must not reverse further than is necessary.

questions

answers

Q. 10.58

Mark one answer

You are parked in a busy high street. What is the safest way to turn your vehicle around to go the opposite way?

■ Find a quiet side road to turn round in

■ Drive into a side road and reverse into the main road

■ Get someone to stop the traffic

■ Do a U-turn

Answer

☑ **Find a quiet side road to turn round in**

Make sure you carry out the manoeuvre without causing a hazard to other vehicles. Choose a place to turn which is safe and convenient for you and for other road users.

Q. 10.59

Mark one answer

When you are NOT sure that it is safe to reverse your vehicle you should

■ use your horn

■ rev your engine

■ get out and check

■ reverse slowly

Answer

☑ **get out and check**

If you can't see all around your vehicle get out and have a look. You could also ask someone reliable outside the vehicle to guide you. A small child could easily be hidden directly behind you. Don't take risks.

Q. 10.60

Mark one answer

When may you reverse from a side road into a main road?

■ Only if both roads are clear of traffic

■ Not at any time

■ At any time

■ Only if the main road is clear of traffic

Answer

☑ **Not at any time**

Don't reverse into a main road from a side road. The main road is likely to be busy and the traffic on it moving quickly. Cut down the risks by using a quiet side road to reverse into.

Q. 10.61

Mark one answer

You want to turn right at a box junction.
There is oncoming traffic. You should

■ wait in the box junction if your exit
is clear

■ wait before the junction until it is clear
of all traffic

■ drive on, you cannot turn right at a box
junction

■ drive slowly into the box junction when
signalled by oncoming traffic

Answer

☑ **wait in the box junction if your
exit is clear**

You can move into the box junction to wait
as long as your exit is clear. The oncoming
traffic will stop when the traffic lights
change, allowing you to proceed.

Q. 10.62

Mark one answer

You are reversing your vehicle into a side
road. When would the greatest hazard to
passing traffic occur?

■ After you've completed the manoeuvre

■ Just before you actually begin to
manoeuvre

■ After you've entered the side road

■ When the front of your vehicle swings
out

Answer

☑ **When the front of your vehicle
swings out**

Always check road and traffic conditions in
all directions before reversing into a side
road. Keep a good look-out throughout the
manoeuvre. Act on what you see and wait if
you need to.

Q. 10.63

Mark two answers

You are driving on a road that has a cycle
lane. The lane is marked by a broken white
line. This means that

■ you should not drive in the lane unless
it is unavoidable

■ you should not park in the lane unless
it is unavoidable

■ you can drive in the lane at any time

■ the lane must be used by motorcyclists
in heavy traffic

Answers

☑ **you should not drive in the lane
unless it is unavoidable**

☑ **you should not park in the lane
unless it is unavoidable**

Where signs or road markings show lanes
are for cyclists only, leave them free. Do not
drive or park in a cycle lane unless it is
unavoidable.

questions   *answers*

Q. 10.64

Mark one answer

Where is the safest place to park your vehicle at night?

- ☐ In a garage
- ☐ On a busy road
- ☐ In a quiet car park
- ☐ Near a red route

Answer

☑ **In a garage**

If you have a garage, use it!

Your car is less likely to be a victim of car crime if it's in your garage.

In winter the windows will be free from ice.

Q. 10.65

Mark one answer

To help keep your vehicle secure at night where should you park?

- ☐ Near a police station
- ☐ In a quiet road
- ☐ On a red route
- ☐ In a well lit area

Answer

☑ **In a well lit area**

Whenever possible park in an area which will be well lit at night.

Q. 10.66

Mark one answer

You are in the right hand lane of a dual carriageway. You see signs showing that the right lane is closed 800 yards ahead. You should

GET IN LANE

800 yards

- ☐ keep in that lane until you reach the queue
- ☐ move to the left immediately
- ☐ wait and see which lane is moving faster
- ☐ move to the left in good time

Answer

☑ **move to the left in good time**

Keep a look-out for traffic signs. If you're directed to change lanes, do so in good time. Don't

- push your way into traffic in another lane
- leave changing lanes until the last moment.

Q. 10.67

Mark one answer

You are driving on an urban clearway. You may stop only to

■ set down and pick up passengers

■ use a mobile telephone

■ ask for directions

■ load or unload goods

Answer

☑ **set down and pick up passengers**

Urban clearways may be in built-up areas and their times of operation will be clearly signed. You should stop only for as long as is reasonable to pick up or set down passengers. You should ensure that you are not causing an obstruction for other traffic.

Q. 10.68

Mark one answer

You are looking for somewhere to park your vehicle. The area is full EXCEPT for spaces marked 'disabled use'. You can

■ use these spaces when elsewhere is full

■ park if you stay with your vehicle

■ use these spaces, disabled or not

■ not park there unless permitted

Answer

☑ **not park there unless permitted**

It is illegal to park in a parking space reserved for disabled users.

These spaces are provided for people with limited mobility, who may need extra space to get in and out of their vehicle.

Q. 10.69

Mark one answer

Your vehicle is parked on the road at night. When must you use sidelights?

■ Where there are continuous white lines in the middle of the road

■ Where the speed limit exceeds 30 mph

■ Where you are facing oncoming traffic

■ Where you are near a bus stop

Answer

☑ **Where the speed limit exceeds 30 mph**

When parking at night, park in the direction of the traffic. This will enable other road users to see the reflectors on the rear of your vehicle.

You must use your sidelights when parking on a road, or in a lay-by on a road, where the speed limit is over 30 mph.

questions   *answers*

Q. 10.70

Mark three answers

On which THREE occasions MUST you stop your vehicle?

- ☐ When involved in an accident
- ☐ At a red traffic light
- ☐ When signalled to do so by a police officer
- ☐ At a junction with double broken white lines
- ☐ At a pelican crossing when the amber light is flashing and no pedestrians are crossing

Answers

- ☑ **When involved in an accident**
- ☑ **At a red traffic light**
- ☑ **When signalled to do so by a police officer**

You MUST stop when signalled to do so by

- a police officer
- a traffic warden
- a school crossing patrol
- a red traffic light.

You must also stop if you are involved in accident which causes damage or injury to any other person, vehicle, animal or property.

Q. 10.71

Mark one answer

You are on a road that is only wide enough for one vehicle. There is a car coming towards you. What should you do?

- ☐ Pull into a passing place on your right
- ☐ Force the other driver to reverse
- ☐ Pull into a passing place if your vehicle is wider
- ☐ Pull into a passing place on your left

Answer

- ☑ **Pull into a passing place on your left**

Pull into the nearest passing place on the left if you meet another vehicle in a narrow road. If the nearest passing place is on the right, wait opposite it.

Q. 10.72

Mark one answer

What MUST you have to park in a disabled space?

■ An orange or blue badge

■ A wheelchair

■ An advanced driver certificate

■ A modified vehicle

Answer

☑ **An orange or blue badge**

Don't park in a space reserved for disabled people unless you or your passenger are a disabled badge holder. The badge must be displayed in your vehicle in the bottom left-hand corner of the windscreen.

Q. 10.73

Mark one answer

You are driving at night with full beam headlights on. A vehicle is overtaking you. You should dip your lights

■ some time after the vehicle has passed you

■ before the vehicle starts to pass you

■ only if the other driver dips their headlights

■ as soon as the vehicle passes you

Answer

☑ **as soon as the vehicle passes you**

On full beam your lights could dazzle the driver in front. Make sure that your light beam falls short of the vehicle in front.

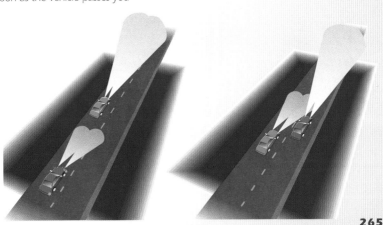

questions   *answers*

Q. 10.74

Mark one answer

When may you drive a motor car in this bus lane?

☐ Outside its hours of operation

☐ To get to the front of a traffic queue

☐ You may not use it at any time

☐ To overtake slow-moving traffic

Answer

✓ **Outside its hours of operation**

Some bus lanes only operate during peak hours and other vehicles may use them outside these hours. Make sure you check the sign for the hours of operation before driving in a bus lane.

Q. 10.75

Mark one answer

Signals are normally given by direction indicators and

☐ brake lights

☐ side lights

☐ fog lights

☐ interior lights

Answer

✓ **brake lights**

Your brake lights will give an indication to traffic behind that you're slowing down. Good anticipation will allow you time to check your mirrors before slowing.

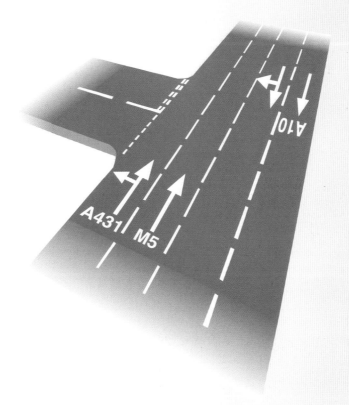

Section 11

Road and traffic signs

This section looks at road and traffic signs.

The questions will ask you about

- **Road signs**

  these tell you about the road ahead.

- **Speed limits**

  signs showing speed limits.

- **Road markings**

  directions may be painted on the road surface.

- **Regulations**

  these can be shown by means of a road sign.

questions

answers

Q. 11.1

Mark one answer

You MUST obey signs giving orders. These signs are mostly in

■ green rectangles

■ red triangles

■ blue rectangles

■ red circles

Answer

☑ **red circles**

Traffic signs can be divided into three classes – those giving orders, those warning and those informing.

Warning signs are usually triangular and direction signs are generally rectangular. One noteable exeption to these classes is the eight-sided 'stop' sign.

Q. 11.2

Mark one answer

Traffic signs giving orders are generally which shape?

Answer

Road signs in the shape of a circle give orders. Those with a red circle are mostly prohibitive. The 'stop' sign is octagonal to give it greater prominence. Signs giving orders must always be obeyed.

questions

answers

Q. 11.3

Mark one answer

Which type of sign tells you NOT to do something?

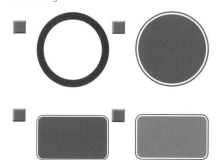

Answer

☑

Signs in the shape of a circle give orders. A sign with a red circle means that you aren't allowed to do something. Study *Know Your Traffic Signs* to ensure that you understand what the different traffic signs mean.

Q. 11.4

Mark one answer

What does this sign mean?

■ Maximum speed limit with traffic calming

■ Minimum speed limit with traffic calming

■ '20 cars only' parking zone

■ Only 20 cars allowed at any one time

Answer

☑ **Maximum speed limit with traffic calming**

If you're in places where there are likely to be pedestrians such as outside schools, near parks, residential areas and shopping areas, you should be extra-cautious and keep your speed down.

Many local authorities have taken measures to slow traffic down by creating traffic calming measures such as speed humps. They are there for a reason; slow down.

questions answers

Q. 11.5

Mark one answer

Which sign means no motor vehicles are allowed?

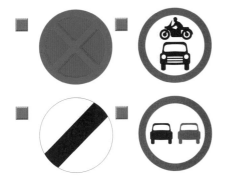

Answer

You would generally see this sign at the approach to a pedestrian-only zone.

Q. 11.6

Mark one answer

Which of these signs means no motor vehicles?

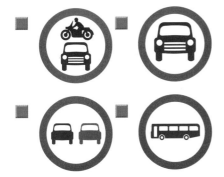

Answer

If you are driving a motor vehicle or riding a motorcycle you must not travel past this sign. This area has been designated for use by pedestrians.

questions *answers*

Q. 11.7

Mark one answer

What does this sign mean?

- New speed limit 20 mph
- No vehicles over 30 tonnes
- Minimum speed limit 30 mph
- End of 20 mph zone

Answer

 End of 20 mph zone

Where you see this sign the 20 mph restriction ends. Check all around for possible hazards and only increase your speed if it's safe to do so.

Q. 11.8

Mark one answer

What does this sign mean?

- No overtaking
- No motor vehicles
- Clearway (no stopping)
- Cars and motorcycles only

Answer

☑ **No motor vehicles**

A sign will indicate which types of vehicles are prohibited from certain roads. Make sure that you know which signs apply to the vehicle you're using.

Q. 11.9

Mark one answer

What does this sign mean?

- No parking
- No road markings
- No through road
- No entry

Answer

☑ **No entry**

'No entry' signs are used in places such as one-way streets to prevent vehicles driving against the traffic. To ignore one would be dangerous, both for yourself and other road users, as well as being against the law.

Q. 11.10

Mark one answer

What does this sign mean?

- Bend to the right
- Road on the right closed
- No traffic from the right
- No right turn

Answer

☑ **No right turn**

The 'no right turn' sign may be used to warn road users that there is a 'no entry' prohibition on a road to the right ahead.

questions

answers

Q. 11.11

Mark one answer

Which sign means 'no entry'?

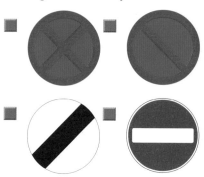

Answer

Look out for traffic signs. Disobeying or not seeing a sign could be dangerous. It may also be an offence for which you could be prosecuted.

Q. 11.12

Mark one answer

What does this sign mean?

- Route for trams only
- Route for buses only
- Parking for buses only
- Parking for trams only

Answer

☑ **Route for trams only**

Avoid blocking tram routes. Trams are fixed on their route and can't manoeuvre around other vehicles and pedestrians. Modern trams travel quickly and are quiet so you might not hear them approaching.

Q. 11.13

Mark one answer

Which type of vehicle does this sign apply to?

- ■ Wide vehicles
- ■ Long vehicles
- ■ High vehicles
- ■ Heavy vehicles

Answer

☑ **High vehicles**

The triangular shapes above and below the dimensions indicate a height restriction that applies to the road ahead.

Q. 11.14

Mark one answer

Which sign means NO motor vehicles allowed?

Answer

☑

This sign is used to enable pedestrians to walk free from traffic. It's often found in shopping areas.

questions   *answers*

Q. 11.15

Mark one answer

What does this sign mean?

■ You have priority

■ No motor vehicles

■ Two-way traffic

■ No overtaking

Answer

 No overtaking

Road signs that prohibit overtaking are placed in locations where passing the vehicle in front is dangerous. If you see this sign don't attempt to overtake. The sign is there for a reason and you must obey it.

Q. 11.16

Mark one answer

What does this sign mean?

■ Keep in one lane

■ Give way to oncoming traffic

■ Do not overtake

■ Form two lanes

Answer

☑ **Do not overtake**

If you're behind a slow-moving vehicle be patient. Wait until the restriction no longer applies and you can overtake safely.

Q. 11.17

Mark one answer

Which sign means no overtaking?

Answer

This sign indicates that overtaking here is not allowed and you could face prosecution if you ignore this prohibition.

Q. 11.18

Mark one answer

What does this sign mean?

- ▪ Waiting restrictions apply
- ▪ Waiting permitted
- ▪ National speed limit applies
- ▪ Clearway (no stopping)

Answer

☑ **Waiting restrictions apply**

There will be a plate or additional sign to tell you when the restrictions apply.

questions

answers

Q. 11.19

Mark one answer

What does this sign mean?

- End of restricted speed area
- End of restricted parking area
- End of clearway
- End of cycle route

Answer

☑ **End of restricted parking area**

Even though you have left the restricted area, make sure that you park where you won't endanger other road users or cause an obstruction.

Q. 11.20

Mark one answer

Which sign means 'no stopping'?

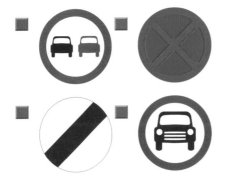

Answer

Stopping where this clearway restriction applies is likely to cause congestion. Allow the traffic to flow by obeying the signs.

Q. 11.21

Mark one answer

What does this sign mean?

- ■ Roundabout
- ■ Crossroads
- ■ No stopping
- ■ No entry

Answer

 No stopping

This sign is in place to ensure a clear route for traffic. Don't stop except in an emergency.

Q. 11.22

Mark one answer

You see this sign ahead. It means

- ■ national speed limit applies
- ■ waiting restrictions apply
- ■ no stopping
- ■ no entry

Answer

 no stopping

Clearways are stretches of road where you aren't allowed to stop unless in an emergency. You'll see this sign. Stopping where these restrictions apply may be dangerous and likely to cause an obstruction. Restrictions might apply for several miles and this may be indicated on the sign.

questions   *answers*

Q. 11.23

Mark one answer

What does this sign mean?

■ Distance to parking place ahead

■ Distance to public telephone ahead

■ Distance to public house ahead

■ Distance to passing place ahead

Answer

☑ **Distance to parking place ahead**

If you intend to stop and rest this sign allows you time to reduce speed and pull over safely.

Q. 11.24

Mark one answer

What does this sign mean?

■ Vehicles may not park on the verge or footway

■ Vehicles may park on the left-hand side of the road only

■ Vehicles may park fully on the verge or footway

■ Vehicles may park on the right-hand side of the road only

Answer

☑ **Vehicles may park fully on the verge or footway**

In order to keep roads free from parked cars, there are some areas where you're allowed to park on the verge. Only do this where you see the sign. Parking on verges or footways anywhere else could lead to a fine.

Q. 11.25

Mark one answer

What does this traffic sign mean?

- No overtaking allowed
- Give priority to oncoming traffic
- Two way traffic
- One-way traffic only

Answer

✓ **Give priority to oncoming traffic**

Priority signs are normally shown where the road is narrow and there isn't enough room for two vehicles to pass, such as at

- a narrow bridge
- roadworks
- a width restriction.

Make sure that you know who has priority. Comply with the sign and don't force your way through. Show courtesy and consideration to other road users.

Q. 11.26

Mark one answer

What is the meaning of this traffic sign?

- End of two-way road
- Give priority to vehicles coming towards you
- You have priority over vehicles coming towards you
- Bus lane ahead

Answer

✓ **You have priority over vehicles coming towards you**

Don't force your way through. Show courtesy and consideration to other road users. Although you have priority, make sure oncoming traffic is going to give way before you continue.

questions

Q. 11.27

Mark one answer

What MUST you do when you see this sign?

▪ Stop, ONLY if traffic is approaching

▪ Stop, even if the road is clear

▪ Stop, ONLY if children are waiting to cross

▪ Stop, ONLY if a red light is showing

Answer

 Stop, even if the road is clear

'Stop' signs are situated at junctions where visibility is restricted or there is heavy traffic. They must be obeyed: you must stop.

Take good all-round observation before moving off.

Q. 11.28

Mark one answer

What does this sign mean?

▪ No overtaking

▪ You are entering a one-way street

▪ Two-way traffic ahead

▪ You have priority over vehicles from the opposite direction

Answer

 You have priority over vehicles from the opposite direction

Don't force your way through if oncoming vehicles fail to give way. If necessary, slow down and give way to avoid confrontation or an accident.

Q. 11.29

Mark one answer

What shape is a STOP sign at a junction?

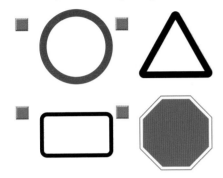

Answer

To make it easy to recognise, the 'stop' sign is the only sign of this shape. You must stop and make effective observation before proceeding.

Q. 11.30

Mark one answer

At a junction you see this sign partly covered by snow. What does it mean?

- Cross roads
- Give way
- Stop
- Turn right

Answer

☑ **Stop**

The STOP sign is the only road sign that is octagonal. This is so that it can be recognised and obeyed even if it is obscured, for example by snow.

questions

answers

Q. 11.31

Mark one answer

Which shape is used for a GIVE WAY sign?

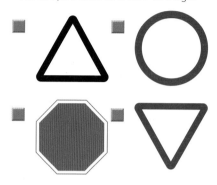

Answer

Other warning signs are the same shape and colour, but the 'give way' sign is the only triangular one that points downwards. When you see this sign you must give way to traffic on the road which you are about to enter.

Q. 11.32

Mark one answer

What does this sign mean?

- Service area 30 miles ahead
- Maximum speed 30 mph
- Minimum speed 30 mph
- Lay-by 30 miles ahead

Answer

☑ **Minimum speed 30 mph**

This sign is shown where slow-moving vehicles would impede the flow of traffic. However, if you need to slow down to avoid a potential accident, do so.

Q. 11.33

Mark one answer

Which of these signs means turn left ahead?

Answer

Blue circles tell you what you must do and this sign gives a clear instruction. Turn left ahead.

You should be looking out for signs at all times and know what they mean.

Q. 11.34

Mark one answer

What does this sign mean?

Answer

☑ **Mini roundabout**

When you see this sign, look out for any direction signs and judge whether you need to signal your intentions. Do this in good time so that other road users approaching the roundabout know what you're planning to do.

■ Buses turning

■ Ring road

■ Mini roundabout

■ Keep right

questions

answers

Q. 11.35

Mark one answer

What does this sign mean?

Answer

☑ **Pass either side to get to the same destination**

These signs are often seen in one-way streets that have more than one lane. When you see this sign, use the route that's the most convenient and doesn't require a late change of direction.

■ Give way to oncoming vehicles

■ Approaching traffic passes you on both sides

■ Turn off at the next available junction

■ Pass either side to get to the same destination

Q. 11.36

Mark one answer

What does this sign mean?

Answer

☑ **Route for trams**

Take extra care when you encounter trams. Look out for road markings and signs that alert you to them. Modern trams are very quiet and you may not hear them approaching.

■ Route for trams

■ Give way to trams

■ Route for buses

■ Give way to buses

Q. 11.37

Mark one answer

What does a circular traffic sign with a blue background do?

■ Give warning of a motorway ahead
■ Give directions to a car park
■ Give motorway information
■ Give an instruction

Answer

☑ **Give an instruction**

Signs with blue circles give a positive instruction. These are often found in urban areas and include signs for mini-roundabouts and directional arrows.

Q. 11.38

Mark one answer

Which of these signs means that you are entering a one-way street?

■  ■

■  ■

Answer

If the road has two lanes you can use either lane and overtake on either side. Use the lane that's more convenient for your destination unless road markings indicate otherwise.

questions   *answers*

Q. 11.39

Mark one answer

Where would you see a contraflow bus and cycle lane?

- On a dual carriageway
- On a roundabout
- On an urban motorway
- On a one-way street

Answer

 On a one-way street

In a contraflow lane the traffic permitted to use it travels in the opposite direction to traffic in the other lanes on the road.

Q. 11.40

Mark one answer

What does this sign mean?

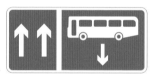

- Bus station on the right
- Contraflow bus lane
- With-flow bus lane
- Give way to buses

Answer

 Contraflow bus lane

There will also be markings on the road surface to indicate the bus lane. You must not use this lane for parking or overtaking.

Q. 11.41

Mark one answer

What does this sign mean?

- With-flow bus and cycle lane
- Contraflow bus and cycle lane
- No buses and cycles allowed
- No waiting for buses and cycles

Answer

✓ **With-flow bus and cycle lane**

Buses, taxis and cycles are permitted to travel in this lane in the same direction as other traffic. They will be on your left. There may be times shown on the sign to indicate when the lane is in operation.

Q. 11.42

Mark one answer

What does a sign with a brown background show?

- Tourist directions
- Primary roads
- Motorway routes
- Minor routes

Answer

☑ **Tourist directions**

Signs with a brown background give directions to places of interest. They will often be seen on the motorway directing you along the easiest route to the attraction.

Q. 11.43

Mark one answer

This sign means

- tourist attraction
- beware of trains
- level crossing
- beware of trams

Answer

☑ **tourist attraction**

These signs indicate places of interest and are designed to guide you by the easiest route. They are particularly useful if you are unfamiliar with the area.

questions   *answers*

Q. 11.44

Mark one answer

What are triangular signs for?

- To give warnings
- To give information
- To give orders
- To give directions

Answer

 To give warnings

This type of sign will warn you of hazards ahead.

Make sure you look at each sign that you pass on the road, so that you do not miss any vital instructions or information.

Q. 11.45

Mark one answer

What does this sign mean?

- Turn left ahead
- T-junction
- No through road
- Give way

Answer

 T-junction

The width of the arms indicate whether a road is a minor one or a major one.

Look well ahead so that you can see road signs early enough for you to be able to anticipate the signed hazard, for example a road junction.

Q. 11.46

Mark one answer

What does this sign mean?

■ Multi-exit roundabout

■ Risk of ice

■ Six roads converge

■ Place of historical interest

Answer

☑ **Risk of ice**

It will take up to ten times longer to stop when it's icy. Where there is a risk of icy conditions you need to be aware of this and take extra care.

If you think the road may be icy don't brake or steer harshly as your tyres could lose their grip on the road.

Q. 11.47

Mark one answer

What does this sign mean?

■ Crossroads

■ Level crossing with gate

■ Level crossing without gate

■ Ahead only

Answer

☑ **Crossroads**

The priority through the junction is shown by the broader line. You need to be aware of the hazard posed by traffic crossing or pulling out onto a major road.

Q. 11.48

Mark one answer

What does this sign mean?

■ Ring road

■ Mini-roundabout

■ No vehicles

■ Roundabout

Answer

☑ **Roundabout**

As you approach a roundabout look well ahead and check all signs. Decide which exit you wish to take and move into the correct position as you approach the roundabout, signalling as required.

Q. 11.49

Mark four answers

Which FOUR of these would be indicated by a triangular road sign?

- Road narrows
- Ahead only
- Low bridge
- Minimum speed
- Children crossing
- T-junction

Answers

- ☑ **Road narrows**
- ☑ **Low bridge**
- ☑ **Children crossing**
- ☑ **T-junction**

Warning signs are there to make you aware of potential hazards on the road ahead. Act on the signs so you are prepared and can take whatever action is necessary.

Q. 11.50

Mark one answer

What does this sign mean?

- Cyclists must dismount
- Cycles are not allowed
- Cycle route ahead
- Cycle in single file

Answer

- ☑ **Cycle route ahead**

Where there's a cycle route ahead, a sign will show a bicycle in a red warning triangle. Watch out for children on bicycles and cyclists rejoining the main road.

Q. 11.51

Mark one answer

Which sign means that pedestrians may be walking along the road?

Answer

When you pass pedestrians in the road, leave plenty of room. You might have to use the right-hand side of the road, so look well ahead, as well as in your mirrors, before pulling out. Take great care if there is a bend in the road obscuring your view ahead.

Q. 11.52

Mark one answer

Which of these signs warn you of a pedestrian crossing?

Answer

Look well ahead and check the pavements and surrounding areas for pedestrians. Look for anyone walking towards the crossing. Check your mirrors for traffic behind, in case you have to slow down or stop.

questions

answers

Q. 11.53

Mark one answer

What does this sign mean?

■ No footpath ahead

■ Pedestrians only ahead

■ Pedestrian crossing ahead

■ School crossing ahead

Answer

 Pedestrian crossing ahead

There are many signs relating to pedestrians that you need to be aware of. You will find these in *The Highway Code* and *Know Your Traffic Signs*. Some of the signs look similar but give different warnings. Make sure you know what they all mean so that you're prepared for any potential hazard.

Q. 11.54

Mark one answer

What does this sign mean?

■ School crossing patrol

■ No pedestrians allowed

■ Pedestrian zone – no vehicles

■ Pedestrian crossing ahead

Answer

✓ **Pedestrian crossing ahead**

Look well ahead and be ready to stop for any pedestrians crossing the road. Also check the pavements for anyone who looks like they might step into the road.

Q. 11.55

Mark one answer

Which of these signs means there is a double bend ahead?

Answer

Triangular signs give you a warning of hazards ahead. They are there to give you time to prepare for the hazard, for example by adjusting your speed.

Q. 11.56

Mark one answer

What does this sign mean?

Answer

✓ **Give way to trams**

Obey the 'give way' signs. Trams are unable to steer around you if you misjudge when it is safe to enter the junction.

■ Wait at the barriers

■ Wait at the crossroads

■ Give way to trams

■ Give way to farm vehicles

questions   *answers*

Q. 11.57

Mark one answer

What does this sign mean?

Humpback bridge

Humps in the road

Entrance to tunnel

Soft verges

Answer

☑ **Humps in the road**

These have been put in place to slow the traffic down. They're usually found in residential areas. Slow down to an appropriate speed.

Q. 11.58

Mark one answer

What does this sign mean?

Low bridge ahead

Tunnel ahead

Ancient monument ahead

Accident black spot ahead

Answer

☑ **Tunnel ahead**

When approaching a tunnel switch on your dipped headlights and reduce your speed. Be aware that your eyes might need to adjust to the sudden darkness.

Q. 11.59

Mark one answer

What does this sign mean?

Two-way traffic straight ahead

Two-way traffic crossing a one-way street

Two-way traffic over a bridge

Two-way traffic crosses a two-way road

Answer

☑ **Two-way traffic crossing a one-way street**

Be prepared for traffic approaching from junctions on either side of you. Try to avoid unnecessary changing of lanes just before the junction.

Q. 11.60

Mark one answer

Which sign means 'two-way traffic crosses a one-way road'?

Answer

Traffic could be joining the road you're in from either direction. Unless you need to turn, don't change lanes as you approach the junction.

Q. 11.61

Mark one answer

Which of these signs means the end of a dual carriageway?

Answer

If you're travelling in the right-hand lane, prepare and move over into the left-hand lane as soon as it's safe to do so.

questions *answers*

Q. 11.62

Mark one answer

What does this sign mean?

■ End of dual carriageway

■ Tall bridge

■ Road narrows

■ End of narrow bridge

Answer

☑ **End of dual carriageway**

Don't leave moving into the left-hand lane until the last moment. Plan ahead and don't rely on other traffic letting you in.

Q. 11.63

Mark one answer

What does this sign mean?

■ Two-way traffic ahead across a one-way street

■ Traffic approaching you has priority

■ Two-way traffic straight ahead

■ Motorway contraflow system ahead

Answer

☑ **Two-way traffic straight ahead**

This sign may be at the end of a dual carriageway or a one-way street. It is there to warn you of oncoming traffic.

Q. 11.64

Mark one answer

What does this sign mean?

■ Crosswinds

■ Road noise

■ Airport

■ Adverse camber

Answer

☑ **Crosswinds**

A warning sign with a picture of a windsock will indicate there may be strong crosswinds. This sign is often found on exposed roads.

Q. 11.65

Mark one answer

What does this traffic sign mean?

⬛ Slippery road ahead

⬛ Tyres liable to punctures ahead

⬛ Danger ahead

⬛ Service area ahead

Answer

☑ **Danger ahead**

This sign is there to alert you to the likelihood of danger ahead. It may be accompanied by a plate indicating the type of hazard. Be ready to reduce your speed and take avoiding action.

Q. 11.66

Mark one answer

You are about to overtake when you see this sign. You should

⬛ overtake the other driver as quickly as possible

⬛ move to the right to get a better view

⬛ switch your headlights on before overtaking

⬛ hold back until you can see clearly ahead

Answer

☑ **hold back until you can see clearly ahead**

You won't be able to see any hazards that might be hidden in the dip. As well as oncoming traffic the dip may conceal

• cyclists

• horse riders

• parked vehicles

• pedestrians

in the road.

Q. 11.67

Mark one answer

What does this sign mean?

▮ Level crossing with gate or barrier

▮ Gated road ahead

▮ Level crossing without gate or barrier

▮ Cattle grid ahead

Answer

☑ **Level crossing with gate or barrier**

Some crossings have gates but no attendant or signals. You should

* stop
* look both ways
* listen and make sure that there is no train approaching.

If there is a telephone, contact the signal operator to make sure that it's safe to cross.

Q. 11.68

Mark one answer

What does this sign mean?

▮ No trams ahead

▮ Oncoming trams

▮ Trams crossing ahead

▮ Trams only

Answer

☑ **Trams crossing ahead**

This sign warns you to beware of trams. If you don't usually drive in a town where there are trams remember to look out for them at junctions and look for tram rails, signs and signals.

Q. 11.69

Mark one answer

What does this sign mean?

▮ Adverse camber

▮ Steep hill downwards

▮ Uneven road

▮ Steep hill upwards

Answer

☑ **Steep hill downwards**

This sign will give you an early warning that the road ahead will slope downhill. Prepare to alter your speed and gear. Looking at the sign from left to right will show you whether the road slopes uphill or downhill.

Q. 11.70

Mark one answer

What does this sign mean?

- Uneven road surface
- Bridge over the road
- Road ahead ends
- Water across the road

Answer

☑ **Water across the road**

This sign is found where a shallow stream crosses the road. Heavy rainfall could increase the flow of water. If the water looks too deep or the stream has spread over a large distance, stop and find another route.

Q. 11.71

Mark one answer

What does this sign mean?

- Humpback bridge
- Traffic calming hump
- Low bridge
- Uneven road

Answer

☑ **Humpback bridge**

You will need to slow down. At humpback bridges your view ahead will be restricted and the road will often be narrow on the bridge. If the bridge is very steep be prepared to sound your horn to warn others of your approach. Going over too fast over the bridge is highly dangerous to other road users and could even cause your wheels to leave the road, with a resulting loss of control.

Q. 11.72

Mark one answer

What does this sign mean?

- Turn left for parking area
- No through road on the left
- No entry for traffic turning left
- Turn left for ferry terminal

Answer

☑ **No through road on the left**

If you intend to take a left turn this sign shows you that you can't get through to another route using the left-turn junction ahead.

questions

answers

Q. 11.73

Mark one answer

What does this sign mean?

■ T-junction

■ No through road

■ Telephone box ahead

■ Toilet ahead

Answer

☑ **No through road**

You will not be able to find a through route to another road. Use this road only for access.

Q. 11.74

Mark one answer

Which sign means 'no through road'?

Answer

☑

This sign is found at the entrance to a road that can only be used for access.

Q. 11.75

Mark one answer

Which of the following signs informs you that you are coming to a No Through Road?

Answer

This sign is found at the entrance to a road that can only be used for access.

Q. 11.76

Mark one answer

What does this sign mean?

- ☐ Direction to park and ride car park
- ☐ No parking for buses or coaches
- ☐ Directions to bus and coach park
- ☐ Parking area for cars and coaches

Answer

✓ **Direction to park and ride car park**

To ease the congestion in town centres, some cities and towns provide park and ride schemes. These allow you to park in a designated area and ride by bus into the centre.

Park and ride schemes are usually cheaper and easier than car parking in the town centre.

Q. 11.77

Mark one answer

You are driving through a tunnel and you see this sign. What does it mean?

- Direction to emergency pedestrian exit
- Beware of pedestrians, no footpath ahead
- No access for pedestrians
- Beware of pedestrians crossing ahead

Answer

☑ **Direction to emergency pedestrian exit**

If you find yourself having to evacuate a tunnel, do so as quickly as you can. Follow the signs, directing you to the nearest exit point. If there are several people using the exit, don't panic but try to leave in a calm and orderly manner.

Q. 11.78

Mark one answer

Which is the sign for a ring road?

Answer

Ring roads are designed to relieve congestion in towns and city centres.

Q. 11.79

Mark one answer

What does this sign mean?

◼ Route for lorries
◼ Ring road
◼ Rest area
◼ Roundabout

Answer

✓ **Ring road**

Ring road signs direct traffic around major towns and cities. Ring roads help the traffic to flow and ease congestion in town centres.

Q. 11.80

Mark one answer

What does this sign mean?

◼ Hilly road
◼ Humps in road
◼ Holiday route
◼ Hospital route

Answer

✓ **Holiday route**

In some areas where the volume of traffic increases during the summer months these signs show a route that diverts traffic away from town centres. This helps the traffic to flow and decreases congestion.

Q. 11.81

Mark one answer

What does this sign mean?

◼ The right-hand lane ahead is narrow
◼ Right-hand lane for buses only
◼ Right-hand lane for turning right
◼ The right-hand lane is closed

Answer

✓ **The right-hand lane is closed**

Yellow and black temporary signs may be used to inform you of roadworks or lane restrictions. Look well ahead. If you have to change lanes, do so in good time.

questions   *answers*

Q. 11.82

Mark one answer

What does this sign mean?

- Change to the left lane
- Leave at the next exit
- Contraflow system
- One-way street

Answer

☑ **Contraflow system**

If you use the right-hand lane in a contraflow system, you'll be travelling with no permanent barrier between you and the oncoming traffic. Observe speed limits and keep a good distance from the vehicle ahead.

Q. 11.83

Mark three answers

To avoid an accident when entering a contraflow system, you should

- reduce speed in good time
- switch lanes anytime to make progress
- choose an appropriate lane early
- keep the correct separation distance
- increase speed to pass through quickly
- follow other motorists closely to avoid long queues

Answers

☑ **reduce speed in good time**

☑ **choose an appropriate lane early**

☑ **keep the correct separation distance**

In a contraflow system you will be travelling close to oncoming traffic and sometimes in narrow lanes. You should

- obey the temporary signs governing speed limits
- get into the correct lane in good time
- keep a safe separation distance from the vehicle ahead.

questions

answers

Q. 11.84

Mark one answer

What does this sign mean?

☐ Leave motorway at next exit

☐ Lane for heavy and slow vehicles

☐ All lorries use the hard shoulder

☐ Rest area for lorries

Answer

✓ **Lane for heavy and slow vehicles**

Where there's a long, steep, uphill gradient on a motorway, a crawler lane may be provided. This helps the traffic to flow by diverting the slower heavy vehicles into a dedicated lane on the left.

Q. 11.85

Mark one answer

You are approaching a red traffic light. The signal will change from red to

☐ red and amber, then green

☐ green, then amber

☐ amber, then green

☐ green and amber, then green

Answer

✓ **red and amber, then green**

If you know which light is going to show next you can plan your approach accordingly. This can help prevent excessive braking or hesitation at the junction.

questions   *answers*

Q. 11.86

Mark one answer

A red traffic light means

▪ you should stop unless turning left

▪ stop, if you are able to brake safely

▪ you must stop and wait behind the stop line

▪ proceed with caution

Answer

☑ **you must stop and wait behind the stop line**

Learn the sequence of traffic lights.

* RED means stop and wait behind the stop line.

* RED-AND-AMBER also means stop. Don't go until the green light shows.

* GREEN means you may go if your way is clear. Don't proceed if your exit road is blocked, and don't block the junction. Look out for pedestrians.

* AMBER means stop at the stop line. You may go if the amber light appears after you've crossed the stop line or you're so close to it that to pull up might cause an accident.

Q. 11.87

Mark one answer

At traffic lights, amber on its own means

▪ prepare to go

▪ go if the way is clear

▪ go if no pedestrians are crossing

▪ stop at the stop line

Answer

☑ **stop at the stop line**

If the lights have been on green for a while they're likely to change to red as you approach. Be ready for this so that you're able to stop in time.

questions   answers

Q. 11.88

Mark one answer

You are approaching traffic lights. Red and amber are showing. This means

▪ pass the lights if the road is clear

▪ there is a fault with the lights – take care

▪ wait for the green light before you pass the lights

▪ the lights are about to change to red

Answer

☑ **wait for the green light before you pass the lights**

Be aware that other traffic might still be clearing the junction. Make sure the way is clear before continuing.

Q. 11.89

Mark one answer

You are at a junction controlled by traffic lights. When should you NOT proceed at green?

▪ When pedestrians are waiting to cross

▪ When your exit from the junction is blocked

▪ When you think the lights may be about to change

▪ When you intend to turn right

Answer

☑ **When your exit from the junction is blocked**

As you approach the lights look into the road you wish to take. Only proceed if your exit road is clear. If the road is blocked hold back, even if you have to wait for the next green signal.

questions　　*answers*

Q. 11.90

Mark one answer

You are in the left-hand lane at traffic lights. You are waiting to turn left. At which of these traffic lights must you NOT move on?

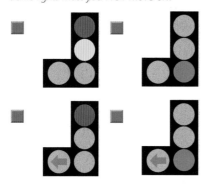

Answer

At some junctions there may be a separate signal for different lanes. These are called 'filter' lights. They're designed to help traffic flow at major junctions. Make sure that you're in the correct lane and proceed if the way is clear and the green light shows for your lane.

Q. 11.91

Mark one answer

What does this sign mean?

☐ Traffic lights out of order

☐ Amber signal out of order

☐ Temporary traffic lights ahead

☐ New traffic lights ahead

Answer

☑ **Traffic lights out of order**

Where traffic lights are out of order you might see this sign. Proceed with caution as nobody has priority at the junction.

Q. 11.92

Mark one answer

When traffic lights are out of order, who has priority?

■ Traffic going straight on

■ Traffic turning right

■ Nobody

■ Traffic turning left

Answer

☑ **Nobody**

When traffic lights are out of order you should treat the junction as an unmarked crossroads. Be cautious as you may need to give way or stop. Keep a look out for traffic attempting to cross the junction at speed.

Q. 11.93

Mark three answers

These flashing red lights mean STOP. In which THREE of the following places could you find them?

■ Pelican crossings

■ Lifting bridges

■ Zebra crossings

■ Level crossings

■ Motorway exits

■ Fire stations

Answers

☑ **Lifting bridges**

☑ **Level crossings**

☑ **Fire stations**

You must always stop when the red lights are flashing, whether or not the way seems to be clear.

questions   *answers*

Q. 11.94

Mark one answer

What do these zigzag lines at pedestrian crossings mean?

Answer

☑ **No parking at any time**

The approach to and exit from a pedestrian crossing is marked with zigzag lines. You must not

- park on them or
- overtake the leading vehicle when approaching the crossing.

Parking here would block the view for pedestrians and the approaching traffic.

◼ No parking at any time

◼ Parking allowed only for a short time

◼ Slow down to 20 mph

◼ Sounding horns is not allowed

Q. 11.95

Mark one answer

When may you cross a double solid white line in the middle of the road?

Answer

☑ **To pass a road maintenance vehicle travelling at 10 mph or less**

You may cross the solid white line to pass a stationary vehicle, pedal cycle, horse or road maintenance vehicle if they are travelling at 10 mph or less. You may also cross the solid line to enter into a side road or access a property.

◼ To pass traffic that is queuing back at a junction

◼ To pass a car signalling to turn left ahead

◼ To pass a road maintenance vehicle travelling at 10 mph or less

◼ To pass a vehicle that is towing a trailer

Q. 11.96

Mark one answer

What does this road marking mean?

▪ Do not cross the line

▪ No stopping allowed

▪ You are approaching a hazard

▪ No overtaking allowed

Answer

 You are approaching a hazard

Road markings will warn you of a hazard ahead. A single, broken line along the centre of the road, with long markings and short gaps, is a hazard warning line. Don't cross it unless you can see that the road is clear well ahead.

Q. 11.97

Mark one answer

This marking appears on the road just before a

▪ no entry sign

▪ give way sign

▪ stop sign

▪ no through road sign

Answer

 give way sign

Where you see this road marking you must give way to traffic on the main road. It might not be used at junctions where there is relatively little traffic. However, if there is a double broken line across the junction the 'give way' rules still apply.

questions   *answers*

Q. 11.98

Mark one answer

Where would you see this road marking?

■ At traffic lights
■ On road humps
■ Near a level crossing
■ At a box junction

Answer

 **On road humps**

Due to the dark colour of the road, changes in level aren't easily seen. White triangles painted on the road surface give you an indication of where there are road humps.

Q. 11.99

Mark one answer

Which is a hazard warning line?

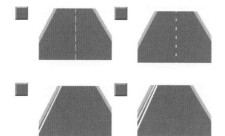

Answer

You need to know the difference between the normal centre line and a hazard warning line. If there is a hazard ahead, the markings are longer and the gaps shorter. This gives you advanced warning of an unspecified hazard ahead.

questions   answers

Q. 11.100

Mark one answer

At this junction there is a stop sign with a solid white line on the road surface. Why is there a stop sign here?

- Speed on the major road is de-restricted
- It is a busy junction
- Visibility along the major road is restricted
- There are hazard warning lines in the centre of the road

Answer

☑ **Visibility along the major road is restricted**

If your view is restricted at a road junction you must stop. There may also be a 'stop' sign. Don't emerge until you're sure there's no traffic approaching.

IF YOU DON'T KNOW, DON'T GO.

Q. 11.101

Mark one answer

You see this line across the road at the entrance to a roundabout. What does it mean?

- Give way to traffic from the right
- Traffic from the left has right of way
- You have right of way
- Stop at the line

Answer

☑ **Give way to traffic from the right**

Slow down as you approach the roundabout checking for traffic coming from the right. If you need to stop and give way, stay behind the broken line until it is safe to emerge onto the roundabout.

questions *answers*

Q. 11.102

Mark one answer

Where would you find this road marking?

■ At a railway crossing

■ At a junction

□ On a motorway

■ On a pedestrian crossing

Answer

☑ **At a junction**

This marking indicates the direction in which the traffic should flow at a mini-roundabout.

Q. 11.103

Mark one answer

How will a police officer in a patrol vehicle normally get you to stop?

■ Flash the headlights, indicate left and point to the left

■ Wait until you stop, then approach you

■ Use the siren, overtake, cut in front and stop

■ Pull alongside you, use the siren and wave you to stop

Answer

 Flash the headlights, indicate left and point to the left

You must obey signals given by the police. If a police officer in a patrol vehicle wants you to pull over they will indicate this without causing danger to you or other traffic.

Q. 11.104

Mark one answer

There is a police car following you. The police officer flashes the headlights and points to the left. What should you do?

■ Turn at the next left

■ Pull up on the left

■ Stop immediately

■ Move over to the left

Answer

☑ **Pull up on the left**

You must pull up on the left as soon as it's safe to do so and switch off your engine.

questions   answers

Q. 11.105

Mark one answer

You approach a junction. The traffic lights are not working. A police officer gives this signal. You should

- turn left only
- turn right only
- stop level with the officer's arm
- stop at the stop line

Answer

✓ **stop at the stop line**

If a police officer or traffic warden is directing traffic you must obey them. They will use the arm signals shown in *The Highway Code*. Learn what these mean and act accordingly.

Q. 11.106

Mark one answer

The driver of the car in front is giving this arm signal. What does it mean?

- The driver is slowing down
- The driver intends to turn right
- The driver wishes to overtake
- The driver intends to turn left

Answer

✓ **The driver intends to turn left**

There might be an occasion where another driver uses an arm signal. This may be because the vehicle's indicators are obscured by other traffic. In order for such signals to be effective all drivers should know the meaning of them.

Be aware that the 'left turn' signal might look similar to the 'slowing down' signal.

questions *answers*

Q. 11.107

Mark one answer

Where would you see these road markings?

▪ At a level crossing
▪ On a motorway slip road
▪ At a pedestrian crossing
▪ On a single-track road

Answer

☑ **On a motorway slip road**

When driving on a motorway or slip road, you must not enter into an area marked with chevrons and bordered by a solid white line for any reason, except in an emergency.

Q. 11.108

Mark one answer

When may you NOT overtake on the left?

▪ On a free-flowing motorway or dual carriageway
▪ When the traffic is moving slowly in queues
▪ On a one-way street
▪ When the car in front is signalling to turn right

Answer

☑ **On a free-flowing motorway or dual carriageway**

You should normally overtake on the right but there are some occasions when you may overtake on the left. These include when traffic is moving slowly in queues, or when a vehicle ahead is positioned to turn right and there's room to pass on the left.

On motorways and dual carriageways, do not overtake on the left if traffic is flowing freely.

Q. 11.109

Mark one answer

What does this motorway sign mean?

▪ Change to the lane on your left
▪ Leave the motorway at the next exit
▪ Change to the opposite carriageway
▪ Pull up on the hard shoulder

Answer

☑ **Change to the lane on your left**

On the motorway, signs sometimes show temporary warnings due to traffic or weather conditions. They may be used to indicate

- lane closures
- temporary speed limits
- weather warnings.

Q. 11.110

Mark one answer

What does this motorway sign mean?

- Temporary minimum speed 50 mph
- No services for 50 miles
- Obstruction 50 metres (164 feet) ahead
- Temporary maximum speed 50 mph

Answer

☑ **Temporary maximum speed 50 mph**

Look out for signs above your lane or on the central reservation. These will give you important information or warnings about the road ahead. Due to the high speeds of motorway traffic these signs may light up some distance from any hazard. Don't ignore the signs just because the road looks clear to you.

Q. 11.111

Mark one answer

What does this sign mean?

- Through traffic to use left lane
- Right-hand lane T-junction only
- Right-hand lane closed ahead
- 11 tonne weight limit

Answer

☑ **Right-hand lane closed ahead**

Move over as soon as you see the sign and it's safe to do so. Don't stay in a lane that is closed ahead until the last moment to beat a queue of traffic.

Q. 11.112

Mark one answer

On a motorway this sign means

- move over onto the hard shoulder
- overtaking on the left only
- leave the motorway at the next exit
- move to the lane on your left

Answer

☑ **move to the lane on your left**

It is important to know and obey temporary signs on the motorway: they are there for a reason. You may not be able to see the hazard straight away, as the signs give warnings well in advance, due to the speed of traffic on the motorway.

questions   *answers*

Q. 11.113

Mark one answer

What does '25' mean on this motorway sign?

Nottingham
A46
25

◻ The distance to the nearest town

◻ The route number of the road

◻ The number of the next junction

◻ The speed limit on the slip road

Answer

☑ **The number of the next junction**

Before you set out on your journey use a road map to plan your route. When you see advance warning of your junction, make sure you get into the correct lane in plenty of time. Last-minute harsh braking and cutting across lanes at speed is extremely hazardous.

Q. 11.114

Mark one answer

The right-hand lane of a three-lane motorway is

◻ for lorries only

◻ an overtaking lane

◻ the right-turn lane

◻ an acceleration lane

Answer

☑ **an overtaking lane**

You should stay in the left-hand lane of a motorway unless overtaking. The right-hand lane of a motorway is an overtaking lane and not a 'fast lane'.

After overtaking, move back to the left when it is safe to do so.

Q. 11.115

Mark one answer

Where can you find reflective amber studs on a motorway?

◻ Separating the slip road from the motorway

◻ On the left-hand edge of the road

◻ On the right-hand edge of the road

◻ Separating the lanes

Answer

☑ **On the right-hand edge of the road**

At night or in poor visibility reflective studs on the road help you to judge your position on the carriageway.

Q. 11.116

Mark one answer

Where on a motorway would you find green reflective studs?

- Separating driving lanes
- Between the hard shoulder and the carriageway
- At slip road entrances and exits
- Between the carriageway and the central reservation

Answer

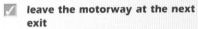 **At slip road entrances and exits**

Knowing the colours of the reflective studs on the road will help you judge your position in foggy conditions or when visibility is poor.

Q. 11.117

Mark one answer

You are travelling along a motorway. You see this sign. You should

- leave the motorway at the next exit
- turn left immediately
- change lane
- move onto the hard shoulder

Answer

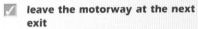 **leave the motorway at the next exit**

You'll see this sign if the motorway is closed ahead. Pull into the nearside lane as soon as it is safe to do so. Don't leave it to the last moment.

Q. 11.118

Mark one answer

What does this sign mean?

- [ ] No motor vehicles
- [ ] End of motorway
- [ ] No through road
- [ ] End of bus lane

Answer

☑ **End of motorway**

When you leave the motorway make sure that you check your speedometer. You may be going faster than you realise. Slow down and look out for speed limit signs.

Q. 11.119

Mark one answer

Which of these signs means that the national speed limit applies?

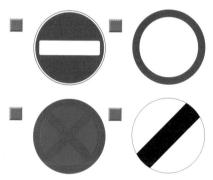

Answer

☑

You should know the speed limit for the road that you're travelling on and the vehicle that you're driving. The different speed limits are shown in *The Highway Code*.

Q. 11.120

Mark one answer

What is the maximum speed on a single carriageway road?

- ◾ 50 mph
- ◾ 60 mph
- ◾ 40 mph
- ◾ 70 mph

Answer

☑ **60 mph**

If you're travelling on a dual carriageway that becomes a single carriageway road reduce your speed gradually so that you aren't exceeding the limit as you enter. There might not be a sign to remind you of the limit, so make sure you know what the speed limits are for different types of roads and vehicles.

Q. 11.121

Mark one answer

What does this sign mean?

- ◾ End of motorway
- ◾ End of restriction
- ◾ Lane ends ahead
- ◾ Free recovery ends

Answer

☑ **End of restriction**

Temporary restrictions on motorways are shown on signs which have flashing amber lights. At the end of the restriction you will see this sign without any flashing lights.

Q. 11.122

Mark one answer

This sign is advising you to

- ◾ follow the route diversion
- ◾ follow the signs to the picnic area
- ◾ give way to pedestrians
- ◾ give way to cyclists

Answer

☑ **follow the route diversion**

When a diversion route has been put in place, drivers are advised to follow a symbol which may be a triangle, square, circle or diamond shape on a yellow background.

Q. 11.123

Mark one answer

Why would this temporary speed limit sign be shown?

■ To warn of the end of the motorway

■ To warn you of a low bridge

■ To warn you of a junction ahead

■ To warn of road works ahead

Answer

☑ **To warn of road works ahead**

In the interests of road safety, temporary speed limits are imposed at all major road works. Signs like this, giving advanced warning of the speed limit, are normally placed about three quarters of a mile ahead of where the speed limit comes into force.

Q. 11.124

Mark one answer

This traffic sign means there is

■ a compulsory maximum speed limit

■ an advisory maximum speed limit

■ a compulsory minimum speed limit

■ an advised separation distance

Answer

☑ **a compulsory maximum speed limit**

The sign gives you an early warning of a speed restriction. If you are travelling at a higher speed, slow down in good time. You could come across queuing traffic due to roadworks or a temporary obstruction.

Q. 11.125

Mark one answer

You see this sign at a crossroads. You should

☐ maintain the same speed

☐ carry on with great care

☐ find another route

☐ telephone the police

Answer

 carry on with great care

When traffic lights are out of order treat the junction as an unmarked crossroad. Be very careful as no one has priority and be prepared to stop.

Q. 11.126

Mark one answer

You are signalling to turn right in busy traffic. How would you confirm your intention safely?

☐ Sound the horn

☐ Give an arm signal

☐ Flash your headlights

☐ Position over the centre line

Answer

 Give an arm signal

In some situations you may feel your indicators cannot be seen by other road users. If you think you need to make your intention more clearly seen, give the arm signal shown in *The Highway Code*.

Q. 11.127

Mark one answer

What does this sign mean?

☐ Motorcycles only

☐ No cars

☐ Cars only

☐ No motorcycles

Answer

 No motorcycles

You must comply with all traffic signs and be especially aware of those signs which apply specifically to the type of vehicle you are using.

questions *answers*

Q. 11.128

Mark one answer

You are on a motorway. You see this sign on a lorry that has stopped in the right-hand lane. You should

☐ move into the right-hand lane

☐ stop behind the flashing lights

☐ pass the lorry on the left

☐ leave the motorway at the next exit

Answer

 pass the lorry on the left

Sometimes work is carried out on the motorway without closing the lanes. When this happens, signs are mounted on the back of lorries to warn other road users of roadworks ahead.

Q. 11.129

Mark one answer

You are on a motorway. Red flashing lights appear above your lane only. What should you do?

☐ Continue in that lane and look for further information

☐ Move into another lane in good time

☐ Pull onto the hard shoulder

☐ Stop and wait for an instruction to proceed

Answer

 Move into another lane in good time

Flashing red lights above your lane show that your lane is closed. You should move into another lane as soon as you can do so safely.

Q. 11.130

Mark one answer

A red traffic light means

■ you must stop behind the white stop line

■ you may go straight on if there is no other traffic

■ you may turn left if it is safe to do so

■ you must slow down and prepare to stop if traffic has started to cross

Answer

☑ **you must stop behind the white stop line**

The white line is generally positioned so that pedestrians have room to cross in front of waiting traffic. Don't move off while pedestrians are crossing even if the lights change to green.

Q. 11.131

Mark one answer

The driver of this car is giving an arm signal. What are they about to do?

■ Turn to the right

■ Turn to the left

■ Go straight ahead

■ Let pedestrians cross

Answer

☑ **Turn to the left**

In some situations drivers may need to give arm signals, in addition to indicators, to make their intentions clear. For arm signals to be effective, all road users should know their meaning.

questions   *answers*

Q. 11.132

Mark one answer

Which arm signal tells you that the car you are following is going to turn left?

Answer

There may be occasions when drivers need to give an arm signal in addition to an indicator. For example

- in bright sunshine
- at a complex road layout
- when stopping at a pedestrian crossing
- to confirm an indicator
- when turning right just after passing a parked vehicle.

You should understand what each arm signal means. If you give arm signals, make them clear, correct and decisive.

Q. 11.133

Mark one answer

When may you sound the horn?

- To give you right of way
- To attract a friend's attention
- To warn others of your presence
- To make slower drivers move over

Answer

☑ **To warn others of your presence**

Don't use the horn aggressively.

You MUST NOT sound it

- between 11.30 pm and 7 am
- when you are stationary, unless a moving vehicle poses a danger.

Q. 11.134

Mark one answer

You must not use your horn when you are stationary

- unless a moving vehicle may cause you danger
- at any time whatsoever
- unless it is used only briefly
- except for signalling that you have just arrived

Answer

☑ **unless a moving vehicle may cause you danger**

Only sound you horn when stationary if you think there is a risk of an accident.

Don't use it to attract someone's attention, as this causes unnecessary noise and could be misleading to other road users.

Q. 11.135

Mark one answer

What does this sign mean?

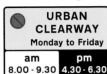

- You can park on the days and times shown
- No parking on the days and times shown
- No parking at all from Monday to Friday
- End of the urban clearway restrictions

Answer

☑ **No parking on the days and times shown**

Urban clearways are provided to keep traffic flowing at busy times. You may stop only briefly to set down or pick up passengers. Times of operation will vary from place to place so always check the signs.

Q. 11.136

Mark one answer

What does this sign mean?

- Quayside or river bank
- Steep hill downwards
- Uneven road surface
- Road liable to flooding

Answer

☑ **Quayside or river bank**

You should be careful in these locations as the road surface is likely to be wet and slippery. There may be a steep drop to the water, and there may not be a barrier along the edge of the road.

questions *answers*

Q. 11.137

Mark one answer

You see this amber traffic light ahead. Which light(s) will come on next?

- Red alone
- Red and amber together
- Green and amber together
- Green alone

Answer

☑ **Red alone**

At junctions controlled by traffic lights you must stop behind the white line until the lights change to green. Red and amber lights showing together also mean stop.

You may proceed when the light is green unless your exit road is blocked or pedestrians are crossing in front of you.

If you're approaching traffic lights that are visible from a distance and the light has been green for some time they are likely to change. Be ready to slow down and stop.

Q. 11.138

Mark one answer

The white line painted in the centre of the road means

- oncoming vehicles have priority over you
- you should give priority to oncoming vehicles
- there is a hazard ahead of you
- the area is a national speed limit zone

Answer

☑ **there is a hazard ahead of you**

A long white line with short gaps means that you are approaching a hazard. If you do need to cross it, make sure that the road is clear well ahead.

Q. 11.139

Mark one answer

Which sign means you have priority over oncoming vehicles?

Answer

Even though you have priority, be prepared to give way if complying with the sign is likely to cause an accident, congestion or confrontation.

Q. 11.140

Mark one answer

You see this signal overhead on the motorway. What does it mean?

- Leave the motorway at the next exit
- All vehicles use the hard shoulder
- Sharp bend to the left ahead
- Stop all lanes ahead closed

Answer

 Leave the motorway at the next exit

You will see this sign if there has been an incident ahead and the motorway is closed. You must obey the sign. Make sure that you prepare to leave as soon as you see the warning sign.

Don't pull over at the last moment or cut across other traffic.

questions   *answers*

Q. 11.141

Mark one answer

A white line like this along the centre of the road is a

- bus lane marking
- hazard warning
- give way marking
- lane marking

Answer

✓ **hazard warning**

The centre of the road is usually marked by a broken white line, with lines that are shorter than the gaps. When the lines become longer than the gaps this is a hazard warning line. Look well ahead for these, especially when you are planning to overtake or turn off.

Q. 11.142

Mark one answer

What is the purpose of these yellow criss-cross lines on the road?

- To make you more aware of the traffic lights
- To guide you into position as you turn
- To prevent the junction from becoming blocked
- To show you where to stop when the lights change

Answer

✓ **To prevent the junction from becoming blocked**

You must not enter a box junction until your exit road or lane is clear. The exception to this is if you want to turn right and are only prevented from doing so by oncoming traffic or by other vehicles waiting to turn right.

questions   answers

Q. 11.143

Mark one answer

What is the reason for the yellow criss-cross lines painted on the road here?

▪ To mark out an area for trams only

▪ To prevent queuing traffic from blocking the junction on the left

▪ To mark the entrance lane to a car park

▪ To warn you of the tram lines crossing the road

Answer

☑ **To prevent queuing traffic from blocking the junction on the left**

Yellow 'box junctions' like this are often used where it's busy. Their purpose is to keep the junction clear for crossing traffic. Don't enter the painted area unless your exit is clear. The exception to this is when you are turning right and are only prevented from doing so by oncoming traffic or by other vehicles waiting to turn right.

Q. 11.144

Mark one answer

What is the reason for the area marked in red and white along the centre of this road?

▪ It is to separate traffic flowing in opposite directions

▪ It marks an area to be used by overtaking motorcyclists

▪ It is a temporary marking to warn of the roadworks

▪ It is separating the two sides of the dual carriageway

Answer

☑ **It is to separate traffic flowing in opposite directions**

Areas of 'hatched markings' such as these are to separate traffic streams which could be a danger to each other. They are often seen on bends or where the road becomes narrow. If the area is bordered by a solid white line, you must not enter it except in an emergency.

questions *answers*

Q. 11.145

Mark one answer

Other drivers may sometimes flash their headlights at you. In which situation are they allowed to do this?

- To warn of a radar speed trap ahead
- To show that they are giving way to you
- To warn you of their presence
- To let you know there is a fault with your vehicle

Answer

 To warn you of their presence

If other drivers flash their headlights this isn't a signal to show priority. The flashing of headlights has the same meaning as sounding the horn – it's a warning of their presence.

Q. 11.146

Mark three answers

At roadworks which of the following can control traffic flow?

- A STOP–GO board
- Flashing amber lights
- A police officer
- Flashing red lights
- Temporary traffic lights

Answers

 A STOP–GO board

A police officer

Temporary traffic lights

As you approach the warning signs you should be considering what actions you need to take. You might have to slow right down or stop. Obey any instructions you are given and don't try to beat any lights by speeding up.

Q. 11.147

Mark one answer

You are approaching a zebra crossing where pedestrians are waiting. Which arm signal might you give?

Answer

A 'slowing down' signal will indicate your intentions to oncoming and following vehicles. Be aware that pedestrians might start to cross as soon as they see this signal.

questions   answers

Q. 11.148

Mark one answer

The white line along the side of the road

■ shows the edge of the carriageway

■ shows the approach to a hazard

■ means no parking

■ means no overtaking

Answer

☑ **shows the edge of the carriageway**

A continuous white line is used on many roads to indicate the edge of the carriageway. This can be useful when visibility is restricted. The line is discontinued at junctions, lay-bys and entrances and exits from private drives.

Q. 11.149

Mark one answer

You see this white arrow on the road ahead. It means

■ entrance on the left

■ all vehicles turn left

■ keep left of the hatched markings

■ road bending to the left

Answer

☑ **keep left of the hatched markings**

Don't attempt to overtake here, as there might be unseen hazards over the brow of the hill. Keep to the left.

questions *answers*

Q. 11.150

Mark one answer

How should you give an arm signal to turn left?

Answer

There may be occasions where other road users are unable to see your indicator, such as in bright sunlight or at a busy, complicated junction. In these cases a hand signal will help others to understand your intentions.

Q. 11.151

Mark one answer

You are waiting at a T-junction. A vehicle is coming from the right with the left signal flashing. What should you do?

■ Move out and accelerate hard

■ Wait until the vehicle starts to turn in

■ Pull out before the vehicle reaches the junction

■ Move out slowly

Answer

☑ **Wait until the vehicle starts to turn in**

Other road users may give misleading signals. When you're waiting at a junction don't emerge until you're sure of their intentions.

Q. 11.152

Mark one answer

When may you use hazard warning lights when driving?

- [ ] Instead of sounding the horn in a built-up area between 11.30 pm and 7 am
- [ ] On a motorway or unrestricted dual carriageway, to warn of a hazard ahead
- [ ] On rural routes, after a warning sign of animals
- [ ] On the approach to toucan crossings where cyclists are waiting to cross

Answer

 On a motorway or unrestricted dual carriageway, to warn of a hazard ahead

When there's queuing traffic ahead and you have to slow down and even stop, showing your hazard warning lights will alert following traffic to the hazard.

Don't forget to switch them off as the queue forms behind you.

Q. 11.153

Mark one answer

You are driving on a motorway. There is a slow-moving vehicle ahead. On the back you see this sign. You should

- [ ] pass on the right
- [ ] pass on the left
- [ ] leave at the next exit
- [ ] drive no further

Answer

 pass on the left

If a vehicle displaying this sign is in your lane you will have to pass it on the left. Use your mirrors and signal. When it's safe move into the lane on your left.

You should always look well ahead so that you can spot any hazards early, giving yourself time to react safely.

questions   answers

Q. 11.154

Mark one answer

You should NOT normally stop on these markings near schools

■ except when picking up children

■ under any circumstances

■ unless there is nowhere else available

■ except to set down children

Answer

☑ **under any circumstances**

At schools you must NOT stop on yellow zigzag lines for any length of time, not even to set down or pick up children or other passengers.

Q. 11.155

Mark one answer

Why should you make sure that your indicators are cancelled after turning?

■ To avoid flattening the battery

■ To avoid misleading other road users

■ To avoid dazzling other road users

■ To avoid damage to the indicator relay

Answer

☑ **To avoid misleading other road users**

Leaving your indicators on could confuse other road users and may even lead to an accident.

Be aware that if you haven't taken a sharp turn your indicators may not self-cancel and you will need to turn them off manually.

Q. 11.156

Mark one answer

You are driving in busy traffic. You want to pull up on the left just after a junction on the left. When should you signal?

■ As you are passing or just after the junction

■ Just before you reach the junction

■ Well before you reach the junction

■ It would be better not to signal at all

Answer

☑ **As you are passing or just after the junction**

You need to signal to let other drivers know your intentions. However, if you indicate too early they may think you are turning left into the junction. Correct timing of the signal is very important to avoid misleading others.

Section 12

Documents

This section looks at the documents needed for drivers and their vehicles.

The questions will ask you about

- **Licences**

  you must know what the law requires.

- **Insurance**

  you must have the cover you need to drive.

- **MOT test certificate**

  you should be aware of the safety checks required to gain an MOT certificate.

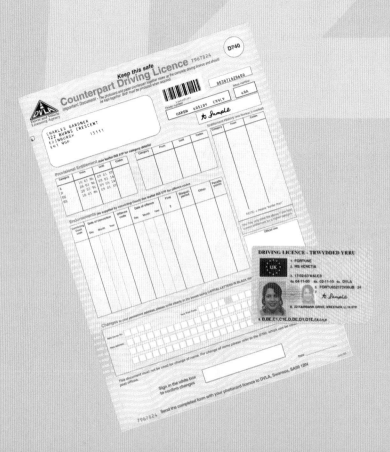

questions

answers

Q. 12.1

Mark one answer

An MOT certificate is normally valid for

- three years after the date it was issued
- 10,000 miles
- one year after the date it was issued
- 30,000 miles

Answer

☑ **one year after the date it was issued**

Make a note of the date that your MOT certificate expires. Some garages remind you that your vehicle is due an MOT but not all do.

Q. 12.2

Mark one answer

A cover note is a document issued before you receive your

- driving licence
- insurance certificate
- registration document
- MOT certificate

Answer

☑ **insurance certificate**

Sometimes an insurance company will issue a temporary insurance certificate called a cover note. It gives you the same insurance cover as your certificate, but lasts for a limited period, usually one month.

Q. 12.3

Mark one answer

NI EXEMPT

A police officer asks to see your documents. You do not have them with you. You may produce them at a police station within

- five days
- seven days
- 14 days
- 21 days

Answer

☑ **seven days**

You don't have to carry the documents for your vehicle around with you. If a police officer asks to see them and you don't have them with you, you may produce them at a police station within seven days.

questions

answers

Q. 12.4

Mark two answers

You have just passed your practical test. You do not hold a full licence in another category. Within two years you get six penalty points on your licence. What will you have to do?

- [ ] Retake only your theory test
- [ ] Retake your theory and practical tests
- [ ] Retake only your practical test
- [ ] Reapply for your full licence immediately
- [ ] Reapply for your provisional licence

Answers

- [x] **Retake your theory and practical tests**
- [x] **Reapply for your provisional licence**

If you accumulate six or more penalty points within two years of gaining your first full licence it will be revoked. The six or more points include any gained due to offences you committed before passing your test.

If this happens you may only drive as a learner until you pass both the theory and practical tests again.

Q. 12.5

Mark one answer

To drive on the road learners MUST

- [ ] have NO penalty points on their licence
- [ ] have taken professional instruction
- [ ] have a signed, valid provisional licence
- [ ] apply for a driving test within 12 months

Answer

- [x] **have a signed, valid provisional licence**

Before you drive on the road you must have a provisional licence, displaying your signature, in the category of vehicle that you're driving. It isn't valid without a signature.

Q. 12.6

Mark one answer

Before driving anyone else's motor vehicle you should make sure that

- [ ] the vehicle owner has third party insurance cover
- [ ] your own vehicle has insurance cover
- [ ] the vehicle is insured for your use
- [ ] the owner has left the insurance documents in the vehicle

Answer

- [x] **the vehicle is insured for your use**

Driving a vehicle without insurance cover is illegal. If you cause injury to anyone or damage to property it could be very expensive and you could also be subject to a criminal prosecution.

You can arrange insurance cover with

- an insurance company
- a broker
- some motor manufacturers or dealers.

Q. 12.7

Mark one answer

Your car needs an MOT certificate. If you drive without one this could invalidate your

■ vehicle service record

■ insurance

■ road tax disc

■ vehicle registration document

Answer

 insurance

If your vehicle requires an MOT certificate, it is illegal to drive it without one that is valid. As well as it being illegal, the vehicle may also be unsafe for use on the road and could endanger you, any passengers and other road users.

Without a valid MOT certificate your insurance is invalid.

Q. 12.8

Mark one answer

NI EXEMPT

When is it legal to drive a car over three years old without an MOT certificate?

■ Up to seven days after the old certificate has run out

■ When driving to an MOT centre to arrange an appointment

■ Just after buying a secondhand car with no MOT

■ When driving to an appointment at an MOT centre

Answer

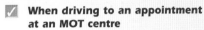 **When driving to an appointment at an MOT centre**

Any car over three years old must have a valid MOT certificate before it can be used on the road. The only time a car is exempt is when it's being driven to an appointment at an MOT testing station.

Q. 12.9

Mark two answers

To supervise a learner driver you must

■ have held a full licence for at least 3 years

■ be at least 21

■ be an approved driving instructor

■ hold an advanced driving certificate

Answers

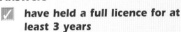 **have held a full licence for at least 3 years**

■ **be at least 21**

Don't just take someone's word that they are qualified to supervise you. The person who sits alongside you while you are learning should be a responsible adult and an experienced driver.

questions

answers

Q. 12.10

Mark one answer

The cost of your insurance may be reduced if

■ your car is large and powerful

■ you are using the car for work purposes

■ you have penalty points on your licence

■ you are over 25 years old

Answer

☑ **you are over 25 years old**

Provided you haven't had previous accidents or committed any driving offences, your insurance should be less costly as you get beyond the age of 25. This is because statistics show that most accidents are caused by, or involve, drivers who are young or inexperienced, or both.

Q. 12.11

Mark one answer

How old must you be to supervise a learner driver?

■ 18 years old

■ 19 years old

■ 20 years old

■ 21 years old

Answer

☑ **21 years old**

As well as being at least 21 years old you must hold a full EC/EEA driving licence for the category of vehicle being driven and have held that licence for at least three years.

Q. 12.12

Mark one answer

A newly qualified driver must

■ display green 'L' plates

■ not exceed 40 mph for 12 months

■ be accompanied on a motorway

■ have valid motor insurance

Answer

☑ **have valid motor insurance**

It is your responsibility to make sure you are properly insured for the vehicle you are driving.

questions

Q. 12.13

Mark one answer

What is the legal minimum insurance cover you must have to drive on public roads?

- Third party, fire and theft
- Fully comprehensive
- Third party only
- Personal injury cover

Q. 12.14

Mark three answers

You have third party insurance. What does this cover?

- Damage to your own vehicle
- Damage to your vehicle by fire
- Injury to another person
- Damage to someone's property
- Damage to other vehicles
- Injury to yourself

Q. 12.15

Mark two answers

For which TWO of these must you show your motor insurance certificate?

- When you are taking your driving test
- When buying or selling a vehicle
- When a police officer asks you for it
- When you are taxing your vehicle
- When having an MOT inspection

answers

Answer

✓ **Third party only**

The minimum insurance required by law is third party cover. This covers others involved in an accident but not damage to your vehicle. Basic third party insurance won't cover theft or fire damage.

Check with your insurance company for advice on the best cover for you and make sure that you read the policy carefully.

Answers

✓ **Injury to another person**

✓ **Damage to someone's property**

✓ **Damage to other vehicles**

Third party insurance doesn't cover damage to your own vehicle or injury to yourself. If you have an accident and your vehicle is damaged you might have to carry out the repairs at your own expense.

Answers

✓ **When a police officer asks you for it**

✓ **When you are taxing your vehicle**

When you take out motor insurance you'll be issued with a certificate. This contains details explaining who and what is insured. You'll have to produce your insurance certificate when you're paying your vehicle excise duty (road tax).

If a police officer asks for your insurance certificate and you don't have it with you, you may produce it at a police station within a specified period.

questions

answers

Q. 12.16

Mark one answer

Vehicle excise duty is often called 'Road Tax' or 'The Tax Disc'. You must

- keep it with your registration document
- display it clearly on your vehicle
- keep it concealed safely in your vehicle
- carry it on you at all times

Answer

☑ **display it clearly on your vehicle**

The tax disc should be displayed at the bottom of the windscreen on the nearside (left-hand side). This allows it to be easily seen from the kerbside. It must be current, and you can't transfer the disc from vehicle to vehicle.

Q. 12.17

Mark one answer

NI EXEMPT

Motor cars must FIRST have an MOT test certificate when they are

- one year old
- three years old
- five years old
- seven years old

Answer

☑ **three years old**

The vehicle you drive must be roadworthy and in good condition. If it's over three years old it must have a valid MOT test certificate.

The MOT test ensures that a vehicle meets minimum legal standards in terms of safety, components and environmental impact at the time it is tested.

Q. 12.18

Mark one answer

Your vehicle needs a current MOT certificate. You do not have one. Until you do have one you will not be able to renew your

- driving licence
- vehicle insurance
- road tax disc
- vehicle registration document

Answer

☑ **road tax disc**

When you renew your road tax disc you need to produce a current, valid MOT certificate for your vehicle.

Q. 12.19

Mark three answers

Which THREE pieces of information are found on a vehicle registration document?

- Registered keeper
- Make of the vehicle
- Service history details
- Date of the MOT
- Type of insurance cover
- Engine size

Answers

- ☑ **Registered keeper**
- ☑ **Make of the vehicle**
- ☑ **Engine size**

Every vehicle used on the road has a registration document. This is issued by the Driver and Vehicle Licensing Agency (DVLA) or Driver and Vehicle Licensing Northern Ireland (DVLNI). The document states the vehicle's

- date of first registration
- registration number
- previous keeper
- registered keeper
- make of vehicle
- engine size and chassis number
- year of manufacture
- colour.

Q. 12.20

Mark three answers

You have a duty to contact the licensing authority when

- you go abroad on holiday
- you change your vehicle
- you change your name
- your job status is changed
- your permanent address changes
- your job involves travelling abroad

Answers

- ☑ **you change your vehicle**
- ☑ **you change your name**
- ☑ **your permanent address changes**

The licensing authority need to keep their records up to date. They send out a reminder when your road tax is due and need your current address to send this to.

Every vehicle in the country is registered, so it's possible to trace its history.

questions   *answers*

Q. 12.21

Mark three answers

You must notify the licensing authority when

- [ ] your health affects your driving
- [ ] your eyesight does not meet a set standard
- [ ] you intend lending your vehicle
- [ ] your vehicle requires an MOT certificate
- [ ] you change your vehicle

Answers

- ☑ **your health affects your driving**
- ☑ **your eyesight does not meet a set standard**
- ☑ **you change your vehicle**

The Driver and Vehicle Licensing Agency (DVLA) hold the records of all vehicles and drivers in Great Britain (DVLNI in Northern Ireland). They need to know of any change in circumstances so that they can keep their records up to date.

Your health might affect your ability to drive safely. Don't risk endangering your own safety or that of other road users.

Q. 12.22

Mark two answers

Your vehicle is insured third party only. This covers

- [ ] damage to your vehicle
- [ ] damage to other vehicles
- [ ] injury to yourself
- [ ] injury to others
- [ ] all damage and injury

Answers

- ☑ **damage to other vehicles**
- ☑ **injury to others**

This type of insurance cover is usually cheaper than fully comprehensive. However, it does not cover any damage to your own vehicle or property. It only covers damage and injury to others.

Q. 12.23

Mark one answer

Your motor insurance policy has an excess of £100. What does this mean?

- [ ] The insurance company will pay the first £100 of any claim
- [ ] You will be paid £100 if you do not have an accident
- [ ] Your vehicle is insured for a value of £100 if it is stolen
- [ ] You will have to pay the first £100 of any claim

Answer

- ☑ **You will have to pay the first £100 of any claim**

This is a method used by insurance companies to keep annual premiums down. Generally, the higher the excess you choose to pay, the lower the annual premium you will be charged.

Q. 12.24
Mark one answer

When you apply to renew your vehicle excise licence (tax disc) you must produce

■ a valid insurance certificate

■ the old tax disc

■ the vehicle handbook

■ a valid driving licence

Answer
☑ **a valid insurance certificate**

Tax discs can be renewed at most post offices, your nearest vehicle registration office or by post to the licensing authority. Make sure you take all the relevant documents with your application.

Q. 12.25
Mark one answer

What is the legal minimum insurance cover you must have to drive on public roads?

■ Fire and theft

■ Theft only

■ Third party

■ Fire only

Answer
☑ **Third party**

Third party insurance is the minimum cover you must have to be able to drive on public roads. It only covers damage and/or injury that you may cause to other people or property. It does not cover you if you are injured or any damage to your vehicle or property.

Q. 12.26
Mark three answers

Which THREE of the following do you need before you can drive legally?

■ A valid driving licence with signature

■ A valid tax disc displayed on your vehicle

■ A vehicle service record

■ Proper insurance cover

■ Breakdown cover

■ A vehicle handbook

Answers
☑ **A valid driving licence with signature**

☑ **A valid tax disc displayed on your vehicle**

☑ **Proper insurance cover**

Make sure that you have a valid driving licence and proper insurance cover before driving any vehicle. These are legal requirements, as is displaying a valid tax disc in the vehicle.

questions   *answers*

Q. 12.27
Mark one answer

NI EXEMPT

The cost of your insurance may reduce if you

- ☐ are under 25 years old
- ☐ do not wear glasses
- ☐ pass the driving test first time
- ☐ take the Pass Plus scheme

Answer

☑ **take the Pass Plus scheme**

The cost of insurance varies with your age and how long you have been driving. Usually, the younger you are the more expensive it is, especially if you are under 25 years of age.

The Pass Plus scheme provides additional training to newly qualified drivers. Pass Plus is recognised by many insurance companies and taking this extra training could give you reduced insurance premiums, as well as improving your skills and experience.

Q. 12.28
Mark one answer

NI EXEMPT

Which of the following may reduce the cost of your insurance?

- ☐ Having a valid MOT certificate
- ☐ Taking a Pass Plus course
- ☐ Driving a powerful car
- ☐ Having penalty points on your licence

Answer

☑ **Taking a Pass Plus course**

The aim of the Pass Plus course is to build up your skills and experience. It is recognised by some insurance companies, who reward people completing the scheme with cheaper insurance premiums.

Q. 12.29
Mark one answer

NI EXEMPT

The Pass Plus scheme has been created for new drivers. What is its' main purpose?

- ☐ To allow you to drive faster
- ☐ To allow you to carry passengers
- ☐ To improve your basic skills
- ☐ To let you drive on motorways

Answer

☑ **To improve your basic skills**

New drivers are more vulnerable on the road and more likely to be involved in accidents. The Pass Plus scheme has been designed to improve your skills and help widen your driving experience.

Accidents

This section looks at what to do in the event of an accident.

The questions will ask you about

- **First aid**

  knowing what to do if someone is injured.

- **Warning devices**

  knowing how to warn other road users of an accident.

- **Reporting procedures**

  knowing where and when to report an accident.

- **Safety regulations**

  knowing what to do if a vehicle carrying hazardous loads is involved in an accident.

Q. 13.1
Mark one answer

At the scene of an accident you should

- ■ not put yourself at risk
- ■ go to those casualties who are screaming
- ■ pull everybody out of their vehicles
- ■ leave vehicle engines switched on

Answer

☑ **not put yourself at risk**

It's important that people at the scene of an accident do not create a further risk to themselves or other road users. If the accident has occurred on a motorway or major road, traffic will be approaching at speed. Do not put yourself at risk when trying to help casualties or warning other road users.

Q. 13.2
Mark four answers

You are the first to arrive at the scene of an accident. Which FOUR of these should you do?

- ■ Leave as soon as another motorist arrives
- ■ Switch off the vehicle engine(s)
- ■ Move uninjured people away from the vehicle(s)
- ■ Call the emergency services
- ■ Warn other traffic

Answers

☑ **Switch off the vehicle engine(s)**

☑ **Move uninjured people away from the vehicle(s)**

☑ **Call the emergency services**

☑ **Warn other traffic**

At an accident scene you can help in practical ways, even if you don't know how to do first aid. Make sure you do not put yourself or anyone else in danger.

The safest way to warn other traffic is by switching on your hazard warning lights.

Q. 13.3
Mark one answer

An accident has just happened. An injured person is lying in the busy road. What is the FIRST thing you should do to help?

- ■ Treat the person for shock
- ■ Warn other traffic
- ■ Place them in the recovery position
- ■ Make sure the injured person is kept warm

Answer

☑ **Warn other traffic**

You could do this by

- displaying an advance warning sign, if you have one (but not on a motorway)
- switching on hazard warning lights
- any other means that does not put you or anyone else at risk.

questions *answers*

Q. 13.4

Mark three answers

You are the first person to arrive at an accident where people are badly injured. Which THREE should you do?

- ■ Switch on your own hazard warning lights

- ■ Make sure that someone telephones for an ambulance

- ■ Try and get people who are injured to drink something

- ■ Move the people who are injured clear of their vehicles

- ■ Get people who are not injured clear of the scene

Answers

- ☑ **Switch on your own hazard warning lights**

- ☑ **Make sure that someone telephones for an ambulance**

- ☑ **Get people who are not injured clear of the scene**

If you're the first person to arrive at the scene of an accident, the risk of further collision and fire are the first concerns.

Switching off vehicle engines will reduce the risk of fire. Your hazard warning lights will let approaching traffic know that there's a need for caution.

Make sure that the emergency services are contacted, as you can't assume this has already been done.

Q. 13.5

Mark one answer

You arrive at the scene of a motorcycle accident. The rider is injured. When should the helmet be removed?

- ■ Only when it is essential
- ■ Always straight away
- ■ Only when the motorcyclist asks
- ■ Always, unless they are in shock

Answer

- ☑ **Only when it is essential**

If a motorcyclist has been injured in an accident, it's important not to remove their helmet unless it is necessary to do so to keep them alive.

Q. 13.6

Mark three answers

You arrive at a serious motorcycle accident. The motorcyclist is unconscious and bleeding. Your main priorities should be to

- try to stop the bleeding
- make a list of witnesses
- check the casualty's breathing
- take the numbers of the vehicles involved
- sweep up any loose debris
- check the casualty's airways

Answers

- ☑ **try to stop the bleeding**
- ☑ **check the casualty's breathing**
- ☑ **check the casualty's airways**

At a road accident, first deal with the danger of further collisions and fire.

Injuries should be dealt with in the following order

- Airway
- Breathing
- Circulation and bleeding.

Q. 13.7

Mark one answer

You arrive at an accident. A motorcyclist is unconscious. Your FIRST priority is the casualty's

- breathing
- bleeding
- broken bones
- bruising

Answer

- ☑ **breathing**

At the scene of an accident you must make sure there is no danger from further collisions or fire before attempting to give first aid to any casualties.

The first priority when dealing with an unconscious person is to make sure they can breathe. This may involve clearing their airway if they're having difficulty or you can see that there is some obstruction.

Q. 13.8

Mark three answers

At an accident a casualty is unconscious. Which THREE of the following should you check urgently?

- Circulation
- Airway
- Shock
- Breathing
- Broken bones

Answers

- ☑ **Circulation**
- ☑ **Airway**
- ☑ **Breathing**

An unconscious casualty may have difficulty breathing. Check that their airway is clear by tilting the head back gently and unblock it if necessary. Then make sure they are breathing.

If there is bleeding, stem the flow by placing clean material over any wounds but without pressing on any objects in the wound.

questions

answers

Q. 13.9

Mark three answers

You arrive at the scene of an accident. It has just happened and someone is unconscious. Which of the following should be given urgent priority to help them?

- Clear the airway and keep it open
- Try to get them to drink water
- Check that they are breathing
- Look for any witnesses
- Stop any heavy bleeding
- Take the numbers of vehicles involved

Answers

- ☑ **Clear the airway and keep it open**
- ☑ **Check that they are breathing**
- ☑ **Stop any heavy bleeding**

Once emergency first aid has been administered, stay with the casualty; make sure someone rings for an ambulance.

Q. 13.10

Mark three answers

At an accident someone is unconscious. Your main priorities should be to

- sweep up the broken glass
- take the names of witnesses
- count the number of vehicles involved
- check the airway is clear
- make sure they are breathing
- stop any heavy bleeding

Answers

- ☑ **check the airway is clear**
- ☑ **make sure they are breathing**
- ☑ **stop any heavy bleeding**

Remember this procedure by saying ABC which stands for Airway, Breathing, Circulation.

Q. 13.11

Mark three answers

You have stopped at the scene of an accident to give help. Which THREE things should you do?

- Keep injured people warm and comfortable
- Keep injured people calm by talking to them reassuringly
- Keep injured people on the move by walking them around
- Give injured people a warm drink
- Make sure that injured people are not left alone

Answers

- ☑ **Keep injured people warm and comfortable**
- ☑ **Keep injured people calm by talking to them reassuringly**
- ☑ **Make sure that injured people are not left alone**

If you stop at the scene of an accident to give help and there are casualties, don't move injured people unless there is a risk of further danger. Make sure no one gives casualties anything to eat or drink.

Q. 13.12
Mark three answers

You arrive at the scene of an accident. It has just happened and someone is injured. Which THREE of the following should be given urgent priority?

- Stop any severe bleeding
- Get them a warm drink
- Check that their breathing is OK
- Take numbers of vehicles involved
- Look for witnesses
- Clear their airway and keep it open

Answers

✓ **Stop any severe bleeding**

✓ **Check that their breathing is OK**

✓ **Clear their airway and keep it open**

Your first priority is to make sure the casualty's airway is clear and they are breathing. Then stem any bleeding using clean material.

Make sure someone calls the emergency services: they are the experts.

If you feel you are not capable of carrying out first aid, you could consider getting some training. It might save a life.

Q. 13.13
Mark two answers

At an accident a casualty has stopped breathing. You should

- remove anything that is blocking the mouth
- keep the head tilted forwards as far as possible
- raise the legs to help with circulation
- try to give the casualty something to drink
- keep the head tilted back as far as possible

Answers

✓ **remove anything that is blocking the mouth**

✓ **keep the head tilted back as far as possible**

Unblocking the airway and gently tilting the head back will help the casualty to breathe. They will then be in the correct position if mouth-to-mouth resuscitation is required.

questions · answers

Q. 13.14

Mark four answers

You are at the scene of an accident. Someone is suffering from shock. You should

- ☐ reassure them constantly
- ☐ offer them a cigarette
- ☐ keep them warm
- ☐ avoid moving them if possible
- ☐ loosen any tight clothing
- ☐ give them a warm drink

Answers

- ☑ **reassure them constantly**
- ☑ **keep them warm**
- ☑ **avoid moving them if possible**
- ☑ **loosen any tight clothing**

The effects of trauma may not be immediately obvious. Prompt treatment can help to minimise the effects of shock.

- Lay the casualty down
- Loosen tight clothing
- Call an ambulance
- Check their breathing and pulse.

Q. 13.15

Mark one answer

Which of the following should you NOT do at the scene of an accident?

- ☐ Warn other traffic by switching on your hazard warning lights
- ☐ Call the emergency services immediately
- ☐ Offer someone a cigarette to calm them down
- ☐ Ask drivers to switch off their engines

Answer

- ☑ **Offer someone a cigarette to calm them down**

Keeping casualties or witnesses calm is important, but never offer a cigarette because of the risk of fire.

Don't offer an injured person anything to eat or drink. They may have internal injuries or need surgery.

Q. 13.16

Mark two answers

There has been an accident. The driver is suffering from shock. You should

- ☐ give them a drink
- ☐ reassure them
- ☐ not leave them alone
- ☐ offer them a cigarette
- ☐ ask who caused the accident

Answers

- ☑ **reassure them**
- ☑ **not leave them alone**

Be aware that they could have an injury that is not immediately obvious. Stay with casualties and talk to them to reassure them.

Q. 13.17

Mark three answers

You are at the scene of an accident. Someone is suffering from shock. You should

- offer them a cigarette
- offer them a warm drink
- keep them warm
- loosen any tight clothing
- reassure them constantly

Answers

- ✓ **keep them warm**
- ✓ **loosen any tight clothing**
- ✓ **reassure them constantly**

People who seem to be unhurt may be suffering from shock. Try to reassure everyone involved in the accident and make sure no one runs into further danger from traffic.

Q. 13.18

Mark one answer

You have to treat someone for shock at the scene of an accident. You should

- reassure them constantly
- walk them around to calm them down
- give them something cold to drink
- cool them down as soon as possible

Answer

- ✓ **reassure them constantly**

Stay with the casualty and talk to them quietly and firmly to calm and reassure them.

Avoid moving them unnecessarily in case they are injured. Keep them warm, but don't give them anything to eat or drink.

Q. 13.19

Mark one answer

You arrive at the scene of a motorcycle accident. No other vehicle is involved. The rider is unconscious, lying in the middle of the road. The first thing you should do is

- move the rider out of the road
- warn other traffic
- clear the road of debris
- give the rider reassurance

Answer

- ✓ **warn other traffic**

The motorcyclist is in an extremely vulnerable position, exposed to further danger from traffic. Approaching vehicles need advance warning in order to slow right down and safely take avoiding action.

Don't put yourself or anyone else at risk. Use the hazard warning lights on your vehicle to alert other road users to the danger.

questions   answers

Q. 13.20

Mark one answer

At an accident a small child is not breathing. When giving mouth to mouth you should breathe

- sharply
- gently
- heavily
- rapidly

Answer

☑ **gently**

If a young child has stopped breathing, first check that the airway is clear, then begin mouth to mouth resuscitation. Breathe very gently and continue the resuscitation procedure until they can breathe without help.

Q. 13.21

Mark three answers

To start mouth to mouth on a casualty you should

- tilt their head forward
- clear the airway
- turn them on their side
- tilt their head back
- pinch the nostrils together
- put their arms across their chest

Answers

☑ **clear the airway**

☑ **tilt their head back**

☑ **pinch the nostrils together**

It's important to ensure that the airways are clear before you start mouth to mouth resuscitation. Gently tilt their head back and use your finger to check for and remove any obvious obstruction in the mouth.

Q. 13.22

Mark one answer

When you are giving mouth to mouth you should only stop when

- you think the casualty is dead
- the casualty can breathe without help
- the casualty has turned blue
- you think the ambulance is coming

Answer

☑ **the casualty can breathe without help**

Don't give up. Look for signs of recovery and check the casualty's pulse. Continue resuscitation until the casualty is breathing unaided.

Avoid moving them unless it's necessary for their safety.

Q. 13.23

Mark one answer

You arrive at the scene of an accident. There has been an engine fire and someone's hands and arms have been burnt. You should NOT

- douse the burn thoroughly with cool liquid

- lay the casualty down

- remove anything sticking to the burn

- reassure them constantly

Answer

☑ **remove anything sticking to the burn**

This could cause further damage and infection to the wound. Your first priorities are to cool the burn and check the patient for shock.

Q. 13.24

Mark one answer

You arrive at an accident where someone is suffering from severe burns. You should

- apply lotions to the injury

- burst any blisters

- remove anything stuck to the burns

- douse the burns with cool liquid

Answer

☑ **douse the burns with cool liquid**

Try to find fluid that is clean, cold and non-toxic. Its coolness will help take the heat out of the burn and relieve the pain. Keep the wound doused for at least ten minutes.

If blisters appear don't attempt to burst them as this could lead to infection.

Q. 13.25

Mark two answers

You arrive at the scene of an accident. A pedestrian has a severe bleeding wound on their leg, although it is not broken. What should you do?

- Dab the wound to stop bleeding

- Keep both legs flat on the ground

- Apply firm pressure to the wound

- Raise the leg to lessen bleeding

- Fetch them a warm drink

Answers

☑ **Apply firm pressure to the wound**

☑ **Raise the leg to lessen bleeding**

As soon as you can, apply a pad of clean material to the wound with a bandage or a clean length of cloth. Raising the leg will lessen the flow of blood.

Avoid tying anything tightly round the leg, as any restriction to blood circulation for more than a short period of time can result in long-term injury.

questions

answers

Q. 13.26

Mark one answer

You arrive at the scene of an accident. A passenger is bleeding badly from an arm wound. What should you do?

- Apply pressure over the wound and keep the arm down
- Dab the wound
- Get them a drink
- Apply pressure over the wound and raise the arm

Answer

☑ **Apply pressure over the wound and raise the arm**

If possible, lay the casualty down. Apply firm pressure to the wound using clean material. Raising the arm above the level of the heart will also help to stem the flow of blood.

Q. 13.27

Mark one answer

You arrive at the scene of an accident. A pedestrian is bleeding heavily from a leg wound but the leg is not broken. What should you do?

- Dab the wound to stop the bleeding
- Keep both legs flat on the ground
- Apply firm pressure to the wound
- Fetch them a warm drink

Answer

☑ **Apply firm pressure to the wound**

Lifting and supporting the casualty's leg, so that the wound is higher than their heart, should also help reduce the flow of blood.

Q. 13.28

Mark one answer

At an accident a casualty is unconscious but still breathing. You should only move them if

- an ambulance is on its way
- bystanders advise you to
- there is further danger
- bystanders will help you to

Answer

☑ **there is further danger**

At an accident only move a casualty if they are in danger where they are. Moving a casualty unnecessarily could cause further injury.

Q. 13.29

Mark one answer

At an accident you suspect a casualty has back injuries. The area is safe. You should

▪ offer them a drink

▪ not move them

▪ raise their legs

▪ offer them a cigarette

Answer

 not move them

Talk to the casualty and keep them calm. Do not attempt to move them as this could cause further injury.

Call an ambulance at the first opportunity.

Q. 13.30

Mark one answer

At an accident it is important to look after the casualty. When the area is safe, you should

▪ get them out of the vehicle

▪ give them a drink

▪ give them something to eat

▪ keep them in the vehicle

Answer

 keep them in the vehicle

Don't move casualties who are trapped in vehicles unless they are in danger.

Q. 13.31

Mark one answer

A tanker is involved in an accident. Which sign would show that the tanker is carrying dangerous goods?

▪ LONG VEHICLE ▪

▪ ▪

Answer

There will be an orange label on the side and rear of the lorry. Look at this carefully and report what it says when you phone the emergency services.

Full details of hazard warning plates are given in *The Highway Code*.

questions   *answers*

Q. 13.32

Mark three answers

The police may ask you to produce which three of these documents following an accident?

- Vehicle registration document
- Driving licence
- Theory test certificate
- Insurance certificate
- MOT test certificate
- Road tax disc

Answers

- ☑ **Driving licence**
- ☑ **Insurance certificate**
- ☑ **MOT test certificate**

You must stop if you have been involved in a collision which results in any injury or damage.

Q. 13.33

Mark one answer

At a railway level crossing the red light signal continues to flash after a train has gone by. What should you do?

- Phone the signal operator
- Alert drivers behind you
- Wait
- Proceed with caution

Answer

- ☑ **Wait**

You must always obey red flashing stop lights. If a train passes but the lights continue to flash, another train will be passing soon. Cross only when the lights go off and the barriers open.

Q. 13.34

Mark one answer

You see a car on the hard shoulder of a motorway with a HELP pennant displayed. This means the driver is most likely to be

- a disabled person
- first aid trained
- a foreign visitor
- a rescue patrol person

Answer

- ☑ **a disabled person**

If a disabled driver's vehicle breaks down and they are unable to walk to an emergency phone, they are advised to stay in their car and switch on the hazard warning lights. They may also display a 'Help' pennant in their vehicle.

Q. 13.35

Mark one answer

On the motorway the hard shoulder should be used

- to answer a mobile phone
- when an emergency arises
- for a short rest when tired
- to check a road atlas

Answer

✓ **when an emergency arises**

Pull onto the hard shoulder and use the emergency telephone to report your problem. The telephone connects you to police control and lets them know your exact location. They will inform the appropriate emergency services for you.

Never cross the carriageway to use the telephone on the other side.

Q. 13.36

Mark two answers

For which TWO should you use hazard warning lights?

- When you slow down quickly on a motorway because of a hazard ahead
- When you have broken down
- When you wish to stop on double yellow lines
- When you need to park on the pavement

Answers

✓ **When you slow down quickly on a motorway because of a hazard ahead**

✓ **When you have broken down**

Hazard warning lights are fitted to all modern cars and some motorcycles. They should only be used to warn other road users of a hazard ahead.

Q. 13.37

Mark one answer

When are you allowed to use hazard warning lights?

- When stopped and temporarily obstructing traffic
- When travelling during darkness without headlights
- When parked for shopping on double yellow lines
- When travelling slowly because you are lost

Answer

✓ **When stopped and temporarily obstructing traffic**

You must not use hazard warning lights when moving, except when slowing suddenly on a motorway or unrestricted dual carriageway to warn the traffic behind.

Never use hazard warning lights to excuse dangerous or illegal parking.

questions

answers

Q. 13.38

Mark one answer

You are on a motorway. A large box falls onto the road from a lorry. The lorry does not stop. You should

- [ ] go to the next emergency telephone and inform the police
- [ ] catch up with the lorry and try to get the driver's attention
- [ ] stop close to the box until the police arrive
- [ ] pull over to the hard shoulder, then remove the box

Answer

☑ **go to the next emergency telephone and inform the police**

Lorry drivers are sometimes unaware of objects falling from their vehicles. If you see something fall off a lorry onto the motorway, watch to see if the driver pulls over. If they don't stop, do not attempt to retrieve it yourself. You should

- pull over onto the hard shoulder near an emergency telephone
- report the hazard to the police.

Q. 13.39

Mark one answer

There has been an accident. A motorcyclist is lying injured and unconscious. Why should you usually not attempt to remove their helmet?

- [ ] Because they may not want you to
- [ ] This could result in more serious injury
- [ ] They will get too cold if you do this
- [ ] Because you could scratch the helmet

Answer

☑ **This could result in more serious injury**

When someone is injured, any movement which is not absolutely necessary should be avoided since it could make injuries worse. Unless it is essential, it's generally safer to leave a motorcyclists helmet in place.

Q. 13.40

Mark one answer

After an accident, someone is unconscious in their vehicle. When should you call the emergency services?

- [ ] Only as a last resort
- [ ] As soon as possible
- [ ] After you have woken them up
- [ ] After checking for broken bones

Answer

☑ **As soon as possible**

It is important to make sure that emergency services arrive on the scene as soon as possible. When a person is unconscious, they could have serious injuries that are not immediately obvious.

Q. 13.41

Mark one answer

An accident casualty has an injured arm. They can move it freely, but it is bleeding. Why should you get them to keep it in a raised position?

- ☐ Because it will ease the pain
- ☐ It will help them to be seen more easily
- ☐ To stop them touching other people
- ☐ It will help to reduce the bleeding

Answer

☑ **It will help to reduce the bleeding**

If a casualty is bleeding heavily, raise the limb to a higher position. This will help to reduce the blood flow.

Before raising the limb you should make sure that it is not broken.

Q. 13.42

Mark one answer

You are going through a congested tunnel and have to stop. What should you do?

- ☐ Pull up very close to the vehicle in front to save space
- ☐ Ignore any message signs as they are never up to date
- ☐ Keep a safe distance from the vehicle in front
- ☐ Make a U-turn and find another route

Answer

☑ **Keep a safe distance from the vehicle in front**

It's important to keep a safe distance from the vehicle in front at all times. This still applies in congested tunnels even if you are moving very slowly or have stopped. If the vehicle in front breaks down you may need room to manoeuvre past it.

Q. 13.43

Mark one answer

You are going through a tunnel. What should you look out for that warns of accidents or congestion?

- ☐ Hazard warning lines
- ☐ Other drivers flashing their lights
- ☐ Variable message signs
- ☐ Areas marked with hatch markings

Answer

☑ **Variable message signs**

Follow the instructions given by the signs or by tunnel officials.

In congested tunnels a minor accident can soon turn into a major incident with serious or even fatal results.

questions   answers

Q. 13.44

Mark one answer

You are going through a tunnel. What systems are provided to warn of any accidents or congestion?

- Double white centre lines
- Variable message signs
- Chevron 'distance markers'
- Rumble strips

Answer
☑ **Variable message signs**

Take notice of any instructions given on variable message signs or by tunnel officials. They will warn you of any accidents or congestion ahead and advise on what action to take.

Q. 13.45

Mark one answer

While driving, a warning light on your vehicle's instrument panel comes on. You should

- continue if the engine sounds alright
- hope that it is just a temporary electrical fault
- deal with the problem when there is more time
- check out the problem quickly and safely

Answer
☑ **check out the problem quickly and safely**

Make sure you know what the different warning lights mean. An illuminated warning light could mean that your car is unsafe to drive. Don't take risks. If you aren't sure about the problem get a qualified mechanic to check it.

Q. 13.46

Mark one answer

You have broken down on a two-way road. You have a warning triangle. You should place the warning triangle at least how far from your vehicle?

- 5 metres (16 feet)
- 25 metres (82 feet)
- 45 metres (147 feet)
- 100 metres (328 feet)

Answer
☑ **45 metres (147 feet)**

Carry an advance warning triangle in your vehicle. They fold flat and don't take up much room. Use it to warn other road users if your vehicle has broken down or there's been an accident.

Place your warning triangle at least 45 metres (147 feet) from your vehicle on the same side of the road.

You may need to place it further back if the vehicle is hidden by, for example, a bend, hill or dip in the road.

Q. 13.47

Mark three answers

You break down on a level crossing. The lights have not yet begun to flash. Which THREE things should you do?

- ■ Telephone the signal operator
- ■ Leave your vehicle and get everyone clear
- ■ Walk down the track and signal the next train
- ■ Move the vehicle if a signal operator tells you to
- ■ Tell drivers behind what has happened

Answers

- ☑ **Telephone the signal operator**
- ☑ **Leave your vehicle and get everyone clear**
- ☑ **Move the vehicle if a signal operator tells you to**

If your vehicle breaks down on a level crossing, your first priority is to get everyone out of the vehicle and clear of the crossing. Then use the railway telephone, if there is one, to tell the signal operator. If you have time before the train arrives, move the vehicle clear of crossing, but only do this if alarm signals are not on.

Q. 13.48

Mark one answer

Your vehicle has broken down on an automatic railway level crossing. What should you do FIRST?

- ■ Get everyone out of the vehicle and clear of the crossing
- ■ Phone the signal operator so that trains can be stopped
- ■ Walk along the track to give warning to any approaching trains
- ■ Try to push the vehicle clear of the crossing as soon as possible

Answer

- ☑ **Get everyone out of the vehicle and clear of the crossing**

Ensure that everyone is well clear of the crossing. In the event of an accident, debris could be scattered over some distance in various directions.

Q. 13.49

Mark two answers

Your tyre bursts while you are driving. Which TWO things should you do?

- ■ Pull on the handbrake
- ■ Brake as quickly as possible
- ■ Pull up slowly at the side of the road
- ■ Hold the steering wheel firmly to keep control
- ■ Continue on at a normal speed

Answers

- ☑ **Pull up slowly at the side of the road**
- ☑ **Hold the steering wheel firmly to keep control**

A tyre bursting can lead to a loss of control, especially if you're travelling at high speed. Using the correct procedure should help you to stop the vehicle safely.

questions

answers

Q. 13.50

Mark two answers

Which TWO things should you do when a front tyre bursts?

- Apply the handbrake to stop the vehicle
- Brake firmly and quickly
- Let the vehicle roll to a stop
- Hold the steering wheel lightly
- Grip the steering wheel firmly

Answers

☑ **Let the vehicle roll to a stop**

☑ **Grip the steering wheel firmly**

Try not to react by applying the brakes harshly. This could lead to further loss of steering control. Indicate your intention to pull up at the side of the road and roll to a stop.

Q. 13.51

Mark one answer

Your vehicle has a puncture on a motorway. What should you do?

- Drive slowly to the next service area to get assistance
- Pull up on the hard shoulder. Change the wheel as quickly as possible
- Pull up on the hard shoulder. Use the emergency phone to get assistance
- Switch on your hazard lights. Stop in your lane

Answer

☑ **Pull up on the hard shoulder. Use the emergency phone to get assistance**

Pull up on the hard shoulder and make your way to the nearest emergency telephone to call for assistance.

Do not attempt to repair your vehicle while it is on the hard shoulder because of the risk posed by traffic passing at high speeds.

Q. 13.52

Mark three answers

Which of these items should you carry in your vehicle for use in the event of an accident?

- Road map
- Can of petrol
- Jump leads
- Fire extinguisher
- First Aid kit
- Warning triangle

Answers

☑ **Fire extinguisher**

☑ **First Aid kit**

☑ **Warning triangle**

Used correctly, this equipment can provide invaluable help in the event of an accident or breakdown. It could even save a life.

Q. 13.53

Mark one answer

You are in an accident on a two way road. You have a warning triangle with you. At what distance before the obstruction should you place the warning triangle?

■ 25 metres (82 feet)

■ 45 metres (147 feet)

■ 100 metres (328 feet)

■ 150 metres (492 feet)

Answer

 45 metres (147 feet)

If there's a bend or hump in the road place the triangle so that approaching traffic slows down before the bend. You must give traffic enough time to react to the warning.

Use your hazard warning lights as well as a warning triangle, especially in the dark.

Q. 13.54

Mark one answer

You have broken down on a two way road. You have a warning triangle. It should be displayed

■ on the roof of your vehicle

■ at least 150 metres (492 feet) behind your vehicle

■ at least 45 metres (147 feet) behind your vehicle

■ just behind your vehicle

Answer

 at least 45 metres (147 feet) behind your vehicle

If you need to display a warning triangle make sure that it can be clearly seen by other road users.

Place it on the same side of the road as the broken down vehicle and away from any obstruction that would make it hard to see.

Q. 13.55

Mark one answer

You have stalled in the middle of a level crossing and cannot restart the engine. The warning bell starts to ring. You should

■ get out and clear of the crossing

■ run down the track to warn the signal operator

■ carry on trying to restart the engine

■ push the vehicle clear of the crossing

Answer

 get out and clear of the crossing

Try to stay calm, especially if you have passengers on board. If you can't restart your engine before the warning bells ring, leave the vehicle and get yourself and any passengers well clear of the crossing.

questions   answers

Q. 13.56

Mark one answer

You are on the motorway. Luggage falls from your vehicle. What should you do?

☐ Stop at the next emergency telephone and contact the police

☐ Stop on the motorway and put on hazard lights whilst you pick it up

☐ Walk back up the motorway to pick it up

☐ Pull up on the hard shoulder and wave traffic down

Answer

☑ **Stop at the next emergency telephone and contact the police**

If any object falls onto the motorway carriageway from your vehicle pull over onto the hard shoulder near an emergency telephone and phone for assistance. Don't

• stop on the carriageway

• attempt to retrieve anything.

Q. 13.57

Mark two answers

You are on a motorway. When can you use hazard warning lights?

☐ When a vehicle is following too closely

☐ When you slow down quickly because of danger ahead

☐ When you are towing another vehicle

☐ When driving on the hard shoulder

☐ When you have broken down on the hard shoulder

Answers

☑ **When you slow down quickly because of danger ahead**

☑ **When you have broken down on the hard shoulder**

Hazard warning lights will warn the traffic travelling behind you that there is a hazard ahead.

Q. 13.58

Mark four answers

You are involved in an accident with another vehicle. Someone is injured. Your vehicle is damaged. Which FOUR of the following should you find out?

- ■ Whether the driver owns the other vehicle involved
- ■ The other driver's name, address and telephone number
- ■ The make and registration number of the other vehicle
- ■ The occupation of the other driver
- ■ The details of the other driver's vehicle insurance
- ■ Whether the other driver is licensed to drive

Answers

- ☑ **Whether the driver owns the other vehicle involved**
- ☑ **The other driver's name, address and telephone number**
- ☑ **The make and registration number of the other vehicle**
- ☑ **The details of the other driver's vehicle insurance**

Try to keep calm and don't rush. Ensure that you have all the details before you leave the accident scene.

Q. 13.59

Mark three answers

You have broken down on a motorway. When you use the emergency telephone you will be asked

- ■ for the number on the telephone that you are using
- ■ for your driving licence details
- ■ for the name of your vehicle insurance company
- ■ for details of yourself and your vehicle
- ■ whether you belong to a motoring organisation

Answers

- ☑ **for the number on the telephone that you are using**
- ☑ **for details of yourself and your vehicle**
- ☑ **whether you belong to a motoring organisation**

Have these details ready before you use the emergency telephone and be sure to give the correct information.

For your own safety always face the traffic when you speak on a roadside telephone.

questions   *answers*

Q. 13.60

Mark one answer

NI EXEMPT

You lose control of your car and damage a garden wall. No one is around. What must you do?

- Report the accident to the police within 24 hours
- Go back to tell the house owner the next day
- Report the accident to your insurance company when you get home
- Find someone in the area to tell them about it immediately

Answer

☑ **Report the accident to the police within 24 hours**

If the property owner is not available at the time, you must inform the police of the accident. This should be done as soon as possible, and within 24 hours.

Q. 13.61

Mark one answer

Your engine catches fire. What should you do first?

- Lift the bonnet and disconnect the battery
- Lift the bonnet and warn other traffic
- Call the breakdown service
- Call the fire brigade

Answer

☑ **Call the fire brigade**

If you suspect a fire in the engine compartment you should pull up as safely and as quickly as possible. DO NOT open the bonnet as this will fuel the fire further.

Get any passengers out of the vehicle and dial 999 immediately to contact the fire brigade.

Q. 13.62

Mark one answer

Before driving through a tunnel what should you do?

- Switch your radio off
- Remove any sunglasses
- Close your sunroof
- Switch on windscreen wipers

Answer

☑ **Remove any sunglasses**

If you are wearing sunglasses you should remove them before driving into a tunnel. If you don't, your vision will be restricted, even in tunnels that appear to be well-lit.

Q. 13.63

Mark one answer

You are driving through a tunnel and the traffic is flowing normally. What should you do?

- Use parking lights
- Use front spot lights
- Use dipped headlights
- Use rear fog lights

Answer

☑ **Use dipped headlights**

Before entering a tunnel you should switch on your dipped headlights, as this will allow you to see and be seen. In many tunnels it is a legal requirement.

Don't wear sunglasses while driving in a tunnel. You may wish to tune your radio into a local channel.

Q. 13.64

Mark one answer

Before entering a tunnel it is good advice to

- put on your sunglasses
- check tyre pressures
- change to a lower gear
- tune your radio to a local channel

Answer

☑ **tune your radio to a local channel**

On the approach to many tunnels a sign will indicate a local radio frequency that you can tune into. This should give a warning of any accidents or congestion in the tunnel ahead.

Accidents in tunnels can lead to many casualties. Getting an advance warning of problems could save your life and others.

Q. 13.65

Mark one answer

You are driving through a tunnel. Your vehicle breaks down. What should you do?

- Switch on hazard warning lights
- Remain in your vehicle
- Wait for the police to find you
- Rely on CCTV cameras seeing you

Answer

☑ **Switch on hazard warning lights**

If your vehicle breaks down in a tunnel it could present a danger to other traffic. First switch on your hazard warning lights and then call for help from an emergency telephone point.

Don't rely on being found by the police or being seen by a CCTV camera. The longer the vehicle stays in an exposed position, the more danger it poses to other drivers.

questions   *answers*

Q. 13.66

Mark one answer

Your vehicle breaks down in a tunnel. What should you do?

- Stay in your vehicle and wait for the Police

- Stand in the lane behind your vehicle to warn others

- Stand in front of your vehicle to warn oncoming drivers

- Switch on hazard lights then go and call for help immediately

Answer

☑ **Switch on hazard lights then go and call for help immediately**

A broken down vehicle in a tunnel can cause serious congestion and danger to other road users. If your vehicle breaks down, get help without delay. Switch on your hazard warning lights, then go to an emergency telephone point to call for help.

Q. 13.67

Mark one answer

You have an accident while driving through a tunnel. You are not injured but your vehicle cannot be driven. What should you do first?

- Rely on other drivers phoning for the Police

- Switch off the engine and switch on hazard lights

- Take the names of witnesses and other drivers

- Sweep up any debris that is in the road

Answer

☑ **Switch off the engine and switch on hazard lights**

If you are involved in an accident in a tunnel be aware of the danger this can cause to other traffic. Put on your hazard warning lights straight away and switch off your engine. Then call for help from an emergency telephone point.

Q. 13.68

Mark one answer

When driving through a tunnel you should

- Look out for variable message signs

- Use your air conditioning system

- Switch on your rear fog lights

- Always use your windscreen wipers

Answer

☑ **Look out for variable message signs**

A minor incident in a tunnel can quickly turn into a major disaster. Variable message signs are provided to warn of any incidents or congestion. Follow their advice.

Q. 13.69

Mark two answers

What TWO safeguards could you take
against fire risk to your vehicle?

■ Keep water levels above maximum

■ Carry a fire extinguisher

■ Avoid driving with a full tank of petrol

■ Use unleaded petrol

■ Check out any strong smell of petrol

■ Use low octane fuel

Answers

☑ **Carry a fire extinguisher**

☑ **Check out any strong smell of petrol**

The fuel in your vehicle can be a dangerous
fire hazard. Never

- use a naked flame near the vehicle if
  you can smell fuel

- smoke when refuelling your vehicle.

Section 14

Vehicle loading

This section looks at the safety of loads.

The questions will ask you about

- **Stability**

    you need to make sure that your load doesn't affect the stability of your vehicle.

- **Towing regulations**

    you need to be aware of the effects of towing a caravan or trailer and the rules that apply.

Q. 14.1

Mark two answers

You are towing a small trailer on a busy three-lane motorway. All the lanes are open. You must

- not exceed 60 mph
- not overtake
- have a stabiliser fitted
- use only the left and centre lanes

Answers

- ☑ **not exceed 60 mph**
- ☑ **use only the left and centre lanes**

You should be aware of the motorway regulations for vehicles towing trailers. These state that a vehicle towing a trailer must not

- use the right-hand lane of a three-lane motorway unless directed to do so, for example, at roadworks or due to a lane closure
- exceed 60 mph.

Q. 14.2

Mark one answer

Any load that is carried on a roof rack MUST be

- securely fastened when driving
- carried only when strictly necessary
- as light as possible
- covered with plastic sheeting

Answer

☑ **securely fastened when driving**

The safest way to carry items on the roof is in a specially designed roof box. This will help to keep your luggage secure and dry, and also has less wind resistance than loads carried on a roof rack.

Q. 14.3

Mark one answer

You are planning to tow a caravan. Which of these will mostly help to aid the vehicle handling?

- A jockey-wheel fitted to the towbar
- Power steering fitted to the towing vehicle
- Anti-lock brakes fitted to the towing vehicle
- A stabiliser fitted to the towbar

Answer

☑ **A stabiliser fitted to the towbar**

Towing a caravan or trailer affects the way the tow vehicle handles. It is highly recommended that you take a caravan manoeuvring course. These are provided by various organisations for anyone wishing to tow a trailer.

questions   *answers*

Q. 14.4

Mark one answer

If a trailer swerves or snakes when you are towing it you should

- [ ] ease off the accelerator and reduce your speed
- [ ] let go of the steering wheel and let it correct itself
- [ ] brake hard and hold the pedal down
- [ ] increase your speed as quickly as possible

Answer

- [x] **ease off the accelerator and reduce your speed**

Strong winds or buffeting from large vehicles can cause a trailer or caravan to snake or swerve. If this happens, ease off the accelerator. Don't

- brake harshly
- steer sharply
- increase your speed.

Q. 14.5

Mark one answer

How can you stop a caravan snaking from side to side?

- [ ] Turn the steering wheel slowly to each side
- [ ] Accelerate to increase your speed
- [ ] Stop as quickly as you can
- [ ] Slow down very gradually

Answer

- [x] **Slow down very gradually**

Keep calm and don't brake harshly or you could lose control completely.

Q. 14.6

Mark two answers

On which TWO occasions might you inflate your tyres to more than the recommended normal pressure?

- [ ] When the roads are slippery
- [ ] When driving fast for a long distance
- [ ] When the tyre tread is worn below 2mm
- [ ] When carrying a heavy load
- [ ] When the weather is cold
- [ ] When the vehicle is fitted with anti-lock brakes

Answers

- [x] **When driving fast for a long distance**
- [x] **When carrying a heavy load**

Check the vehicle handbook; this should give you guidance on the correct tyre pressures for your vehicle.

If you are carrying a heavy load in the rear of your vehicle, you may need to adjust the headlight aim as well as the tyre pressures.

Q. 14.7

Mark one answer

A heavy load on your roof rack will

- improve the road holding
- reduce the stopping distance
- make the steering lighter
- reduce stability

Answer

 **reduce stability**

A heavy load on your roof rack will reduce the stability of the vehicle because it moves the centre of gravity away from that designed by the manufacturer. Be aware of this when you negotiate bends and corners.

If you change direction at speed, your vehicle and/or load could become unstable and you could lose control.

Q. 14.8

Mark one answer

Are passengers allowed to ride in a caravan that is being towed?

- Yes if they are over fourteen
- No not at any time
- Only if all the seats in the towing vehicle are full
- Only if a stabilizer is fitted

Answer

 **No not at any time**

Riding in a towed caravan is highly dangerous. The safety of the entire unit is dependent on the stability of the trailer. Moving passengers would make the caravan unstable and could cause loss of control.

Q. 14.9

Mark one answer

You are towing a caravan along a motorway. The caravan begins to swerve from side to side. What should you do?

- Ease off the accelerator slowly
- Steer sharply from side to side
- Do an emergency stop
- Speed up very quickly

Answer

 **Ease off the accelerator slowly**

Try not to brake or steer heavily as this will only make matters worse and you could lose control altogether. Keep calm and regain control by easing off the accelerator.

questions   *answers*

Q. 14.10

Mark one answer

A trailer must stay securely hitched-up to the towing vehicle. What additional safety device can be fitted to the trailer braking system?

- Stabiliser
- Jockey wheel
- Corner steadies
- Breakaway cable

Answer

☑ **Breakaway cable**

In the event of a towbar failure the cable activates the trailer brakes, then snaps. This allows the towing vehicle to get free of the trailer and out of danger.

Q. 14.11

Mark two answers

Overloading your vehicle can seriously affect the

- gearbox
- steering
- handling
- battery life
- journey time

Answers

☑ **steering**

☑ **handling**

Any load will have an effect on the handling of your vehicle and this becomes worse as you increase the load. Any change in the centre of gravity or weight the vehicle is carrying will affect its braking and handling on bends.

You need to be aware of this when carrying passengers, heavy loads, fitting a roof rack or towing a trailer.

Q. 14.12

Mark one answer

Who is responsible for making sure that a vehicle is not overloaded?

- The driver of the vehicle
- The owner of the items being carried
- The person who loaded the vehicle
- The licensing authority

Answer

☑ **The driver of the vehicle**

Your vehicle must not be overloaded. Carrying heavy loads will affect control and handling characteristics. If your vehicle is overloaded and it causes an accident you'll be responsible.

Q. 14.13

Mark one answer

Which of these is a suitable restraint for a child under three years?

- ■ A child seat
- ■ An adult holding a child
- ■ An adult seat belt
- ■ A lap belt

Answer

 A child seat

The driver is responsible for ensuring that children under three wear suitable child restraints. If the child is in the front seat a restraint must be used. If the child is in the rear seat, a restraint must be used if available. Suitable forms of restraint include a harness or baby carrier. Any harness or booster seat used should be appropriate to the child's size and weight.

Q. 14.14

Mark one answer

A child under three years is being carried in your vehicle. They should be secured in a restraint. Which of these is suitable?

- ■ An adult holding a child
- ■ A lap belt
- ■ A baby carrier
- ■ An adult seat belt

Answer

☑ **A baby carrier**

If a child of 14 or under is a passenger in your car, you as the driver are responsible for them wearing a suitable restraint.

For a child under three years old, a harness or child seat would also be suitable restraints. These should be appropriate to the child's size and weight.

Useful information

This part of the book gives information you may find useful. It includes

- Acceptable forms of photo ID

  which types of identity are acceptable and who can make a statement and sign a photo to confirm your identity

- Theory test centres in Great Britain and Northern Ireland

  where you can take your theory test

- Service standards

  how we judge our performance

- Complaints guide

  what to do if you have any complaints about the theory test

- Compensation code

  when you can receive compensation and what compensation you can claim.

Acceptable forms of photo ID

Forms of photographic identification acceptable at both theory and practical tests are as follows

- your passport, or document of like nature. Your passport doesn't have to be a British one, or current

- *cheque guarantee card or credit card bearing your photograph and signature

- an employer's identity or workplace pass bearing your photograph and name or signature, or both

- Trade Union Card bearing your photograph and signature

- Student Union Card with reference to either the NUS or an education establishment or a course reference number. The card must bear your photograph and name or signature, or both

- School Bus Pass bearing the name of the issuing authority and your photograph and signature

- *card issued by a Railway Authority or other authorised body for the purchase of reduced-price railway tickets (e.g. a Young Person's Railcard), bearing the name of the issuing authority and your photograph and signature

- *Gun Licence, including a Firearm or Shotgun Certificate, which bears your photograph and signature

- *Proof of Age Card issued by the Portman Group bearing your photograph and signature.

Any form of photographic identification presented must be recognisably you and, unless you can bring associated paperwork like a marriage certificate, must be in the same name as you booked your test.

If you don't have any of these you can bring a signed photograph, together with a statement like the one shown opposite that it's a true likeness of you. Both the statement and the back of the photograph must be signed by the same person. They can be any of the following

- *Approved Driving Instructor, but not a trainee (pink licence) holder

- *DSA-certified motorcycle instructor

- Member of Parliament

- medical practitioner

- *local authority councillor

- teacher (qualified)

- Justice of the Peace

- civil servant (established)

- police officer

- bank official

- minister of religion

- barrister or solicitor

- *Commissioned Officer in Her Majesty's Forces

- *LGV Trainers on the DSA Voluntary Register of LGV Instructors.

*Not valid in Northern Ireland.

I _____ (name of certifier), certify that this is a true likeness of _____ , who has been known to me for (number) months / years in my capacity as _____

Signed

Dated

Daytime phone no.

LGV Trainer no.

If you have any queries about what photographic evidence we will accept, contact the enquiry line on 0870 0101 372 (0845 600 6700 in Northern Ireland).

Theory test centres in Great Britain and Northern Ireland

England

Aldershot
Barnstaple
Barrow
Basildon
Basingstoke
Bath
Berwick-upon-Tweed
Birkenhead
Birmingham
Blackpool
Bolton
Boston
Bournemouth
Bradford
Brighton
Bristol
Bury St Edmunds
Cambridge
Canterbury
Carlisle
Chelmsford
Cheltenham
Chester
Chesterfield
Colchester
Coventry
Crawley
Derby
Doncaster
Dudley
Durham
Eastbourne
Exeter
Fareham
Gillingham

Gloucester
Grantham
Grimsby
Guildford
Harlow
Harrogate
Hastings
Hereford
Huddersfield
Hull
Ipswich
Isle of Wight
Isles of Scilly
King's Lynn
Leeds
Leicester
Lincoln
Liverpool
London
– Croydon
– Ilford
– Kingston
– Palmers Green
– Southwark
– Staines
– Uxbridge
Lowestoft
Luton
Manchester
Mansfield
Middlesbrough
Milton Keynes
Morpeth
Newcastle
Northampton
Norwich

Nottingham
Oldham
Oxford
Penzance
Peterborough
Plymouth
Portsmouth
Preston
Reading
Redditch
Runcorn
Salford
Salisbury
Scarborough
Scunthorpe
Sheffield
Shrewsbury
Sidcup
Slough
Solihull
Southampton
Southend-on-Sea
Southport
St Helens
Stevenage
Stockport
Stoke-on-Trent
Stratford-upon-Avon
Sunderland
Sutton Coldfield
Swindon
Taunton
Torquay
Truro
Watford
Weymouth

Wigan
Wolverhampton
Worcester
Workington
Worthing
Yeovil
York

Scotland

Aberdeen
Ayr
Dumfries
Dundee
Dunfermline
Edinburgh
Elgin
Fort William
Gairloch
Galashiels
Glasgow Central
Glasgow North-West
Greenock
Helmsdale
Huntly
Inverness
Isle of Arran
Isle of Barra
Isle of Benbecula
Isle of Islay, Bowmore
Isle of Mull, Salen
Isle of Tiree
Kirkwall
Kyle of Lochalsh
Lerwick
Motherwell
Oban
Pitlochry

Portree
Stirling
Stornoway
Stranraer
Tarbert, Argyllshire
Tongue
Ullapool
Wick

Wales

Aberystwyth
Bangor
Builth Wells
Cardiff
Haverfordwest
Merthyr Tydfil
Newport
Rhyl
Swansea

Northern Ireland

Ballymena
Belfast
Londonderry
Newry
Omagh
Portadown

Service standards

We judge our performance against the following standards (printed in our Business Plan) which we review each year

- 90% of customers will be satisfied with the overall level of service we provide
- 95% of calls to booking offices will make contact with our automated call-handling system without receiving an engaged tone
- after a call has gone through our automated call-handling system, we will answer 90% of all incoming calls to booking offices in no more than 20 seconds
- we will give 95% of candidates an appointment at their preferred centre within two weeks of their preferred date
- we will keep 99.5% of appointments
- we will answer 97% of all letters and e-mails within 10 working days
- we will pay 95% of all refunds within 15 days of a valid claim.

Complaints guide

We aim to give our customers the best possible service. Please tell us when

- we've done well
- when you aren't satisfied.

Your comments can help us to improve the service we offer. If you have any questions about your theory test please contact us using the numbers below.

For DSA:
tel: 0870 01 01 372, fax: 0870 01 04 372.

For DVTA (in Northern Ireland):
tel: 0845 600 6700, fax: 0870 01 04 372.

If you have any complaints about how your theory test was carried out, or any aspect of our customer service, please call the Customer Services section on 0870 241 0204. Alternatively you can write to the Customer Services Manager at the following address

Customer Services
Driving Theory Test
PO Box 148
Salford M5 3SY

If you're dissatisfied with the reply you can write to the Managing Director at the same address.

If you're still not satisfied, you can take up your complaint with

The Chief Executive
Driving Standards Agency
56 Stanley House
Talbot Street
Nottingham NG1 5GU

In Northern Ireland you should write to

The Chief Executive
Driver & Vehicle Testing Agency
Balmoral Road
Belfast BT12 6QL

None of this removes your right to take your complaint to your Member of Parliament, who may decide to raise your case personally with the DSA or DVTA Chief Executive, the Minister or the Parliamentary Commissioner for Administration (the Ombudsman). Please refer to our leaflet 'Service standards – putting things right.'

DSA is a Trading Fund and we are required to cover our costs from the driving test fee.

We don't have a quota for test passes or fails and if you demonstrate the standard required, you'll pass your test.

Compensation code

DSA will normally refund the test fee, or rearrange another test at no further cost to you, if

- we cancel your test
- you cancel and give us at least three clear working days' notice
- you keep the test appointment but the test doesn't take place, or isn't finished, for a reason that isn't your fault.

We'll also repay you the expenses that you had to pay on the day of the test if we cancelled your test at short notice. We'll consider reasonable claims for

- the cost of travelling to and from the test centre
- any standard pay or earnings you lost through taking unpaid holiday leave (usually for half a day), after tax and national insurance contributions.

Please write to the address below and send a receipt showing travel costs and an employer's letter, which shows what earnings you lost.

DVTA has a different compensation code. If you think you're entitled to compensation write to

Customer Services
Driving Theory Test
PO Box 148
Salford M5 3SY

This compensation code doesn't affect your existing legal rights.

More official guidance for new drivers to help you to pass your tests:
available from
the Driving Standards Agency and TSO

The Highway Code

The Highway Code is essential reading for everyone. It explains road traffic law and gives guidance as to best driving practice, with particular reference to vulnerable road users such as horse riders, cyclists and the elderly. The current version was prepared to reflect the changes in lifestyle and technology, giving rules for dealing with driver fatigue and recommendations about the use of mobile phones.

ISBN 0 11 552290 5   £1.49

Know Your Traffic Signs

This useful publication illustrates and explains the vast majority of traffic signals, signs and road markings which any road user is likely to encounter.

It is the most comprehensive explanation of road signs available, and is exceptional value for money.

0 11 551612 3   £3.00

The Official Theory Test Practice Papers

If you want to be fully prepared for your car theory test there is no better way than to practice answering the questions. These sample papers are the only official theory test practice papers and are graded just as in the real test.

0 11 552251 4   £4.99

The Official Driving Test

The practical driving test – fully illustrated and written in a clear and easy-to-understand style.

The full syllabus and tests, explained by the experts who set the standards. Help with your practical test and how to become a safer driver. It covers everything the learner needs to prepare for the driving test, from getting on the road to hazard awareness. Includes information about the new safety checks.

0 11 552520 3   £6.99